Heart

Also by Gail Godwin

Heart

A Personal Journey Through Its Myths and Meanings

Gail Godwin

WILLIAM MORROW • 75 YEARS OF PUBLISHING
An Imprint of HarperCollins*Publishers*

HarperCollins books may be purchased for educational, business, or sales promotional use. For information please write: Special Markets Department, HarperCollins Publishers Inc., 10 East 53rd Street, New York, NY 10022.

FIRST EDITION

Designed by Betty Lew

Printed on acid-free paper

Library of Congress Cataloging-in-Publication Data
    Godwin, Gail.
        Heart / by Gail Godwin.—1st ed.
            p. cm.
            ISBN 0-380-97795-8
                1. Heart—Folklore. 2. Heart—Symbolic aspects. 3. Heart in
        literature. 1. Title.
            GR489.4.G63 2001
            700'.453—dc21   00-049009

01   02   03   04   05   QW   10   9   8   7   6   5   4   3   2   1

To Robert,

Heart Companion

Contents

Part Three: Hospitality of Heart

Author's Note

A book like this is under boundless obligation to that noble breed of communicators, the translators. They make it possible for people like me to pluck what I need from the world's gardens of wisdom, from ancient Mesopotamia to modern China, and offer it to readers in handy, casual-looking bouquets. Throughout *Heart*, whenever it has been possible, I name the source who is bringing me Socrates, Jesus, Teresa, Pascal, et al., in English.

I am fortunate in my researcher, Dan Starer, whom I first sent on an errand to the French consulate years ago, when he was just out of college, to find out for me how a French father could impose a marrying codicil on his bachelor son. What Dan found out killed my plot but gained me, and his other eventual writer-clients, a rigorous and intuitive purveyor of information. He has excelled in *Heart*, tracking down handsomely illustrated books by European cardiologists, an unpublished thesis that provides a transliteration of Inanna's descent in her native language, and many other esoteric treasures I wouldn't have known to ask for, but which add spice and zest to the myths and meanings of heart.

Jennifer Hershey, vice president, associate publisher, and editor in chief of Avon Books, took on the editorship of *Heart* when it was in an earlier stage of formation, and she has been a heart-friend and (to regender Henry James's phrase about the ideal critic) a sister to the manuscript. Its final form incorporates almost every one of her suggestions, twelve single-spaced pages of them, ranging from such toughies as "Are religious heart and romantic heart connected?" to such sisterly prods as "What does this concept mean to you, in your life?," "Is there a story that will illustrate this further?," and "Can you be even more openhearted here?"

It was Hamilton Cain who dreamed up the idea of *Heart* and enlisted my agent, John Hawkins, to invite me to write it.

Prologue
The Rhythms That Count

The rhythms that count—the rhythms of life, the rhythms of the spirit—are those that dance and course in life itself. The movement in gestation from conception to birth; the diastole and systole of the heart; the taking of each successive breath; the ebb and flow of tides in response to the pull of the moon and the sun; the wheeling of the seasons from one equinox or one solstice to another—these, not the eternally passing seconds registered on clocks and watches and not the days and months and years that the calendar imposes, define the time that is our true home and habitation, the time we dwell within until our days are ended. If we lose consciousness of them, we become alienated from ourselves. I can think of no better place to overcome such alienation than a garden.

—Allen Lacy, *The Inviting Garden:*
Gardening for the Senses, Mind, and Spirit

I work at home. Before I begin work every day, Ambrose and I take a walk, weather permitting. Ambrose is our Siamese cat, in his twelfth year as I write. Until two years ago, Ambrose had a twin brother, Felix. They were all over each other, snuggling and grooming and wrestling. I often wondered if each cat knew where he stopped and the other began; after all, they had been together since they were cat-embryos floating inside their mother's sac.

Felix's sudden decline and death from cardiomyopathy, an acquired disease of the heart muscle that can come on at any cat-age, made us a very sad household that spring. Since then we have been a family of three: the Resident Composer, who spends most of his day in his downstairs northeast studio; the Resident Writer, who spends most of her day in her upstairs southwest study; and the Resident Cat, who can be found anywhere from his third-floor file cabinet/lookout under the skylight to the concealing high grasses down by the pond.

This July morning, about eight-thirty, was fair and green after rain. I slipped into my rubber loafers, Ambrose emitted his ecstatic walk-cry, and we set off around the northeast side of the house to check things out. Two snails moved at standstill snail pace along a wet bluestone. Just around the corner: not such a pleasant sight on another bluestone. But the tiny dismembered mouse, undoubtedly a residue of Ambrose's previous evening's work, is part of this day, too, and we stop and look—the ants and the flies are already at *their* work—and, in a sense, pay our respects.

Then on to the stone wall, where the chipmunk dives into a crevice at our approach, and past the lavender and vinca and daisies to the big sage plant where, on hot mornings, we have sometimes been fortunate enough to glimpse the garter snake. At the beginning of June, we found the snake draped across a rock beneath the bloom-ing sage; I held Ambrose wriggling in my arms while I looked. In early afternoon I took a work break and went out to look again. Amazing. The snake was still there, in the exact same position. But when I looked closer, I realized it was the ghost of the snake, draped over the rock beneath the sage plant. Marie, my assistant, had just arrived, and she held back the aromatic, velvety gray-green leaves so I could extricate the skin in one piece. Even the outline of the mouth and tail were still intact. How had the snake managed to crawl out of its last year's skin without rupturing even the shape of the mouth? "The birds are going to love this for their nests," said Marie. We carried the thirty-inch skin, light and brittle as filo pastry, inside to show Robert in his studio, then took it back outside and spread it enticingly beside some laurel bushes near a nest site, and the next morning it was gone.

At the end of our walk, Ambrose and I pause at his brother's flat gravestone in the shade garden. It says FELIX in capital letters, like a Latin inscription. When I went to the monument place to pick it up, the young woman who had carved it was working on a stone for a monk at a monastery across the river in West Park. All their stones since 1904 have been marble, she said. When other monasteries of the order are sold, the monks are dug up and reburied at West Park. So she has to make new stones because marble crumbles. All stones are carved alike: at the top, IHS, the first three letters of Ihsus (Jesus, in Greek); then, underneath, the name of the monk, and, below that, his dates of birth, profession, and death.

All stones must be done by hand. "But after the first fifty, it gets easy," she says.

Dearest Felix, you are gone, I wrote in my journal two springs ago. *But I know what I valued about you. These qualities are to be found in others, and Felix, a cat, helped me to recognize what they were. A suppleness within, and toward the other, whether it is a stone wall you've leapt lightly onto, or a human face you press your face lightly against. Even your voice was an inquiring one, ending in a question mark. Open. Approaching. Not closed, demanding, or assertive.*

Qualities of the heart.

Ambrose sits down on the stone, then rolls over until his body covers all the letters of FELIX. Cat-sensuously, he wriggles and undulates above his brother's ashes while I pick white and purple pansies for my study, if the deer have left me any.

I did not take the time to pick flowers for my study until two summers ago, after a lady in town gave me a blue-and-white Portuguese vase for my birthday. The vase is a little rectangular china box from the Museum of Modern Art, with a three-quarter-inch hole in the center of the top and eleven smaller holes on either side. It came filled with pansies from her garden, and I fill it with pansies until the first nasturtiums show their faces in early July.

Two summers ago, I was depleted and grim, in my third year of writing a novel that, from its inception, seemed to ask more of me than I could give. I loved it and grew with it, but in the way a parent loves and grows with a difficult, demanding, yet terribly interesting child. I never thought of giving up on it, but I dreamed of the day it would leave the house. People around me would roll their eyes when, month after month, I excused myself from anything pleasurable or fun with the same old groaning plaint: "I will, I'd *love* to—*as soon as I finish this novel.*" As time wore on, I didn't even have to finish the sentence. Before I got to the word *finish,* they were already nodding and rolling their eyes.

But then Lee Mayer gave me this inviting little vase, and I felt I could handle the small truancy of going outside each morning and picking enough fresh flowers to fill up the twenty-three holes and carrying them upstairs to brighten the windowsill of my study before I sank down on my Scandinavian kneeling chair with a sigh and a prayer for endurance and turned on the computer.

Since then, filling the vase has become part of my morning rhythm. Even in the depth of winter I give myself the present of plopping in fresh water something that has grown out of the earth, a sprig of white pine or hemlock, red berries and thorns, and setting it on the sill beside the computer. Now it is pansy and nasturtium time again, and when I pick the first nasturtiums I always remember a story my literary agent told me.

His mother, Mrs. Hawkins, grew nasturtiums all winter in her greenhouse; they clambered all winter, orange and salmon and golden yellow, up their indoor trellises. One cold winter night, she and her husband were on the way to their chamber orchestra rehearsal. They were too early, so they decided to take a detour to look at a new building down by the river. Suddenly the headlights of their car shone on an older woman whom they knew slightly walking slowly along the road beside the river. As it was so cold, they stopped and offered her a ride home. She accepted. When they let her off at her house, Mrs. Hawkins gave her the jar of nasturtiums she had picked to give "to someone or other" at the rehearsal.

A few weeks later the Hawkinses received a note from the woman saying she had been depressed all winter and was on her way to drown herself in the river. But when they suddenly stopped and offered her a ride and gave her those bright summer flowers in the depth of winter, she took it as a sign from God that she was supposed to go on living.

A woman whose life was saved by a bouquet of nasturtiums. But someone's heart had to be tuned in to the rhythms that count; Marian Hawkins had to understand the value of growing nasturtiums in the wintertime in order for there to *be* such bouquets to give to "someone or other" in need of a reminder of summer. She and her husband had to be the sort of people who were curious enough

about something new to go out of their way to see how it was coming along, the sort of people who without thinking twice would
divert their point-to-point journey a second time to run a solitary
woman home on a cold night. Heart acts are often improvisational
detours from point-to-point plans.

Robert tells me the Italians have a musical notation not found in any
other language: *tempo giusto*, "the right tempo." It means a steady,
normal beat, between 66 and 76 on the metronome. *Tempo giusto* is
the appropriate beat of the human heart.

With Robert's new hand-sized quartz metronome, Marie and I
decide to test out the premise. She takes my pulse: a brisk 72, at the
top end of *tempo giusto*, on the brink of *andante*. I can't find her pulse,
so she guides my fingers to a throbbing place on her neck and we
coordinate it with the clock and the flashing red light on Robert's
metronome. Marie walks five miles every morning and then swims at
the Y and then goes home to lift rocks in her garden until it's time to
come and be my assistant. So she's way down at the low end of *tempo
giusto*, even lower than *adagio*: she's a 64 *larghetto*.

Most afternoons, I shut up shop around three. I save the day's
work on hard drive and floppy disk, climb off my kneeler, blow out
the votive candles in front of my household gods, gather up the coffee cups and juice glasses, and descend the fourteen stairs from my
study to the main floor in order to climb the fourteen stairs on the
other side of the house to the bedroom. If Ambrose is in proximity,
he races ahead of me up the second set of stairs and beats me to the
bed. I stretch out on my back, pull the white eiderdown up to my
chin, and he mounts the snowy mound of my chest and stands fore-

head to forehead with me, marching in place, until I am laid out correctly. Then he makes a sharp right turn, backs up against my face, and heaves himself into position so his warm furry back is under my chin and his heart on my heart. I have tried during these occasions to feel his quicker heartbeat, twice the tempo of mine, but all I can feel is the steady throb of my own, intensified by 9.6 pounds of solid cat lying on top of it.

After Felix died, we asked our veterinarian if we should get another cat for Ambrose. "Ah, it's difficult to predict," he said. He told us about the great Siamese cat he brought home from the Philippines, a cat who became his soul's companion. "Then I worried that he might be lonely and I got a kitten, but it was a mistake. He became grouchy and aloof and would never seek me out when the kitten was around. The two of *them* became friends, but he and I were never as close again."

In his first few weeks alone, Ambrose would go outside, plant his four legs in the gravel, and emit a bloodcurdling yowl that seemed to come from the pit of his being. He's grieving, we said. He still does this occasionally, but as the seasons separate him from the time when he was two cats instead of one, the yowl has become more perfunctory, like a ritual whose reason he no longer remembers.

Now we lie heart-to-heart in profound synchrony. I wonder if I remind him of his mother, or is my human heartbeat too slow? So far, today has been close to paradisal: no machine or appliance has broken down, no repairmen are expected, nobody has asked for a part of our day that we'd rather not give but feel we ought to; no power mower or leaf blower or weed whacker or vacuum cleaner has sent the Resident Cat fleeing to safety beneath the skirts of his third-floor sofa. There has been not a single phone call or fax from anyone urgently requiring something FedExed to them from the Resident Composer or the Resident Writer by no later than noon the next day.

Marie is upstairs on the third floor, putting papers into piles: *Pay Now, Pay Later, Better Look at This, This Can Wait.* Marie is happy; her daughter Kassy just e-mailed from Manhattan that she got a bonus today. Marie will not learn until tonight that Kassy went home from work today and found her apartment robbed.

The first Japanese beetle will not appear on a leaf until tomorrow.

Yes, a moment of holy rest, whose steady beat will imprint itself in our memory cells, to be replayed during more untranquil days.

A *tempo giusto* for the heart bank.

One morning I was curled up in an armchair, a legal pad on my knees, jotting down images and ideas. The novel that had tested my limits was at last in production, the book tour to help promote it was still months away, and I was in that galvanic state of flirtation with a possible next novel. I had just reread Conrad's two novellas *The Heart of Darkness* and *The Secret Sharer,* and their back-to-back combination had set me to fantasizing a woman's journey into a heart of darkness where she would have to confront her shadow. Sort of a modern version of what the ancient Sumerian goddess Inanna, Queen of Heaven, undertook when she set her heart on the Great Below and descended into the underworld to visit her dark sister, Queen Ereshkigal.

The phone rang and John, my agent, said, "Someone's had this delicious, rather quirky idea. It's probably not for you. But I promised I'd run it past you, anyway."

A young editor, working out at his health club that morning, had come up with an idea for a book he thought I should write. "A book about the heart," John said. "Not a medical book, but the ways we've imagined the heart through time in myth and art and popular culture and what those images tell us about the human condition, then and now. It would be informative, but not scholarly. More of a lush, writerly, intimate book with a narrative arc."

"It's a great idea," I said. "I'd love to *read* a book like that. But I don't want to write it."

"No, I didn't think so," said John. "But it *is* a great idea, isn't it?"

I rattled off a list of writers I thought could do it. John wrote the names down.

"It should have world history and religion and psychology and the arts in it, but it shouldn't be a plodding survey," I said. "Whoever writes it should try for a broad, inclusive sweep, with emphasis on the lively, human-interest stuff."

"I agree," said John.

"And there should be personal anecdotes sprinkled around. It shouldn't be just a compilation or an anthology."

"My thought exactly," said John.

"And written from the writer's heart, whoever you get to write it."

"I completely agree," said John.

"And not survey-ish or travelogue-y, either. More like a long conversation with that writer over drinks or tea, about books and lovers and mystics and animals and gardens—all sorts of weird and curious stories about the heart. There should be some medical stories, too, cardiology lore: anything that falls under the rubric of 'the heart,' from pump-pump in the night, to the telltale heart, the heart that has reasons, the heart of the matter, the broken heart . . . the heart of darkness, which I was thinking about when you called: *John, I am not going to do this book!* I was making notes for a new novel when you called."

"Congratulations. Want to talk about it?"

"Not yet."

"Well, I'll let you get back to it. But I promised I'd run this past you."

"When does the editor need an answer?"

"Oh, I think he'd be willing to wait a few days."

"Give me three days," I said. "At least—let me sleep on it. And don't offer it to anyone else, just yet."

My internal reference library, overstimulated by the new idea, kept me awake most of the night. Voices chattered and quipped, declaimed and soliloquized. I kept snapping on the light to take dictation. "Now that my ladder's gone," Yeats confessed, "I must lie down where all the ladders start, in the foul rag-and-bone shop of the heart." "Give me," prayed Saint Francis, "a transformed and undefended heart." "My heart teaches me, night after night," the Psalmist said. "I left my heart in San Francisco," Tony crooned. "Your lips are so near, but where is your heart?" lamented a top ten tune from the fifties. "Blessed are the pure in heart," said Jesus. "Purity of heart is to will one thing," Kierkegaard elaborated. Pharaoh hardened his heart. "Circumcise the foreskin of your hearts," Moses scolded the grumbling Israelites. "He wears a condom on his heart," a Saul Bellow character remarked. "I wish you were not so heartless," said Madame Merle to Gilbert Osmond. "More die of heartbreak than radiation," said Saul Bellow. "Our shared bedroom, my heart," Augustine whispered to God. "Our hearts are restless till they rest in thee." Inanna set her heart on the Great Below and descended into the underworld to visit her sister Ereshkigal, Queen of the Dead. "No, I'll not weep," says Lear, turned out into the night by his daughter Regan. "I have full cause for weeping, but this heart shall break into a hundred thousand flaws or ere I'll weep. . . . Let them anatomize Regan, see what breeds about *her* heart." "Unhappy that I am," said Cordelia, dooming herself, "I cannot heave my heart into my mouth."

"Work of seeing is done," announced Rilke, setting himself a new task in poetry, "now practice heart-work upon those images captive within you." "Do you suppose Oz could give me a heart?" the Tin Woodman asked Dorothy. "Ah, he was a man after my own heart!" "Did not our heart burn within us while he talked with us along the way?" "And she kept all these things and pondered them in her heart." "Break, heart: I prithee, break!"

Sleep, heart: I prithee, sleep! Turn the light off and leave it off.

Heart of the city, heart of the country, heart of the artichoke, my heart's in the highlands, my heart is turned to stone, he's chickenhearted, no, he's lionhearted, her heart is a lonely hunter, from the bottom of my heart, in my heart of hearts, I had a change of heart, did my heart good, to your heart's content, eat your heart out, heart in my mouth, wear my heart on my sleeve, cross my heart, lose my heart, take heart, don't take it to heart, don't lose heart, pour your heart out in a heart-to-heart talk, trap your raccoon in a Havahart trap. Set your heart on it, set your heart against it: the education of the heart, the death of the heart, the afterlife of the heart, the prayer of the heart, work the earth of your heart, but for now let not your heart be troubled, set your heart at rest.

Enough. In the morning, I called John, my agent, then Ambrose and I went for our walk, I picked some nasturtiums for Mrs. Mayer's little Portuguese vase, came up to my study, and knelt on my Scandinavian kneeler. I turned on the computer, and enrolled in the school of the heart.

PART ONE

The Heart Through Time

The utterances of the heart—unlike those of the discriminating intellect—always relate to the whole. The heartstrings sing like an Aeolian harp only to the gentle breath of a premonitory mood, which does not drown the song but listens. What the heart hears are the great things that span our whole lives, the experiences which we do nothing to arrange but which we ourselves suffer.

—C. G. Jung, *The Symbolic Life*

In the chronicle of our species, ever since we acquired speech and symbols, the imaginative place accorded to the heart can tell you a great deal about how a people defines itself and what it holds sacred.

When the Aztecs cut open captive enemy warriors and offered their bloody hearts to the sun god, they believed the heart was the body's sun and the more hearts they sacrificed the more power they were returning to the sun. Before the enemy warrior was killed, they painted him with stripes, tied him to a rope, and gave him a blunt wooden sword; Aztec warriors, armed with real swords and shields, fought him. The longer "the stripe" held out, the braver and more "nutritious" was deemed the meal offered to the sun.

When primitive peoples ate the hearts of particularly brave enemies or animals they had killed, they believed they were ingesting the strength and courage of the owner of that heart.

For the alchemists in the Middle Ages, the heart represented the image of the sun within a human being, just as gold was the image of the sun on earth. Later they understood that their undertaking was also an outward and visible sign for purifying the heart.

For the disciplined practitioner of Buddhist Tantric yoga, the "heart level" represents that advanced achievement of consciousness in an individual where, for the first time, "a light is lit in the heart."

From this point on, one is no longer dependent on reflected light, but can at last see directly for oneself.

For Aztecs, alchemists, and Tantrics alike, the heart-sun-enlightenment connection is paramount in value, though the means of expressing that value evolves from visceral to chemical to symbolic. As our consciousness becomes more differentiated, "what is outside" becomes known as "also inside."

It has been said by many thoughtful people that our era, or the era we are just completing, has represented the nadir of the heart. Since the onset of the Industrial Revolution, we have lived in a culture that increasingly worships decisions of the head alone. The head without the heart is much better equipped to make empirical, technical, product-oriented decisions.

In his unusual and extremely readable autobiography, *Memories, Dreams, Reflections*, dictated and written when he was eighty-one, the Swiss psychiatrist Carl Jung describes his encounter with the Native American chief of the Taos pueblos in New Mexico in 1932.

"I was able to talk with him as I have rarely been able to talk with a European," Jung recalls. "To be sure, he was caught up in his world just as much as a European is in his, but what a world it was! In talk with a European, one is constantly running up on the sand bars of things long known but never understood; with this Indian, the vessel floated freely on deep alien seas. At the same time, one never knows which is more enjoyable: catching sight of new shores, or discovering new approaches to age old knowledge that has been almost forgotten" (Vintage, p. 247).

Chief Ochwiay Biano, which means Mountain Lake, must have sensed a kindred spirit in the Swiss doctor, because he was devastatingly candid with him.

Chief Mountain Lake: "See how cruel the whites look, their lips are thin, their noses sharp, their faces furrowed and distorted by folds. Their eyes have a staring expression; they are always seeking something. What are they seeking? The whites always want something. They are always uneasy and restless. We do not know what they want. We do not understand them. We think that they are all mad."

When Jung asks why he thinks they are all mad, Mountain Lake replies, "They say they think with their heads."

"Why of course," says Jung. "What do you think with?"

"We think here," says Chief Mountain Lake, indicating his heart.

After this exchange, Jung fell into a deep meditation. The Pueblo chief had struck a vulnerable spot. Jung saw image upon image of cruelties wreaked by his forebears: the Roman eagle on the North Sea and the White Nile, "the keenly incised features of Julius Caesar, Scipio Africanus, and Pompey . . . Charlemagne's most glorious forced conversions of the heathen . . . the pillaging, murdering bands of the Crusading armies . . . the peoples of the Pacific islands decimated by firewater, syphilis and scarlet fever carried in the clothes the missionaries forced on them."

Chief Mountain Lake had shown Jung the other face of his own civilization: it was "the face of a bird of prey seeking with cruel intentness for distant quarry. . . ."

What makes this dialogue reported by Jung so relevant is that it is a *living encounter* between a representative of the unconscious "heart-thinking" of the ancients and a modern man of science and pioneer of consciousness who understood that the wisdom of the heart must catch up with our overdeveloped "thinking heads" if we are to survive. We have to preserve the gold in the age-old "knowledge of the heart" and keep making it ever more conscious if we are to protect our growing human possibilities from the keen-featured bird-of-prey mentality that circles above. We must develop a new consciousness of the heart.

In our contemporary bottom-line society, heart-knowledge—based on feeling values, relationship, personal courage, intimations of the ineffable, a passion for transcendence—tends to be mistrusted as impractical, profitless, or nonexistent. Where *is* "the heart," anyway, scoffs the bird-of-prey executive, trudging joylessly on his treadmill, except under your breastbone?

The heart has been reduced once again to the visceral, but this time without any sacred connection to the powers of life and light. No longer do we literally cut our enemies' hearts out and feed them to an out-of-date sun god: we do it the bloodless, sophisticated way, without a flint knife, and feed them to the contemporary god of "market value function," which leads to money and power. Already, back in the 1950s, Erich Fromm was writing about the prevalence of the "marketing personality" in our society, the person who sees self and the selves of others in terms of "market value." In those terms, the poetic heart is lost; the only heart we truly believe in is the one we watch on our angiogram screen and sacrifice butter and ice cream for and feel pumping fast as we plot our profit-and-loss tactics for the morrow. We work these literal hearts hard, the only hearts we have left. We stay so well defended that we hesitate to pursue things passionately enough to risk a broken heart.

Some of us have anesthetized our hearts so thoroughly that it takes the utmost in thrills, the most graphic depiction of horrors, to make *something* in our breasts lurch or recoil: to shock us into a reaction that at least *feels* like feeling.

Having flung down that gauntlet, I invite you to take a broad, anecdotal tour of the heartscape through recorded time to see if we can pinpoint by comparison our present heart location. What have we gained since the cave artist painted a red heart on an elephant? What have we lost since the Industrial Revolution? In what ways have we changed, and in what ways have we remained pretty much the same since King Solomon courted new wives with his love songs, and Vatsayana collected together in his *Kama Sutra* some ancient Hindu recipes for good loving, and a cleric at Eleanor of Aquitaine's court penned the *Rules of Courtly Love*?

"Humanity does not pass through phases as a train passes through stations," wrote C. S. Lewis in *The Allegory of Love: A Study in Medieval Tradition;* "being alive, it has the privilege of always moving yet never leaving anything behind. Whatever we have been, in some sort we are still."

I. The Elephant with a Heart

Around 10,000 B.C. someone found time to draw a picture of a woolly mammoth on a cave wall in Spain. With an economy of line worthy of Paul Klee, this prehistoric artist has lovingly and respectfully rendered the living essence of that extinct creature from its tail to its trunk tip. The elephant, supple, lumbering, true to nature, all but moves. And, just at the spot where its heart would naturally be, the artist has painted a red, heart-shaped spot. This valentine in the Pindal cave near Colombre in Asturias is believed to be the oldest artistic representation of the heart in the world. I like to imagine this individual suddenly infused with those timeless symptoms of creativity: playfulness, awe, curiosity—the leap of ecstasy that comes over our hearts when we suddenly discover in our hectic schedule an unclaimed moment to use as we desire. *What is this great furry being with a back like a mountain? Here, great animal that I fear and kill and eat, my hand makes a memory-image of you. Look! I have created you again. Most important, I've given you a heart.*

II. Heart Shape

Touch your pencil tip to the page, then swing out into a lush upward, leftward curve until you've got the shape of a blade of grass being blown slightly to the right. Then make the line bow down, keeping its arc, until if the grass blade had eyes on its tip it would be looking at the ground. At that point, stop, turn your stopping point into a cleavage, and send the pencil up and out into a mirror image of your shape so far. When you've returned to the top, to your starting point, you've got a heart. At least on paper.

If you're left-handed, you'll probably swing into a lush upward, *rightward* curve, or if you're someone like Paul Klee, for whom the heart shape was a favorite compositional motif and who enjoyed drawing with alternate hands (and sometimes both at the same time), you will start your spry line wherever and come up with lively results. Whoever you are and however you draw it, each heart will have its own personality: one cheeky and plump, one long and skinny-mean with its tail aimed like a weapon, one dense and primal, like the woolly mammoth's on the cave wall, one wispy and floating on its side like a blown leaf giving up the season's ghost.

Some mythologists think that the symbolic shape that looks up at us from our valentines and jewelry and cookie cutters did evolve from a leaf, the ivy leaf, which was a symbol of immortality in ancient times. Because of its year-round greenness and its climbing, nestling, and snuggling propensities, it became a symbol for friendship and fidelity. In ancient Greece, ivy was given to brides and grooms at weddings.

But, getting back to the elephant, I think there is strong evidence that the heart shape we use as our symbol derives from prehistoric "life drawing." The cave artist came from a society that hunted the woolly mammoth and would therefore have seen the dead animal's heart—most likely he'd have eaten pieces of it, pondering as he chewed on the qualities of the creature whose life organ he was ingesting. Our heart organ *is*, roughly, heart-shaped.

Later on, the Pythagorean natural philosopher Philolaus (b. circa 470 B.C.) noted the similarity between the shape of the heart and the shape of the human face. Many artists have drawn and painted faces shaped like hearts and continue to do so.

Another intriguing suggestion has been put forth, that the heart shape with its rounded and cleft top and phallic point is a figurative symbol for the combined male and female principles, the yang and the yin, the bisexual dual nature of the heart, as mentioned by Aristotle.

I lean toward the elephant hypothesis.

III. The Sumerians

He touched [Enkidu's] heart but it did not beat, nor did [Enkidu] lift his eyes again. So Gilgamesh laid a veil, as one veils a bride, over his friend. . . .

Bitterly Gilgamesh wept for his friend Enkidu; [. . .] in his bitterness he cried, "How can I rest, how can I be at peace? Despair is in my heart. What my brother is now, that shall I be when I am dead."

—The Epic of Gilgamesh,
translated by N. K. Sandars

Here, in the oldest-known story in the world, we see the heart already being experienced in its dual sense: as the life-giving center-piece in our breasts that ceases to beat when we are dead, and as the wellspring of our human emotions. The word *heart*—both as indispensable organ and as the imaged locus of our fear, sadness, anger, love, restlessness, discernment, foreboding, pleasure, longing, comfort, pride, despair—is all over this epic, written down on clay tablets around 1850 B.C. by the people who, until several years ago, were thought to have invented writing. (Now, due to recent excavations near Cairo, it looks as if the Egyptians might have preceded them.)

The story begins with "restless-hearted" Gilgamesh abusing his powers as king of the Sumerian walled city of Uruk, which would be Warka in today's Iraq. Out of sheer abundance of energy and unchallenged strength, Gilgamesh high-hands it over everybody. He appropriates other people's sons for his own projects, and his lust leaves no virgin to her lover. At last the gods, who have taken pity on the oppressed Urukians, petition the goddess of creation to create someone for Gilgamesh to match the ardor of his energies: "You made him, Aruru, now create his equal; let it be as like him as his own reflection, his second self, *stormy heart for stormy heart*. Let them contend with each other and leave Uruk in quiet."

Aruru forms a mental image (she uses the god of heaven as a model), washes her hands, pinches off some clay, throws it down in the desert, and creates Enkidu. Soon Gilgamesh is hearing tales from a trapper of a wild, hairy man "unlike any other" who roams with the wild beasts and helps them escape from the traps. At the trapper's beseeching, Gilgamesh sends a harlot—probably a temple prostitute—out into the wilderness to tame Enkidu. After Enkidu lies with her, the beasts will have no more to do with him, "for wisdom was in him and *the thoughts of a man were in his heart*." The harlot then tells Enkidu all about Gilgamesh ("He is like a wild bull and lords it over men"); and Enkidu, aroused by the description, resolves to go into Uruk and fight him. Besides feeling challenged, Enkidu is equally desirous of meeting an equal, *"a comrade who would understand his heart."* Meanwhile, Gilgamesh has dreamed that something like a meteor, made of god-stuff, is flung down from heaven, and "for me its attraction was like the love of woman." He tells his mother the dream and she predicts the coming of Enkidu, whom "you will love as a wife, you will love as yourself."

Enkidu arrives in town, the two men fight, snorting like bulls and breaking doorposts. Here later-uncovered cuneiform fragments bring important new details. Until recently it was assumed from missing lines that Gilgamesh threw Enkidu to the ground. Now new

fragments describe Enkidu forcing Gilgamesh to one knee ("Gilgamesh went down, his foot on the ground, his rage subsided") and
then Enkidu *wins Gilgamesh's heart* by magnanimously praising Gilgamesh rather than gloating as the victor. "There is not another like
you in the world," Enkidu tells Gilgamesh, and the two seal their
friendship with an embrace (or kiss in another translation). (In
another of the later-unearthed tablets, Gilgamesh is on the way to
his marriage when Enkidu comes into town and does not let Gilgamesh into the room with his bride. Enkidu bars the door and the
two men fight.)

After the embrace or kiss, Gilgamesh takes Enkidu home to his
mother, who accepts Enkidu as a son. But their happiness together
in Uruk is brief. Enkidu feels his muscles going soft and becomes
sick at heart. When Gilgamesh comes upon his friend weeping one
day, he decides what they both need is a new challenge. He proposes
they set out together to slay the terrible monster Humbaba, who
guards the pine forest and has a face like coiled intestines. They do
this, each man alternating between bouts of fear and egging the other
on, and return triumphant to Uruk. Gilgamesh dresses in fresh
clothes and attracts the attention of Ishtar, the goddess of Uruk,
who proposes marriage. He insults her, reminding her of the bad
fates all her previous husbands suffered, and she finally persuades
her reluctant father, the god of heaven, to lend her the Bull of
Heaven to sic on Gilgamesh. Gilgamesh and Enkidu slay it, too, and
offer its heart to the sun god (here we have the first written account of a
heart sacrifice).

However, by this point they have irritated too many of the other
gods and Enkidu has a dream that he must die. Forthwith he sickens
and expires. Up to this point, death has been known to Gilgamesh
only in the abstract. Now, with the death of the one he loved,

someone like himself, it becomes a felt experience. ("What sleep is this that seized you? You have grown dark and cannot hear me!") It is at this point, when Gilgamesh *touches Enkidu's heart* and feels no beat in that static organ, that *despair enters his innermost being—his heart.*

The loss he has suffered is unbearable. Fear of death, his own death, becomes his new obsession. In the second half of the epic, Gilgamesh goes on his solitary search for the secret of eternal life. The gods withhold it from him. An old couple, like Noah and his wife, whom the gods granted immortality because they saved all the animals in their boat during the Flood, feel sorry for him and give him a secret root to take home that will make him young again each time he eats it; but while bathing in a pond Gilgamesh leaves the root with his clothes and a wily snake steals it away (and thus becomes able to slough off its old skin every year). Gilgamesh sits down and weeps. "For whose sake has *my heart's blood been spent?* For myself I have gained nothing. Not I, but the snake has joy of it now."

However, that is not quite the end of this old story, new fragments of which continue to come to light. When the boatman who has ferried Gilgamesh to the island of the immortal old couple returns him home to Uruk again, Gilgamesh invites him ashore: "Go up on the wall and walk around. Examine the terrace, look closely at the brickwork! Are not the burnt bricks solid? Did not the seven wise men lay these foundations?"

Like the proud cicerone of a city that was built long before him and will survive after him, Gilgamesh points out to his ferryman how well things have been organized here: "One third of the whole is town, one third is garden and orchard, one third is riverbed, also the precinct of the Ishtar temple: These parts and the precinct comprise Uruk."

This is not the voice of an enraged or defeated man come home to die "with nothing to show for it," but the mature utterance of a man who has exhibited a great capacity for friendship, love, adventure, endurance, joy and sorrow, and pride in human achievements, including his own, that will outlast him. Qualities of the heart.

Gilgamesh is the life's journey of a restless-hearted man "who inspected the edges of the world," who "saw mysteries and knew secret things," who brought back from his travels and tribulations a tale of the days before the Flood. He engraved the whole story on a stone, we are told, and at his death the people weighed out their offerings "for Gilgamesh, the son of Ninsun, *the heart of Uruk.*"

Just this morning, reading in bed before coming to this side of the house to write, I confronted a simple sentence that clarified more than half a century's reading passions. In *How to Read and Why,* Harold Bloom confides that a story by a wise writer (in this instance he's speaking of Chekhov) teaches him implicitly that literature is *a form of the good,* which is why he reads. Of course, I thought, reflecting for the first time that literature and religion have never been separate pursuits for me, nor are they likely ever to be. They lead to the same place, the place of more understanding of where I am and what I'm learning from it; they both make me want to be a better me. The story of Gilgamesh, as it was told and retold, shaped and reshaped, scratched on clay in various versions over millennia, is the story of one human heart living fully in its time, finally conceding its human limits—and becoming a beloved symbol for the heart of a people. That basic story, whether written thousands of years ago, or yesterday, or tomorrow, and called "literature" or "religion," can be equally beneficial in heartening the human in us and humanizing the heart in us.

IV. The Egyptians

O Lord of Amentet (the underworld), I am in thy presence. There is no sin in me, I have not lied wittingly, nor
have I done aught with a false heart. Grant that I may be
like unto those favored ones who are round about thee,
and that I may be an Osiris. . . .
      –Chapter **XXX** B, *The Egyptian Book of the Dead,*
      translated by E. A. Wallis Budge

For a Sumerian, only the gods got to live forever. However, an Egyptian living in the same period believed he had hope of eternal life if,
after death, his heart was weighed before the Egyptian Court of the
Dead and found acceptable. The "trial of the heart" ceremony,
depicted in great detail on ancient papyri in lifelike little pictures
called hieroglyphics, went as follows: the dead man's heart, represented by an urn, was placed on the left-hand scale; an ostrich
feather, symbol of truth and justice, was placed on the right-hand
scale. The jackal-headed Anubis, judge of the dead, kneels ready to
weigh the heart. The monster Ammit, "eater of the dead," part hip-
popotamus, part lion, and part crocodile, stands by, ready to devour
the deceased's heart if it is "found to be wanting."

Without the heart, the deceased cannot enter the company of
the gods.

At this point the deceased makes his "negative confession,"
telling forty-two gods what sins he has *not* committed. The compre-
hensiveness of this ancient moral code, set down on papyri as *The
Book of the Dead,* and known to have been in use by the Egyptians

since 4500 B.C., makes the approximately three-thousand-years-younger Ten Commandments seem rudimentary in comparison. For instance, for the ancient Egyptian, "Thou shalt not steal" meant not only "I have not committed theft," but also "I have not robbed with violence, I have not made light the bushel, I have not purloined the things which belong unto God, I have not carried off food by force, I have not committed fraud, I have not increased my wealth except by means of such things as are mine own possessions." And here are two sins against conservation we might do well to reinstate today: "I have not fouled running water," and "I have not multiplied my speech beyond what should be said."

Because the Egyptian considered his heart to be his inner sun, the source of his being, and also his *ka*, his double who lives inside his body, not only was meticulous care taken to preserve the physical organ after death but his texts abound with "heart idioms" that describe feelings, conditions of the soul, and traits of temperament. "I have not eaten my heart" means I have not lost my temper and become angry. "I have not hastened my heart" means I have not acted without due consideration. To be happy is to be "long of heart"; to be depressed, "short of heart"; a friend is one who "fills the heart"; to hide one's thoughts is to "drown the heart." To "wash the heart" is to satisfy a desire.

After the deceased has made his negative confession, he adds this prayer: "My heart, my mother! My heart, my mother! My heart whereby I came into being! May naught stand up to oppose me in the judgement . . . may there be no parting of thee from me in the presence of him that keepeth the balance." For to be separated from his heart means eternal death. A pivotal chapter in *The Book of the Dead*—the prayer from which I quoted in the epigraph to the Egyptians—is titled "Chapter of Not Allowing the Heart of the Deceased to Fall Away from Him (or Be Driven Away from Him) in the Underworld."

And now his own heart, placed on the scale, will act as witness to his report. If the heart is lighter than the feather of truth and justice, the monster Ammit gets it for his dinner and that is the end of that heart. But if it exactly balances the feather of truth and justice, the deceased may proceed on to join the company of the gods, becoming "an Osiris" as he had prayed to become—which would be comparable to a Christian's getting to join the "body of Christ" if he makes it to Heaven.

As I was relishing the many images and ideas that leapt out at me from the negative confession list of the ancient Egyptians, it struck me that the material could provide a rousing comparative religion session for my adolescent Sunday school class at St. Gregory's, Woodstock. We had recently finished drawing the tablets of the Ten Commandments as they might have looked to Moses; the Hebrew letters, done with stencils, were a great success. Then we went on to illustrate a broken commandment of our own choice. For "Thou shalt not covet," I drew a woman like me in a red nightgown narrowing her angry eyes at someone else's best-selling novel that has just walked into her bedroom on bandy legs. For "Thou shalt have no other gods," one student did a girl in glitter-paint miniskirt and shiny black boots worshiping the Steak Rabbit God, a Disney World-y sirloin creature with rabbit ears posing atop a Greek pedestal.

Just think what one might draw to illustrate, say, negative confession 14 in The Book of the Dead: "Hail Ta-ret (Fiery Foot), who comest forth out of the darkness, I have not eaten my heart." When an old text from another civilization strikes a spark in you, or tickles your funny bone, or makes you want to draw it and add your own contemporary twist to it, there's more than a good chance that something in the material is speaking heart-to-heart from then to now. "Eat your heart out!" we currently say to someone we have bested, someone we know will rage and burn at our victory (as we would at theirs?). A sort of modern curse, really: when this person reaches her weighing-of-the-heart moment, which comes to us all in one way or another, may she balk at number 14 and subsequently be turned into food for the monster.

AN ANCIENT BOY'S HEART

In the five-thousand-year-old text *The Book of the Dead*, the ideogram for the heart is an urn with handles on either side and a stopper on top. The early Egyptians buried the hearts of their pharaohs inside canopic jars of this shape; it was only in later dynasties that the embalmers developed a method for taking out the other organs without removing the heart. The heart, as we know, was the most important organ for the Egyptians: they believed that it was the seat of one's spirit and the center of the will. If the dead person arrived at the Hall of Judgment to be judged by Osiris, the heart would be weighed against the feather of truth. If the heart was heavier, the deceased would be eaten by the Eater of the Dead. If the heart was in balance, the deceased could proceed safely on to become "an Osiris" in the afterworld.

I'm looking right now into a fascinating volume, *Mummies, Disease and Ancient Cultures* (revised second edition, 1998, edited by Aidan Cockburn, Eve Cockburn, and Theodore A. Reyman), in which paleopathologists write about their autopsies on mummies.

In the chapter entitled "ROM I: Mummification for the Common

People," there is an arresting photograph of the well-preserved heart of Nakht, a teenage Egyptian boy, described on his coffin as a weaver, who died in the first half of the twelfth century B.C.

All of the tomb chambers in which Nakht's coffin was found at Deir-el-Bahri in 1904 had been robbed of their aristocratic mummies (along with their cache of fine possessions) long ago in antiquity, thus leaving empty chambers for humbler people in later times to bury their dead. Like many poor families today, Nakht's people had splurged on a fine coffin, in the desirable anthropoid shape of the times. The lid, gaily painted with scenes and inscriptions, portrays the deceased wearing a long blue-striped wig, his forearms and clenched fists carved in relief. Nakht's corpse inside the fancy coffin had simply been washed and wrapped in linen, probably by the family, indicating that there was no money left over for professional mummification. The bandages, some of which had been made from his own clothes, came off all the more easily for the lack of sacral oils; Nakht's body had desiccated naturally, without the aid of the embalmer's draining techniques, in the hot, dry air of Thebes.

Nakht's 3,200-year-old-heart, removed from his thorax by an international team of paleopathologists at the University of Toronto in 1974, has shrunk, but still retains the shape of the heart you see in medical books. In the photograph, its fibrous, porous look resembles a small-scale model of artist Jim Dine's sculpture "Heart of Straw."

What is so engaging about the ROM I chapter, written by the five specialists who took part in the autopsy, is the *heartfulness* that steals into the writing. Affection flickers up from the scientific vocabulary as the members of the team—an Egyptologist and four pathologists—describe the unwrapping of ROM I (the shorthand designation for this particular mummy belonging to the Royal Ontario Museum) and how they set to the task of discovering everything the corpse of this ancient boy could tell them about himself and his short life.

Official records of his time would describe Nakht as a *mnh*, or "stripling," a youth old enough to be employed but still unmarried and living at home. The writers report that the coffin would have cost approximately 31g of silver, about 10 percent of the family's annual income. And then comes the first of the heartful grace notes: "The grieving parents must have been willing to sacrifice a great deal to see their son suitably interred."

Though unfused epiphyses on Nakht's left knee suggested infection and malnutrition during life, all his teeth were in good condition, including the fully developed wisdom teeth, which had not yet had a chance to come through. The whorls and ridges on his fingers and toes were still there, as were his fingernails and toenails. A thin transparent film on his left eye socket still bore eyelashes.

Nakht's heart and brain, both well preserved, were left intact for permanent display. The team then went to work on all other tissues to find out what had cut this young life short. The postmortem revealed calcified ova of several offending parasites that could have produced severe complications. The tapeworm ova implied that Nakht ate meat: a small cyst of *Trichinella spiralis* in a muscle between the ribs testified that Nakht ate pork on at least one occasion, probably on the holy day of Osiris, the only day an Egyptian was allowed to eat pork. Families too poor to afford meat made cakes in the shape of pigs.

Nakht's intact brain later underwent the first CTT scan in paleopathology. This was carried out at the Hospital for Sick Children in

Toronto. No abnormalities were found. Parts of the report subsequently became part of a teaching exhibit on disease in ancient
times.

At the end of the article there is an affectionately worded update.
A test done in 1994 on Nakht's tissues shows "yet another infec-
tious disease in *this young lad* (my italics)." Nakht had had malaria,
possibly in the late stage of his short life.

"What we see in this young boy," the team of specialists concludes, "is an all too common picture of multiple parasitism, any one
of which would be debilitating and possibly fatal, particularly the
malaria. They are surely the cause of death in this youth."

From ROM I to *"this young lad."* A distinct case of heartfelt
research.

Oh, Nakht, we never knew you, but what a long way you've come.

V. The Hebrews

Now YHWH saw that great was humankind's evildo-
ing on earth and every form of their heart's planning was
only evil all the day.
   —Genesis 6:5

Then YHWH was sorry that he had made humankind
on earth and it pained his heart.
   —Genesis 6:6 (*The Five Books of Moses*, translated by
   Everett Fox [The Schocken Bible])

In these, the first two mentions of the heart in the Bible* (God is just getting ready to send the Flood to wipe out his disappointing human creatures), we encounter heart in two senses: as *a deviser of schemes* and *as something that feels*. In the Judaic tradition, heart is the crucible of a person's true essence, whether that essence is noble or wicked or in transformation. And, interestingly, although the Jews were the first people to arrive at an abstract notion of God and thus forbade images of him, he is represented from the very beginning as having a heart like theirs: a central place in him that can be hurt and angered and softened—and changed.

However, God spares Noah and his family, and a male and female of every species. They wait out the Flood on the ark that Noah built from God's instructions. God spares Noah, we are told, because "Noah was a righteous, wholehearted man who walked with God"

---

*There are over a thousand references to the heart in the Bible. A selective plunge into the Book of Psalms alone will give you a sampling of the scope and variety of the "heart phrase" as it is used throughout both Old and New Testaments. Before the day is over, it is likely that you and I will have used one or more of these phrases in conversation.

> Commune with your whole heart upon your bed and be still
> The fool has said in his heart, There is no God
> My heart teaches me, night after night
> Weigh my heart, summon me by night [note the Egyptian echo here]
> They have closed their heart to pity
> You have given him his heart's desire
> My heart within my breast is melting wax**
> May your heart live for ever! [the Psalmist is addressing God]
> Those who have clean hands and a pure heart
> The sorrows of my heart have increased

**"My heart is like wax; it is melted in the midst of my bowels" is from Psalm 22, the first lines of which Jesus is reported to have quoted from the

(Genesis 6:9). Fox translates *tamim* (the Hebrew word designating someone wholly sound, just, complete—the King James version prefers "perfect") as "wholehearted," and points out that God will later use the same vocabulary to make a covenant with Abraham: "Walk in my presence! And be wholehearted!" (Genesis 16:17).

For the ancient Hebrews, heart, *lev,* meant the seat of wisdom and understanding, the inner personality, the whole gamut of emotional life, as well as the collective mind, or mind-set, of the people: the mental heart as well as the fleshly heart—as when the aged Moses, addressing his people for the last time before they, but not he, get to enter Canaan after forty years of wandering in the desert, exhorts them to "circumcise the foreskin of your heart, and be no longer stubborn" (Deuteronomy 10:16). He was saying to them, in a tradition they understood: Our forefather Abraham made a *physical*

---

cross ("My God, my God, why hast thou forsaken me?"). The person in this psalm is in dire distress but nevertheless trying to hold on to a shard of faith. "But be not thou far from me, O Lord," he implores in a later verse. We find a similar notion of *the heart as wax* expressed by Ibn al-Arabi, the Sufi Islamic philosopher (1165–1240), who regarded the mystic's heart as something absolutely pliable and receptive. Just as wax receives the impression of a seal, this softened "heart of wax" is capable of taking whatever shape God imprints on it. Sufi mystics even today are referred to as "men of the heart." For them, spiritual vision is likened to "the heart's eye."

> You speak in my heart and say, "Seek my face"
> Strife is in their hearts
> My heart dances for joy
> Be strong and let your heart take courage
> Teach us to number our days that we may apply our hearts to wisdom
> There is a voice of rebellion deep in the hearts of the wicked
> I wail, because of the groaning of my heart
> My heart is pounding, my strength has failed me

covenant with God when he started the practice of circumcision for our people; now isn't it time, as you enter triumphantly into the land God promised us, to *internalize* that pact by doing the same thing to our *communal heart*?

Hebrews, the name applied to the early Israelites, comes from *ivri*, Hebrew for "those who crossed over," or "the ones from beyond." They were one of the nomadic peoples of Arabia believed by themselves to be directly descended from Noah's son, Shem—thus the name Semites. They tended to be sojourners rather than settlers and colonizers, and their nomadic origins, as later would be the case with Islam, saw God not in one defined place, but following along with them wherever they went. The nomadic way of life encourages frugal packing, and from that standpoint alone it is logical that the two wandering nations who developed monotheism carried only one god

---

My heart was hot within me
He knows the secrets of the heart
My heart is stirring with a noble song
My heart shall meditate on understanding
My heart quakes within me
There is corruption in her heart [the city]
It was you, a man after my own heart [who betrayed me]
His speech is softer than butter, but war was in his heart
My heart is firmly fixed
Reproach has broken my heart and it cannot be healed
Their heart was not steadfast toward him
Whose hearts are set on the pilgrims' way
Harden not your hearts
A crooked heart shall be far from me
My heart is smitten like grass and withered
Thy word I have hidden in mine heart
Their heart is as fat as grease
I will thank you with unfeigned heart
He heals the brokenhearted

in their luggage—and that god moreover invisible: they carried him in their hearts.

The Hebrew people first enter history through the biblical accounts of Abraham, who would have lived about 1800 B.C. in Ur, which was down the Euphrates River just below Uruk, the former kingdom of Gilgamesh. When Abraham was a young married man, his father, Terah, had moved the whole clan northwest from Ur to Haran. The original destination was to have been Canaan (the Palestine of the Bible) but for some reason they stopped and settled in Haran, and it was in Haran that Abraham first heard the call of the one God. This single creative God, who would invite Abraham to have a personal relationship with him ("Walk in my presence! And be wholehearted!") and enter into a covenant with him—moreover, an invisible God with a heart—was a moving and radically new concept. The human mind—and the human heart—took a giant step forward with Abraham's idea, and it is worth exploring how such giant steps can come about in the course of our evolution. What is happening here with Abraham is something we need to understand afresh today and carry forward some more: the invisible God with a heart can only be made manifest in the world by how we act and what we do.

Here are three stories that show Abraham moving toward his realization of this. The stories are from elaborations on scripture, called midrashim. Their function is comparable to those passages in biography where the biographer, using what evidence he has, illustrates possible "hidden moments" in his subject's life.

Taking their cue from a reference in Joshua (24:2–3) about Abraham's father and brother "serving other gods," early Jewish interpreters inferred that the father made his living carving and selling images of the popular Sumerian gods in wood, stone, gold, silver, copper, and iron, and may have worshiped them, or pretended to, for good business relations. It would have been a flourishing business, because the Sumerians had many gods controlling various aspects of their lives: there was a water god, a sky god, a moon god, a sun god, even a silt god. It seems Abraham's brother Nahor had no problem with the father's trade, but in the *midrashim* the idol business struck Abraham as both troubling and absurd, and his skepticism often takes the form of prankish rebellion.

In one story, Abraham serves a lamb dish to some of his father's idols and waits for them to eat. When they don't, Abraham takes an ax and hacks them into pieces, all but the largest. When the father comes in and demands an explanation, Abraham tells him, "I offered some food to your idols, but they quarreled over it, and the largest hacked the lesser ones to pieces."

"Don't mock me," says Terah. "These are only images of wood, made by a man's hands."

"If that's the case," Abraham replies, "how can they eat the food you set before them daily, and how can they answer your prayers?"

In another *midrash*, Faher Terah leaves Abraham to watch the shop for a few minutes. A man comes in to buy an idol and Abraham asks him how old he is. When the man answers fifty, Abraham says, "Fifty years old and you are going to bow down to this idol who was only made this morning?"

In a third story (from the *Apocalypse of Abraham*, translated by James L. Kugel in *The Bible As It Was*), the writer has Abraham himself narrate how he became disillusioned with his father's gods. This time Abraham, alone in his father's sanctuary of idols, discovers that a heavy stone god named Marumat has fallen at the feet of an iron god called Nakhin. "And it came to pass that, when I saw this, my heart was troubled, and I thought that I, Abraham, would be unable to return it to its place all by myself. . . ." Abraham calls his father, and when they are lifting Marumat together, the god's head falls off in Abraham's hands. Terah sends Abraham to fetch a chisel and Abraham watches while his father carves another body, attaches the head that fell off, and then smashes the old body. ("Then I said to myself, 'What are these useless things that my father is doing? Is he not rather a god to his gods, since it is by virtue of his sculpting and shaping, by his skillfulness, that they come into being? It would be more fitting for them to bow down to my father, since they are his handiwork.'")

In these stories, Abraham is confronting his father and the potential idol buyer and then himself with the absurdities of a life in which you sacrifice to *things* the nourishments meant for your fellow human beings and the worship due to God alone. I think of that sofa scene in *American Beauty* when, against all odds in their absurd and poisonous life, Lester and Carolyn Burnham rouse each other's passionate hearts once more—until she sacrifices the miraculous heart-moment to the four-thousand-dollar sofa she's afraid he'll spill beer on.

One can easily imagine how Abraham came to hear God's voice telling him to pack up his household and leave for an unspecified place. After his father died, the Chaldeans couldn't have had much use for someone who refused to worship their gods. The apocryphal Book of Judith says that Abraham was literally driven out of town.

Whatever the truths that led to these stories, Abraham was to hear and obey God for the remainder of his long life, even when God tested his faithfulness to the extreme, once even asking him to sacrifice his beloved son Isaac and intervening only at the last minute.

The five books of the Old Testament* chronicle Abraham's and his descendants' struggle to learn, and to teach others, how to "walk wholeheartedly" with the invisible God. As already mentioned, the aged Moses, recounting to the assembled Israelites their long jour-ney from Egypt before they cross over without him into the Promised Land, exhorts them to circumcise the foreskin of their heart. Moses also predicts their eventual exile into Babylon, where they will serve gods made by human hands of wood and stone, which cannot see or hear or eat or smell, but promises them that in exile they will find Yahweh, their god, "if you search for him with all your heart and with all your being" (Deuteronomy 4:29).

Historically it is uncertain just when the Hebrews entered Canaan—the thirteenth century B.C. is a popular guess. The golden age of Israel was from about 961–921 B.C. under David and Bathsheba's son, Solomon.

At the beginning of his kingship, young Solomon asked God for wisdom (also translated as "an understanding heart") and was given it, but by the end of his forty-year reign, his foreign wives had "turned away his heart after other gods," and "his heart was not

---

*Though I use the common appellation Old Testament, for simplicity's sake, I never forget the rabbi's wife who gently reminded me when I was going on about "the Old Testament," "We only have the one, darling." The correct name for the "Old" Testament is the Hebrew Bible, or the *Tanakh*, which is an acronym for *Torah* (the five books of Moses), *Neviim* (the Prophets), and K (K'tuvim, writings).

The Hebrew Bible is our primary source of information about the ancient Hebrews and their early culture and nationhood. Far from being a "religious manual," it is a collection over time of many materials: the oral sagas of their origins and genealogies, their myths, their poetry, their erotic love songs, their folklore, their philosophical literature (Job). But underlying all of these genres is the idea of God in constant relationship to them and how they are changed by it—*and he is changed by it*—over time.

wholly true to the Lord his God, as was the heart of David his father" (1 Kings 11:4). After Solomon's death the kingdom of Israel was split in half, thus bringing David's legacy to an end. Eventually both fragments fell to invaders, and after the siege of Jerusalem in 597 B.C. the Israelites were deported to Babylon, as had been predicted by Moses seven centuries earlier.

The people of Israel were right back where Abraham started from, twelve centuries earlier: in the land of Gilgamesh on the lower Euphrates. However, a priest named Ezekiel had a vision (so vividly described in Ezekiel 1 that it has been challenging—and defeating—visual artists ever since) and shortly after began prophesying to his fellow exiles. The first prophecies were not cheerful. Israel was to be brought even lower: Jerusalem and the temple of Solomon were to be totally destroyed. And in 586 B.C. these events came to pass.

At which point, Ezekiel's message shifts from doom to hope. The worst had happened. The exiles would return and build another temple. Directions were given by God for this temple in a city that would be called "the Lord is there" (Ezekiel 48:35). That temple still remains to be built (perhaps because it is to be an internalized temple?): a freshwater stream would flow beneath it in such abundance that the brine of the Dead Sea itself would be made sweet. More than the earlier prophets, Ezekiel emphasized the responsibility of each individual to obey God's commands; *it was up to each of us singly to break the chain of past injustices.*

It is through Ezekiel that God makes a startling extension of his covenant. He will not abandon that covenant, but will rebuild it on an even stronger base, the base of "a new heart" that will be able to walk accordingly with God and feel shame when it deviates. His promise amounts to that of a spiritual heart transplant: "A new heart also will I give you, and a new spirit will I put within you; and I will take the stony heart out of your flesh, and I will give you a heart of flesh" (Ezekiel 36:26–28).

Thus the evolving relationship of the Hebrews with their God: a God who could not be seen, but with whom you could walk and talk "heart-to-heart," whether you were a stranger in a strange land, a nomad wandering under the stars, king of your people for a brief span, or a heartbroken exile, waiting for return to the city, whose name will one day be Yahweh Shamah: "the Lord is there."

A new heart that will be able to walk accordingly with God and feel shame when it deviates: that is the kind of new heart I would like to have. That is the goal that goads me most in these evolving prophecies of a nomad people out of whose writings so much of our culture and ethics derives. They knew about the possibility of this new heart all those years ago, one with its own internal checks and balances, walking in the loose embrace of God, yet I feel that I haven't even scratched the surface of such a heart in myself. Why not? If not now, when? What's stopping me? What absurd little gods on pedestals am I feeding and worshiping? What four-thousand-dollar sofas are coming between me and my new heart? What voice in the night haven't I listened to, and what will I have to leave behind—and what might I find—if I set off into such terrifying freedom with only that voice for company?

VI. The Hindus

The Person the size of a thumb abiding within the body
always resides in the hearts of people. With the heart,
with insight, with thought has he been contemplated.
Those who know this become immortal.

—Svetasvatara Upanishad 3:13,
translated by Patrick Olivelle

THE UPANISHADS

The Upanishads, composed from about 600 to 300 B.C. in India,
comprise the oldest speculative literature of the Hindus. They mark
a dramatic breakthrough in human consciousness. Here is where the
enlightened individual self as container of the cosmic consciousness—God at home in you—begins to play a noticeable role. In
their own time, the Upanishads were appended to the earlier sacred
scriptures, the Vedas, to meet seekers' needs for connections
between the human organism and cosmic realities.

Upanishad means "connection" or "equivalence." It later came to
mean "a sitting down close to," as one does with one's guru, because
that was the way these connections were conveyed from master to
disciple. Just as the Hebrew Bible as we know it is a collection of
writings in different genres by a people in the process of discovering
themselves, the Upanishads is compiled from a common stock of old
stories and episodes, hymns, illuminative metaphors, aphorisms, and
dialogues between seekers and holy men. Giving less emphasis to personal gods and goddesses and focusing more on the God to be discovered within the depths of one's being, *as well as the necessary disciplines*

to approach it, the Upanishads point, again and again, to an interior place in ourselves where each of us can meet the ineffable source of being "wherefrom words turn back" (Taittiraya Upanishad 2:4).

In the Upanishads, the divine being already resides in the secret cave of our heart. But our mutual encounter becomes possible only when earthly impurities and bonds have been banished from that heart. The individual spiritual self, *atman*, is also the universal self, *brahman* (which means "holy power," or God); but the individual self is *unaware of this* until spiritual and physical disciplines, known as yoga, bring the union into consciousness. The Upanishads speak of the heart as the "great fulcrum of the cosmos." And the enlightened self, where *atman* and *brahman* can finally meet, "lives in the hub where the arteries meet."

A powerful current of similar thinking and feeling connects the Upanishads with many later "faiths of the heart," ranging from the beliefs of the Islamic Sufis to the preachings of Meister Eckhart, the thirteenth-century Catholic founder of German mysticism (who was condemned as a heretic). The kernel of all these faiths is the same: the God who lives yonder is put aside for the God who is at home in the human heart and radiates his effects outward from that power source.

The Upanishads greatly influenced (and comforted) "the philosopher of pessimism" himself, Arthur Schopenhauer (1788–1860), who was moved to offer them this grandiloquent, oft-quoted blurb: "The Upanishads afford the most rewarding and exalting reading possible in this world: they are the consolation of my life, as they will be of my death." Schopenhauer viewed the world as a place of unsatisfied wants and pains. He had no friends, never married, and was estranged even from his mother. The only escape from worldly disappointment, according to his philosophy, was to negate the will and renounce desire. Yet an important heart-note is struck in his ethics, which are based upon *sympathy*: If we can focus our moral will on someone else's hurt, feel it as our own, then we can at least make an effort to relieve the pain. This act requires a *uniting of head and heart*, as expressed in this passage from the only one of Schopenhauer's works ever to become popular in his lifetime (*Essays from the Parerga and Paralipomena*):

> It is vital to keep one's head, of course; but it is wrong to be so cold-blooded as to prevent the whole person, with heart and head together, from coming into action and being profoundly moved.

I was glad to learn that the lonely old philosopher in retirement did have as his companion a beloved poodle. He named her Atma—the feminine of *atman*, the self that exists as *brahman* in every individual.

When we were back with the Egyptians and their forty-two negative confessions, I referred to a young girl's illustration of the Steak Rabbit God. As we enroll in the school of the heart, we should be like her. When confronting texts from other times and cultures, read for a while with the mind—and then let your mind take a rest and see what in the material leaps out at you on its own, makes you smile, startles you with a contemporary recognition, ignites your imagination. Chances are that something in the material has spoken heart-to-heart to you from then to now. (The result is similar to what happens after you have grown weary of trying to stare an evasive star into focus: you turn away slightly to rest your vision, only to catch the star shining steadily at you out of the corner of your eye.)

Here is a story that leapt out at me from the Upanishads just when I was beginning to despair of ever getting my mind around Hindu beliefs. The following dialogue between a Brahman and a king depicts the place of the heart in ancient Hindu culture and also leaves me with images I can mull over.

There are different versions of the dialogue in the Upanishads. This is the one from the oldest Upanishad, the Brhadaranyaka (2:1), in my much shortened and paraphrased form.

A Brahman (priest and teacher, highest caste) comes on a gracious mission to a king (next caste down) and offers to teach him a formulation of the truth. Good, says the King, I'll give you a thousand cows for such a speech. Then everybody will hail me as a learned king.

The Brahman begins: It is the person up there in the sun that I venerate as *brahman* (God). The King breaks in: Don't start a conversation with me about him! I venerate him (that person in the sun) only as the supreme head and king of all beings. Anyone revering him as such becomes a supreme head and king himself.

The Brahman continues: It is the person up there in the moon that I venerate as *brahman*. The King breaks in: Don't start a conversation with me about him! I already venerate the moon as the great white-robed king Soma. Anyone revering him as such will have abundant soma (hallucinogenic herb) pressed out for him every day.

The Brahman then preaches that he reveres as *brahman* "that person" residing in lightning, space, wind, fire, water, the mirror, the sound drifting behind a man as he walks, the four quarters, the shadow. The King counters each postulate with: Don't start a conversation with me about him! and declares his limited allegiance to the element in question and what he expects to get from it but refuses to locate *brahman* there. Finally the Brahman says: It is the person here in the body that I venerate as *brahman*. To this last the

King retorts: Don't start a conversation with me about him! I venerate him only as the one possessing a body. Anyone who venerates
him as such will possess a body and so will his children.

The learned Brahman finally falls silent.

"Is that all?" the King asks.

"That's all," says the Brahman.

"But that is not enough for knowledge of *brahman*," the King says.

"Let me come to you as your pupil," says the Brahman.

"I'm not sure it's proper for a Brahman to become the pupil of a
king," says the King, "but I'm going to see to it that you perceive this
thing clearly."

Taking the Brahman by the hand, the King leads him to a sleeping
man. "O Soma, great god dressed in white," the King addresses the
sleeping man. "Get up."

Nothing happens until the King prods the sleeping man, who
awakens.

The King then asks the Brahman, "When this man was asleep,
where was the person consisting of the perception? And from where
did he return?"

The Brahman does not know.

The King explains: "When the man was asleep, the person consisting of perception, having gathered the cognitive power of the
man's vital functions into his own cognitive power, *was resting in the
space within the heart*. When that person takes hold of them, then
the man is said to be asleep. During that time, the breath remains in
the grasp of that person consisting of perception, as do the functions
of speech, sight, hearing, and mind. Wherever the man travels in his
dreams, those regions become his worlds. He may appear to become
a king or an eminent Brahman, he may visit the highest or lowest
regions.

"However, when a man is in deep, dreamless sleep, and is not aware of anything at all, this is what happens. There are seventy-two thousand* veins that run from the heart to the pericardium. He slips out of the heart through these veins and rests within the pericardium. He rests there oblivious to everything, just as a young person, or a king, or even an eminent Brahman, is oblivious to everything during sexual bliss."

The King then sums up his lesson for the Brahman. "Just as a spider sends forth its thread, or a fire sends forth many tiny sparks, so indeed do all the vital functions, all the worlds, all the gods, and all beings, spring from this self (*atman*). Its hidden name is 'the real behind the real,' for the real consists of the vital functions, and the self is the real behind the vital functions."

A passage rich in imagery, that. I, in my red nightgown, asleep and dreaming while multiple forms of "that person consisting of perception" soar and descend in Blakean swirls around my pillow into realms sublime and dreadful, into places I've been and places I haven't.

Or: my body in deeper and dreamless sleep, a smaller replica of it curled, *both protectively and protected*, inside the thin membranous space that surrounds my heart, while the *brahman-atman* connection continues to throb with the steady beat of the living organ.

---

*According to Joseph Campbell in his chapter on ancient India in *Oriental Mythology*, this teaching of the nerves or veins going out from the heart, together with its association with the states of dream sleep and of dreamless sleep, shows that the psychosomatic doctrine of yoga was already developed by 700–600 B.C. The mythical importance of the number 72,000 he relates to the 72 five-day weeks of the Mesopotamian calendar and to Plutarch's account of the killing of Osiris (the dead and resurrected Egyptian god who came to stand for each person's Self): in Plutarch, Osiris was clapped into his coffin (i.e., sent into a deep sleep) by 72 associates of Osiris's brother Seth.

And then I awaken, in easy possession of something I had no idea I knew before I went to sleep.

"My heart teaches me, night after night," chanted the Psalmist, and now—from that dialogue between the king and the Brahman in the oldest Upanishad—I understand better how this gets done.

RELIGIOUS HEART/ROMANTIC HEART: THE HINDU CONNECTION

In an introduction to *The Kama Sutra of Vatsayana*, John W. Spellman writes that the texts of Hinduism are like an ocean in which many fish live that eat one another. It surely has felt that way to me. Yet I believe I have found in this often contradictory ancient body of wisdom an answer to one important question: When did the religious heart get separated from the romantic heart? Or were they ever together?

Well, yes, they were—they are. The link is *kama*, the principle of desire. Without desire there would be no creativity, no need to get closer, no need to go out of oneself and make more life, or a larger life. And these needs are common to religion and romance. The Hindus grasped this truth long ago, that *desire is the source of all creation*, a concept that underscores the link between sexual love and godliness. What is a god, but one who creates? This is borne out in all representions of Kama, the young god of love and sexual desire, shooting his flower arrows from a bow of sugarcane strung with a row of bees; *kama* as sexual motif expressing the dynamic aspect of life in the art and architecture of India; *kama* in the amorously entwined couples in temple sculpture and other sacred places.

The connection between sexual desire and the desire to unite with the divine reached a highly developed stage in India. It may have reached as far as anybody has managed to get, before or since. The sex act was (and still is, in the worship of the Shiva lingam today) seen also as a symbolic union in which the participants represent the cosmic principles of creation. That being so, the *Kama Sutra* is more than just a handbook of positions for lovemaking. It is a guide for keeping the principle of desire alive and balanced in the human heart and therefore in the cosmos at large. If the impetus of desire is dead, what can happen? Gardens don't get planted, people don't get explored and loved, songs and poems don't get written, even the poor Creator is entombed in a "holy" sepulcher where nothing is permitted to change or grow.

Before we dip into the *Kama Sutra*, a warmhearted book containing a wealth of human understanding, tenderness, and tact, we need to know the place of *kama* in the four goals of life as defined by the ancient Hindus.

The four goals are: *dharma*, *artha*, *kama*, and *moksa*. *Dharma*, *artha*, and *kama* are to be practiced in this life; *moska* is the goal of ultimate liberation of the soul, or *atman*, from the cycle of rebirths so it can merge into the cosmic soul, *brahman*. Your hope of achieving *moksa* depends on how well you have fulfilled the three earthly goals of *dharma*, *artha*, and *kama*.

Dharma is right conduct, all the acts that pertain to one's moral and spiritual duties. In the first stage of your life, when you are a student, you are taught what these things are. *Artha* is the accumulation of wealth, material goods, security, and success. One of the duties of the householder is to begin each day pondering how to increase both *dharma* and *artha*. *Kama* is the enjoyment of appropriate objects by the five senses, and the consciousness of pleasure that arises from that contact. You are obligated to learn the proper means of enjoyment, and these proper means are contained in the *Kama Sutra*. If a conflict arises between *dharma* and *artha*, you must choose *dharma* over *artha*; if *dharma* is in conflict with *kama*, you sacrifice *kama*. Refreshingly straightforward, isn't it?

But how does this square with the Buddhist principle that desire and attachment cause all the misery and suffering in the world? It doesn't. That's what Spellman meant about Hindu texts being like an ocean full of fish that devour other fish. But for our purposes of heart-reading, we are not obligated to make things "square." We just ramble and see what leaps out at us from the textual foliage.

Here are a few highlights from the *Kama Sutra* that we might add to our heart skills today. Though the book was shelved under Philosophy in my bookstore, it would also be a good candidate for the "how to" and the "decorating" shelves. In the "Social Concepts" section of the *Kama Sutra*, a bachelor, or man about to become a householder, should set up his quarters thus: near water, surrounded by a garden, balmy with rich perfumes, containing a soft bed "pleasing to the sight" with white covering and canopy and a pillow at the top and at the bottom; and nearby, a couch, a stool containing flowers and "fragrant ointments for the night," a lute hanging from a peg made from an elephant tooth, a board for drawing, books, a toy cart, a dice board, some garlands of yellow amaranth flowers, and a pot for spitting. Martha Stewart couldn't have covered the accoutrements better. And yet what a wide-hearted vision of the "necessities" of *kama* compared to our grim lovemaking manuals of today.

Besides the obvious *kama* arts and sciences (singing, dancing, cookery, gardening, composing poems) to be studied by men, young maids, daughters of princes, and courtesans, a person should know how to: tattoo, prepare perfumes, color gems, teach parrots and starlings to speak, read someone's character from his features, play word games, and pay compliments. Every one of the sixty-four skills listed has to do with the enhancement of pleasure, the enjoyment of the gifts of the earth, and close attention to things and people. Heart skills.

Though the *Kama Sutra* dispenses detailed, almost hour-by-hour advice on how to live in society, how to find a wife and treat a wife, how a wife should spend her day and treat her husband, how a courtesan should live and what skills she should know, how a eunuch should behave, and how to attract others to yourself, Westerners tend to think of the *Kama Sutra* as a graphic sex manual alone, especially if they've never looked inside the book itself.* The section specifically dealing with the modes, skills, and ethics of sexual union constitutes less than one-fifth of the text. And that section *is* graphic, in the way you wish more instruction books that come with new household equipment would be—everything is coherently described, step by step, with no steps left out. ("Why can't this be as clear as the *Kama Sutra*?" I burst out yesterday when a friend and I were torturing our brains over the operating manual that came with a cappuccino machine.)

Yet the tone of the *Kama Sutra*'s "On Sexual Union" is always one of accommodation, preparation, and tender regard for the other person's specific needs and pleasures as well as a healthy respect for your own. Skills of the heart, whether in service to a lover, a parrot, an art, or a divine presence, call forth the same attributes of tact, appreciation, sensitivity, and *attention:* all of which are fueled by the desire to be closer to the object in question.

---

*Though I did recently come across a coffee-table volume of the *Kama Sutra*, with everything left out *but* the positions. Page after glossy page of two well-coiffed, well-exercised, very blond, pink, naked people dutifully coupled in close-up poses, their marketing smiles ablaze, with no background "tendernesses" to distract from the main product. No nearby waters, no soft linens, no flowers, no lute, no drawing board . . . no toy cart!

THE CHAKRAS

The Hindus also gave us the mystical physiology of the chakras, seven energy points where body and spirit are believed to intercon-nect. Each chakra ("disk" or "wheel") comes with its symbolic images and reflects a basic attribute of being alive. When all the chakras are opened up and flowing freely into each other, the person is fully conscious and enlightened.

Picture yourself sitting cross-legged, Buddha style. At the base of your spine, coiled between the anus and the genitals, the perineum, is your first chakra, *muladhara* (which means "root support"); its basic purpose is survival, its element is earth, its images are the ele-phant and the coiled serpent; in kundalini yoga, this coiled serpent must be coaxed out of unconsciousness so her root energy can rise through the system and unite with the force of knowledge. (Keep in mind that the chakras are meant as visualization techniques to guide you during the yogic disciplines.) Your second chakra, *svadhisthana* ("sweetness"), is in the lower pelvis; its basic purpose is sexuality and emotions, its animal symbol is a leviathan or water monster, and its element is water. Your third chakra, *manipura* ("fullness of jew-els"), resides in the diaphragm or solar plexus; its element is fire, its symbolic animal is the ram, and its purpose is power, will, and self-definition. It is the locus of vitality, but also of aggression. Contem-porary depth psychologists who see a correspondence between the Hindu chakras and our Western stages of consciousness surmise that our collective culture's prevalent location is at the *manipura* level—with evolutionary spurts toward the next level, *anhata*, the heart chakra.

Your *heart* chakra, *anhata* ("unstruck" or "unruffled"), takes you beyond the generative and survival levels into the region of relationship, compassion, and balance. Here a new thing rises into being, the discovery of your *purusa*, "that person the size of the thumb" described in the Upanishads as living in the heart. This tiny entity represents the first germ of higher consciousness, which can lift you above emotional and survival happenings; the "thumbling in your heart" can behold these turbulences without identifying with them. *Anhata's* element is air (the heart is embedded in the lungs) and its symbolic animal is the gazelle: shy and fleet of foot. Like values, convictions, feelings—heart qualities—the gazelle is elusive and likely to vanish if frightened. When you attain the heart level where the *purusa* dwells, you can envision *atman*, your individual spiritual self, and its connection to *brahman*, the universal self, or God. If you are a yogi, you now know that "I am it." Or, if you come out of another tradition, you could say with St. Paul, "It is not I that lives, but Christ that lives in me." When you reach the heart chakra, your life is not only subjective but objective; you no longer exist exclusively inside your own circumscribed life but partake of a larger one.

The fifth chakra, *visuddha* ("purification"), lies in the throat, the seat of speech; here you are at the gateway of the great liberation; here, like Buddha, your mind becomes illumined. The element of *visuddha* is sound, and the animal is once again the elephant, but in *muladhara* he was supporting the physical earth where you were rooted; in *visuddha* he supports the invisible realm of abstract thought. The purpose of your *visuddha* chakra is communication, to speak and be heard. However, now you have reached the level where you can convey the unseen truths to others. Your sixth chakra, *ajna* (to perceive), lies behind the brow—the so-called "third eye." It is your highest bodily center. Its element is light. Here *atman* is shining like a sun. *Ajna* has no animal symbol, but its shape is envisioned as a winged seed. Its purpose is intuition and psychic perception. In *ajna*, you are detached and objective, your man and woman power are united within you; you are re-created in a new form. The seventh chakra, *sahasrara* ("thousandfold"), is located in the cerebral cortex. Its element is pure thought. Its purpose is transcendence and understanding. In chakra pictures, *sahasrara* is often represented by a penis shape emerging from the top of the person's head.

VII. Siddhartha Gautama: The Buddha (563–483 B.C.)

Siddhartha had begun to feel the seeds of discontent within him. . . . He had begun to suspect that his worthy father and his other teachers, the wise Brahmins, had already . . . poured the sum total of their knowledge into his waiting vessel; and the vessel was not full, his intellect was not satisfied, his soul was not at peace, his heart was not still. . . . And where was Atman to be found, where did He dwell, where did His eternal heart beat, if not within the Self, in the innermost, in the eternal which each person carried within him? But where was this Self, this innermost?

—Herman Hesse, *Siddhartha*,
translated by Hilda Rossner

Hesse's fictional Siddhartha is not the Buddha of history, but a young Indian of the Brahman class who meets the Buddha but can't rest content with being his disciple. Hesse's hero has to find out his own answer to the enigma of his purpose on this earth just as the Buddha himself was compelled to do—and as Hesse himself did. (Hesse's *Siddhartha* exemplifies the perfect match of a novelist's personal struggle with the right material.) This exquisite short novel has become a classic in the Western world, treasured by the young and the not-so-young alike, because its author, a European, was able to embody the universality of the spiritual quest in the sixth-century Indian character bearing the same first name as the Buddha.

I first skimmed *Siddhartha* when my nephew was writing a paper on it in high school. I was ashamed of myself for my slapdash ingestion of this powerful and beautiful story—reading it with a rushed mind rather than a listening heart, so to speak; however, it gave us a basis for some good talk and didn't seem to infect my nephew, who loved the book and could identify with the hero's quest. Then, a year or so later, during an all-night bout (or blessing) of insomnia, I read *Siddhartha* slowly, savoring every word, and it left me with a vivid impression not only of the human spiritual journey whatever the era or the clime, but with a heartfelt grasp of the essentials of what the real Buddha worked out for himself and then took to the road to share with others for forty-five grueling years, until his death at the age of eighty.

"Perhaps the most striking thing about him," Huston Smith writes about Gautama Siddartha Buddha in *The World's Religions*, "was his combination of a cool mind and a warm heart." The cool mind shielded him from sentimentality and the warm heart kept him from indifference. Smith compares his gift for rational thinking to that of Socrates.

Every problem was subjected by the Buddha to cool, dispassionate analysis. As prescribed by the Upanishads-influenced Schopenhauer in his popular *Essays* (keep your head while allowing your heart to be moved), the Buddha was calm and confident in dialogue, yet his objective, critical side was remarkably balanced (writes Smith) by "a Franciscan tenderness so strong as to have caused his message to be subtitled 'a religion of infinite compassion.'" His acceptance of his mission to help and guide the whole desperate world of humanity regardless of personal cost "won India's heart as well as her mind."

In a nutshell, that is what the Buddhist strives for: achieving the rare combination of *a cool mind and a warm heart.*

✍ Practiced in more disparate cultures than any other religion for the last two and a half millennia, Buddhism is about the efforts of a human being to become enlightened and then to help bring about the enlightenment of others: about self-observation and ethical living; about clarity of mind and "infinite compassion." The Buddha preached that we all have it in us to become Buddhas (awakened ones), regardless of our previous lives or our positions in society. When admirers would ask the holy man, "What *are* you? A god? An angel? A saint?" Buddha would reply, "No. I am awake."

For those of us who did not grow up hearing the stories and legends of this great teacher, here is a sketch. Siddhartha Gautama was an Indian prince of the warrior class. (This is one notch below the Brahman, or priest, class.) His father's great wealth prevented him from seeing any suffering. At sixteen, he married a neighboring princess and had a son and lived a luxurious life until one day while riding he came across a decrepit old man. That day the prince learned there was a thing called aging, from which no one was exempt. On another occasion, he rode out and saw a body racked with disease lying by the road, and thus discovered sickness, and on another ride he encountered a corpse and became acquainted with the fact of his ultimate death. This completed the destruction of his sheltered life based on physical securities. Soon afterward he confronted a monk with a shaved head and begging bowl, and this became his call to break completely, at twenty-nine, with his old life and go in search of enlightenment on another plane.

At first he overdid everything. He immersed himself in Hindu philosophy with the foremost Hindu masters of his day. He then joined a band of ascetics and starved himself until he could poke his finger into his stomach and touch the ridges of his spine. After nearly dying, he came up with the principle of "The Middle Way": *give the body what it needs to function optimally.* The final phase of his six-year quest he devoted to rigorous thought combined with the raja yoga the Hindu masters had taught him. One evening, sensing that a breakthrough was near, he ate a bowl of rice and milk and sat down under a banyan tree (a sheltering east Indian fig tree that spreads and sends out adventitious branches to the ground, where they take root). There followed a temptation scene similar to the one Jesus of Nazareth would undergo half a millennium later. The Evil One, in Buddha's case, first paraded voluptuous women past him—unsuccessfully. Next he physically assailed him with torrential rains, hurricanes, and missiles of flaming rocks—to no avail. Then he tried to tempt Buddha with false modesty, challenging his right to attain enlightenment. Finally, when all else had failed, he tried to discourage Buddha: no one would understand him.

"There will be some who understand," the Buddha answered, and the Evil One was vanquished.

For forty-five years thereafter, the Buddha traveled India until he was old and infirm, training monks, counseling the perplexed, comforting the distressed, preaching his Four Noble Truths and the Eightfold Path he had worked out during his six years of withdrawal. Endowed with great practical and organizational abilities, he founded communities that would spread beyond India and eventually make Buddhism the most prevalent religion in all of Asia, and in our century, a revitalizing force in Western religious life. Understanding the principles of creative renewal, he broke up every day's busy schedule with three periods of meditation, and took a three-month annual retreat with his monks during the rainy season. Just like Jesus, he wrote nothing, but has had plenty of interpreters since. In his lifetime, he avoided what he called "the thickets of theorizing," preferring to teach with stories. "Be lamps unto yourselves," he liked to say.

The Four Noble Truths are:

1. Life is colored by suffering and dislocation.
2. The cause of this suffering is "desire for private fulfillment," all those inclinations that increase separateness from others, all those desires for self at the expense of others.
3. The cure? The overcoming of all such desires.
4. How can this be accomplished? By following the Eightfold Path.

What is the Eightfold Path? As a prelude, choose right associations; link yourself up with people whose values you admire. Then:

1. Follow Right Views (the Four Noble Truths).
2. Seek Right Intent. ("Make up your hearts as to what you really want.")
3. Practice Right Speech (veracity and charity).
4. Practice Right Conduct. (Do not kill, steal, lie, be unchaste or drunk.)
5. Practice Right Livelihood. (Do not practice professions that are incompatible with spiritual seriousness.)

6. Practice Right Effort. (Pace yourself. Be like the ox, carrying a heavy load through the mire. Keep going.)

7. Practice Right Mindfulness. (A much-loved Buddhist text opens with the words: "All we are is the result of what we have thought.")

8. Practice Right Concentration. (This refers to the techniques that came out of Hinduism's raja yoga, the disciplines of body and mind that clear our hearts of delusion, craving, and hostility and allow the mind to repose in its true condition.)

It would remain for the Tibetans to perfect the luminous compassion of Buddhism into Vajrayana—"the Diamond Way"—an ultimate level in the school of the heart.

Here is one last story about the warm heart of Buddhism's founder. In his final hours, as he lay dying from dysentery after having eaten a meal of tainted boar's flesh with his friend Cunda the blacksmith, the Buddha worried that Cunda might feel responsible for his death. So he sent a message to the smith that there were two meals in his life that had been exceptional blessings: the first was the meal taken just before his enlightenment under the banyan tree, and the second was the meal taken with his friend Cunda that was now opening the gates of Nirvana for him.

Wouldn't you have liked to know this man?

VIII. The Chinese

In China, whose five-thousand-year-old civilization has outlasted all others so far, the word for heart and mind is the same: *xin*, or *hsin* (depending on whether you're using the modern or old style of transliterating Chinese characters). Not only is the heart the king of bodily organs, but it is also "the thinking heart." True knowledge, Confucius taught, lies in the heart. He created and taught an ethical system that emphasized "human-heartedness," stressing balance in the heart. And in an early collection of Taoist wisdom, *Hsin-Shu (Method of the Heart*, circa 400 B.C.), it is written: "If the heart is in order, then so too are the senses."

In Chinese medicine, whose comprehensive mind-body science is becoming increasingly respected by Western doctors, the *hsin* is the command center, which manifests itself as consciousness and intelligence.

CONFUCIUS (551–478 B.C.)

Confucius, a candid, scholarly man of humble origins who died thinking of himself as a failure, lived at a time when Chinese society was coming unglued. Unquestioned customs and traditions of the Chou dynasty had given way to the lawless horrors of the Period of the Warring States. Rival armies no longer drank together or exchanged polite compliments from their chariots before getting down to the business of battle, nor did they nobly hold their prisoners for ransom afterward. Surprise attacks and mass slaughters had become the modern way. The worst excesses peaked in the century after Confucius's death, but his restorative influence was already infusing the devastated civilization. Huston Smith trenchantly sums up his influence (*The World's Religions*, HarperSanFrancisco, p. 154):

> Though Confucius did not author Chinese culture, he was its supreme editor. Winnowing the past, underscoring here, playing down or discarding there, reordering and annotating throughout, he brought his culture to a focus that has remained remarkably distinct for twenty-five centuries.

But why did the man who is called "the mentor and model of ten thousand generations" think he had failed? Because he did not see the results of his "editing" in his lifetime. No ruler would give him a public office and let him put his ideas into practice. Finally, at sixty-seven, he quit wandering from state to state, offering his unwanted advice, and spent his last five years editing and teaching the classics of China's past. Like Jesus, Confucius showed up at the right time and left behind a new "heart-oriented" system of ethics, though both died without seeing their vision put into practice. It is interesting how Buddha, Confucius, Lao-tzu, Socrates, and Jesus, whose teachings have shaped the world, *never wrote anything down*. Yet they all attracted loving and dedicated disciples who carried on their work.

The prime virtue in the Confucian system is *jen*. *Jen* is the combination of "human being" and "two." It is best translated as "human-heartedness." In the sociable Confucian ethic, one cannot become a person by oneself. *Jen* simultaneously embraces humanity toward others and respect for yourself. If you are a person of *jen*, you have the capacity to measure the feelings of others by your own. In public and private life, this means you have a largeness of heart that seeks to affirm others as you yourself would wish to be affirmed.

The Confucian ideal is *chun tzu*, translated as "humanity at its best," or "the superior person." If you have attained *chun tzu*, you are like an ideal host. Your attitude is not "What can I get from these people?" but "How can I accommodate them?" Because you have your own standards, you can take a gracious initiative rather than cling to convention. You *are* the best of convention because you have assimilated *li*, the social grammar of right behavior. The Confucian *li* covers every aspect of human conduct that fosters a sense of community. It's all there, in the best of the Chinese classics, winnowed and enlivened by Confucius and taught by him to his students: everything from greetings, table manners, gestures of deference, filial behavior, leadership, worship, and leave-taking. Because you have practiced *li* and made it your own, you have a rightness of heart.

> *If there is righteousness in the heart, there will be beauty in*
>   *the character.*
> *If there is beauty in the character, there will be harmony in*
>   *the home.*
> *If there is harmony in the home, there will be order in the*
>   *nation.*
> *If there is order in the nation, there will be peace in the world.*
> —*The Analects of Confucius*, translated by Arthur Waley

For Confucius, how people treated one another in this life took precedence over concerns about otherwordly things. When he was consulted about how best to serve the spirits of the dead, he would answer, "If you aren't able to serve people, how do you expect to serve the spirits?"

The resilience of the Confucian tradition has bounced back refreshed, most recently after the Cultural Revolution of 1966–76, when China's political leaders tried to erase the country's cultural past. The "Anti-Confucius" campaigners organized a nationwide "critique" of the *Analects* to force literate people to realize its outdatedness, but the measure backfired when the enforced readership fell in love with its timeliness all over again.

LAO-TZU (B. ?604 B.C.) AND THE *TAO TE CHING*

The tradition is that Taoism evolved from a man called Lao-tzu, which simply means Old Boy or the Old Fellow. According to legend, the Old Fellow, disgusted by his people's refusal to cultivate the natural goodness he advocated, climbed on a water buffalo and headed west toward Tibet. In Chinese art there are many pictures of this.

Going a step further than Confucius, who gave up trying to influence his country but continued to teach in it, Lao-tzu embarked on self-exile and solitude. However, the gatekeeper at the Hankao Pass sensed something special about him and begged the old man to at least leave behind a record of his beliefs for the civilization he was deserting. Lao-tzu agreed, and returned to the gate three days later with a little book of five thousand characters, which can be read in thirty minutes. The gatekeeper, Yin Hsi, became a famous Taoist worthy. Scholars say the *Tao Te Ching* was not written down until later, but whoever wrote it down, "the little book" fathered by the Old Fellow is still being read and translated two and a half thousand years later. When I began researching the Chinese part of "The Heart Through Time," I found six English translations to choose from at my small Woodstock bookstore, the Golden Notebook, including a new one by Ursula K. Le Guin, who was brought up on the Paul Carus edition of 1898. In her preface, she writes that her father used to mark the chapters in the *Tao Te Ching* that he wanted read at his funeral; and now she has marked the chapters she wants read at hers.

Tao means "the way," or "the path." It also means "the way in which one does something." It is the road traveled and it is also the way we make the journey our own. In the school of philosophy known as Taoism, *tao* means "the way the universe works." To be "in" *tao* is to be in alignment with the natural workings of the universe.

How do we get in alignment? Through creative quietude, or *wu wei*. *Wu wei* is not idle inaction or "doing nothing." It is a suppleness, a yielding up of our striving conscious wills to the resources of a deeper self in tune with *tao*.

> *Do you have the patience to wait*
> *till your mud settles and the water is clear?*
> *Can you remain unmoving*
> *till the right action arises by itself?*
> —*Tao Te Ching*, translated by Stephen Mitchell

In many ways the teachings of the *Tao Te Ching* and the teachings of Confucius approach the righteous heart from opposite viewpoints. Confucians are more practical: "When in doubt, consult the tradition of human-heartedness at its best." Taoists are more mystical: "When in doubt, empty your mind of all thoughts, let your heart be at peace; give yourself up to whatever the moment brings." Confucians work for balance, the Doctrine of the Mean. Taoists respect the dynamic imbalance, from *yin* to *yang* and back, as being the very essence of life—which you might as well get in harmony with, since you exist inside its melody. Together, Taoism and Confucianism balance the Chinese character. "Confucius roams within society, Lao-tzu wanders beyond," the Chinese like to say.

Since Buddhism made its way into China around A.D. 67, that country has been unique in being able to handle three belief systems simultaneously. Here in the West, and in India, religions are exclusive, even competitive. As Huston Smith points out in *The World's Religions*, it makes no sense to think of someone being a Christian, a Muslim, and a Jew all at once, or even a Buddhist and a Hindu. But traditionally every Chinese could be Confucian in ethics and public life, Taoist in private life and hygiene, and Buddhist at the time of death. A Chinese person can wear a Confucian hat, Taoist robes, and Buddhist sandals.

HEART IDEAS IN CHINESE MEDICINE

By the time of Confucius's death, the earliest texts of Chinese medicine—which is also a philosophy—were being collected into a work that would become known by 200 B.C. as the *Huang Ti Nei Ching Su Wen* (*The Yellow Emperor's Classic of Internal Medicine*), a highly inclusive and metaphorical treatise covering every aspect of the patient presenting a physical complaint. At its ideal best today, Chinese medicine is a holistic and *wholehearted* approach to the human organism with all its mental, emotional, behavioral, social, and spiritual complexities. More and more Western doctors are finding it a rich addition to their traditional diagnostic tools.* Whereas Western medicine has up until now tended to address the various systems separately (cardiovascular, gastrointestinal, musculoskeletal, neuro-

*For a readable, insightful, and well-organized presentation of how Chinese medicine is practiced by one Western M.D. and psychiatrist, I recommend Leon Hammer's *Dragon Rises, Red Bird Flies: Psychology and Chinese Medicine* (Station Hill Press, 1990), from which I have gleaned most of the following material.

humeral, endocrinological, lymphatic, reproductive, urinary, respiratory, metabolic, sensory) and to develop theories about the diseases
related to those organs, Chinese medicine looks for connections and
movements between the systems and posits theories about mind-
body health. The doctor studies and treats the person (looking for
that person's special imbalance), and not just the disease. The four
steps of Chinese diagnosis are *looking, listening, asking,* and *touching.*
To be healthy, your five organ systems or spheres of influence (heart,
lungs, spleen, liver, kidneys) have to be in harmony. The most
important of the five is the heart, but it works in conjunction with
the other systems. The first thing a Chinese doctor will do is examine the "heart line" that runs down the center of your tongue,
because the heart is thought to control the tongue and the throat.
Then he will feel your overall pulse and also your heart pulse. If
there is no heart pulse it means the heart is closed.

Each part of a person can fall into various imbalances and dishar-
monies, causing different symptoms. Yin (the receptive) and yang
(the active) being the two contrasting aspects of energy, there can be
yin deficiencies and excesses and yang deficiencies and excesses in
each organ system. Here are some possible imbalances in the Heart
system (capitalized to distinguish the entire concept from the single
organ itself) that can cause trouble:

Keeping in mind that the yin energies of the Heart beget your
insights and the yang energies provide your expression of them, a
person with Heart Yin Deficiency will be rigid and inhibited, unre-
ceptive to new ideas, with common symptoms of set jaw, tight neck
and back, and reduced respiration. A person with Heart Yin Excess
is likely to be easily agitated and fatigued due to heightened receptivity to the inner chaotic world of the unconscious and constant sensory and emotional impingements from the outer world (I recognize

a lot of myself in the description of the Heart Yin Excess type) and also manifests certain physical "armorings against too much input," such as tight neck, rigid spine, and forgetting to breathe. Someone with Heart Yang Deficiency would have difficulty putting his ideas into execution and have periods of feeling worthless and melancholy, whereas someone with Heart Yang Excess might be a compulsive communicator whose productive output is voluminous but lacking in quality or development; this type is prone to anxiety, agoraphobia, and sudden physical collapse because the drained Heart Yin energies haven't had a chance to replenish their receptivity.

This is only the shallowest draft of an ancient healing art. What I like about it, though I haven't yet availed myself of its techniques,* is its abundance of metaphors that help me to visualize the inner workings of my mind-body. I know very well what the cardiological heart is likely to fall prey to: angina, arrhythmia, congestive failure, the Big Attack, but it enlarges my scope of useful knowledge to know that, in Chinese medicine, Heart can be diagnosed as "Heart Full" (always too tired), which leads to "Heart Large" (cardiac failure), "Heart Small" (results from prolonged birth delivery, or a sudden, profound shock; can lead to coronary artery disease), "Heart Tight" (worrying, racing mind, sleeplessness; leads to angina), and "Heart Closed" (energy has become very restricted or stagnant; person is always in some emotional difficulty, and likely to be vengeful or spiteful).

---

*However, Robert's five sessions with a local Chinese doctor and acupuncturist cured the arthritis in his knee after other treatments and medications had failed.

IX. The Japanese

The word Shinto means "the way of the kami" [gods], but man is capable of walking that way. He is not called to an impossible task. The basic attitude toward life is expressed by the word *makoto*. *Makoto* is common both to kami and to men. The term is usually translated as honesty, conscientiousness, or truthfulness. . . . Truth in the sense of *makoto* involves an inner searching of the heart which is just as important as the outer confronting of the situation.

—Floyd H. Ross, *Shinto: The Way of Japan*

A Shinto rite . . . can be defined as an occasion for the recognition and evocation of an awe that inspires gratitude to the source and nature of being. And as such, it is addressed as art (music, gardening, architecture, dance, etc.) to the sensibilities—not to the faculties of definition. . . . And to retain this sense [of gratitude and awe], the faculties remain open, clean, and pure. . . . And to this there is the corollary that the pure heart follows the processes of nature. Man—a natural thing—is not evil inherently, but is in his pure heart, in his natural being, divine. The fundamental terms are "bright heart" (*akaki kokoro*), "pure heart" (*kiyoki kokoro*), "correct heart" (*tadashiki kokoro*), and "straight heart" (*naoki kokoro*). The first denotes the quality of a heart shining brightly as the sun; the second, a heart clear as a white jewel; the third, a heart inclined to justice; and the last, a

heart lovely and without misleading inclinations. All four
unite as *seimei shin*: purity and cheerfulness of spirit.
—Joseph Campbell, *The Masks of God:*
Oriental Mythology

In the above-cited volume, Campbell relates an amusing and reveal-
ing exchange reported to have taken place at the Ninth International
Congress for the History of Religions in 1958, in Tokyo. A Western
sociologist, after having been taken by the Japanese Organizing
Committee to every major Shinto shrine in the country and having
witnessed a number of Shinto rites, grew more and more confused
by this uniquely Japanese form of worship. He had observed the
stately procession of the priests in their white vestments and black
headdresses and black wooden shoes. He had heard the eerie risings
of the spiritlike music, the pluckings of the *koto*, the alternating light
and heavy drumbeats, the wind instruments and great gongs min-
gling with the sounds of wind and pines and sea. He had watched the
heavily garbed dancers, some masked, others not, moving in dream-
like trance against intoned utterances. Then the whole thing would
be over, the ritual done. But what did it all mean?

Finally at a conference lawn party in a Japanese garden of rocks
and lakes and pagodas and paths leading into unforeseen vistas, he
confronted a Shinto priest with his dilemma. I've been to your
Shinto shrines and I've seen quite a few of your ceremonies, he
explained, but I still don't get your ideology or your theology. The
Japanese priest pondered the visiting sociologist's question and then
respectfully answered with a smile, "We do not have ideology. We
do not have theology. We dance."

The Japanese are famous for their ability to assimilate outside
influences and transform them into something uniquely Japanese.

When Buddhism entered their island world in the sixth century (a Korean king sent the emperor of Japan a huge golden Buddha, along with a packet of sutras written in Chinese characters, which provided the comparatively primitive Japanese with a written form for their native language), they soon conjoined it with their traditional folk religion, Shinto. Most Japanese religious households today have two altars: one for the Shinto *kami*, and one for *botoke*, the Buddha. There is even a term in common usage, *kamibotoke*, which embraces the deities of both religions. Kami altars are associated with life and the avoidance of whatever threatens vitality and productivity, Buddha altars with death and the veneration of ancestors or those who are in the process of becoming ancestors. Both Shinto and Buddhist practices follow the annual cycle and the life cycle. Virtually all Japanese marriages are Shinto ceremonies; funerals are almost always Buddhist.

But on the whole, Japanese awe and gratitude for the present moment, a heartfelt obeisance to the smallest and dailiest of artifacts, takes precedence over philosophizing about the transcendent. For instance, there are annual requiem services for lost and broken needles! Japanese worship is grounded in the here and now, the "small moment" in which the secular is made sacred. A clean, unencumbered heart also means a clean, unencumbered house, and the Shinto New Year is observed by cleaning house, yard, and road, paying off debts, and "cleaning the slate," inside and out.

Both Buddhist and Shinto practices in Japan emphasize the creative, playful approach rather than the grim, rational climb toward enlightenment. Earnest Zen novices are teased and baffled, and sometimes slapped, by their masters, or presented with koans— questions or riddles that can't be "solved" but only grown into. Likewise, Zen flower arranging (*ikebana*) and the Zen tea ceremony (*chanoyu*), both activities combining spontaneity with highly organized form, were perfected by Japanese Buddhist monks. If you can't get to Japan to experience a tea ceremony, rent the Hiroshi Teshigahara movie *Rikyu*, based on the novel about the sixteenth-century Buddhist monk who was cultural mentor and confidant to the warlord Hideyoshi, who attempted to invade China and Korea and who ordered Rikyu's death for not approving of his schemes. The film's portrayal of the two men can also be seen as a paradigm for the struggle that goes on within the psyche of this civilization that Campbell has described as "glass hard yet intensely poignant."

HAIKU

> *Father and mother,*
> *long gone, suddenly return*
> *in the pheasant's cry*

> *Nothing in the cry*
> *of cicadas suggests they*
> *are about to die*
> —Bashō (1644–94), *The Essential Bashō*,
> translated by Sam Hamill

The heart concept is central to the practice of haiku, Japan's distinct form of poetry. Though haiku comes from the word *haikai*, which means "sportive" or "playful," it has a precise rule of form: it must be seventeen syllables in a 5/7/5 pattern. Characteristically it is attentive to a specific time and place and season, and it records or implies the evanescence of all existence. Its images arise naturally out of the *kokoro*—the heart-mind; they are *felt and perceived* at the same time.

Even today, Japanese critics evaluate a poem by two standards: its *kokoro* (sincerity, conviction, "heart") and its craft. In his prefatory remarks about Japanese poetry in *The Essential Bashō*, Hamill quotes several critics: One says of a poem, "Plenty of heart, not enough words." Another says, "interesting *kokoro*, but a rather common form." The ideal haiku is not only spare, clean, swift, and resonant; it has *amari-no-kokoro*, a heart-soul quality that reaches beyond the words and leaves an indelible aftertaste.

If you translate a haiku poem, you must keep the 5/7/5 scheme. Thus Bashō's:

> *Neko no tsuma*
> *hetsui no kuzure yori*
> *kayoi keri*

becomes in Sam Hamill's rendering:

> *The housecat's lover*
> *visits her frequently through*
> *the burnt-out oven*

X. The Greeks

THE DURABLE HEART OF
BABY DIONYSUS ZAGREUS

In the pantheon of Greek mythology, Zagreus ("the torn") was the offspring of one of Zeus's famous rapes. Posing as a snake, Zeus wrapped himself around Persephone, queen of the underworld, and she bore him Zagreus, a horned infant. Zeus gave the rule of the world to his son, who immediately climbed on the throne and mimicked his daddy by brandishing a thunderbolt in his tiny hand. Zeus's wife, Hera, was not amused by this illegitimate interloper and enlisted her cronies the Titans, an older generation of out-of-favor gods, to distract the child with rattles and a looking glass. While baby Zagreus was admiring himself in the looking glass, the Titans rushed him, tore him limb from limb, boiled his body with herbs, and ate it, all but the heart, which Zeus's daughter Athena saved and handed over to her father.

Zeus swallowed his son's heart for safekeeping, pulverized the Titans to soot with his lightning bolt (from this soot sprang the human race), did a rerun of his snake seduction with Semele, the goddess of the moon, regenerating his torn son in her womb. Hera got wind of this and disguised herself as an old crone, who tempted the pregnant Semele to ask Zeus to show himself to her in his resplendent god form. Semele asked him and Zeus obliged, whereupon the poor moon goddess was burned to a crisp. Zeus plucked his unborn son from the ashes, fashioned a cozy little pouch for the fetus between his thigh and genitals, and when the full nine months were up, Dionysus "the twice born" emerged from his father's groin. Before Hera could murder the child again, Zeus sent him to be raised in the household of a distant royal couple.

Dionysus became the god of the moon, the night, wine, moisture, ecstasy, orgies, and the Greek theater. Drama, the art form that combines poetry, music, gesture, and spectacle, descends to us directly from Dionysian ritual. The twin masks of tragedy and comedy can be traced to the worship of Dionysus, who personified the duality of human nature. In Dionysian festivals, which filter down to us in

such rituals as Halloween and Mardi Gras, masks were worn to sym-
bolize the surrender of everyday reality and the means of transform-
ing identity.

Periodically, Dionysus went mad. The madness was attributed to
a last-minute curse by Hera, but when you consider all his heart
went through at such an early age, he might have managed it very
well on his own.

THE HEART SEPARATES FROM THE HEAD: THE FATHERS OF PHILOSOPHY

The heart inside him growled low with rage
as a bitch mounting over her weak, defenseless puppies
growls, facing a stranger, bristling for a showdown—
so he growled from his depths, hackles rising at their outrage.
But he struck his chest and curbed his fighting heart:
"Bear up, old heart! You've borne worse, far worse,
that day when the Cyclops, man-mountain, bolted
your hardy comrades down. But you held fast—
Nobody but your cunning pulled you through
the monster's cave you thought would be your death."
—Homer (circa 700 B.C.), *The Odyssey*,
translated by Robert Fagles

The heart, the knot of the veins and the fountain of the
blood which races through all the limbs, was set in the
place of guard, so that when the might of passion was
roused by reason warning that something was amiss due
to an outside cause or to the inner lusts, [the heart]
would signal to everything in the body and thus allow

the principle of the best to have the command over all
of them.

—Plato (427–347 B.C.), *Timaeus*

For nature, when no other more important purpose stands
in her way, places the more honorable part in the more
honorable position; and the heart lies about the center of
the body. . . .

The heart is the perfection of the whole organism. Therefore the principle of the power of perception and the soul's
ability to nourish itself must lie in the heart.

—Aristotle (384–322 B.C.), "On the
Parts of Animals" and "Concerning the
Soul" from *Aristotle Selections*, edited by
W. D. Ross, 1927, Oxford translation

Within the time span of the quotations cited above, the Greeks are
beginning the process—a process still going on today—of differentiating the mind from the heart. From this point on, we are leaving
behind the "whole heart" visions of the ancient world. The heart
drops a few notches and loses pride of place as the centerpiece of consciousness, the undisputed locus of one's character. By the fifth century B.C., the Greeks, devoted to logic and reason and physical proofs,
had begun debating on *exactly where in the body* the soul was located.
Alcmeon of Crotona, one of Pythagoras' pupils, situated the soul in
the gray mass of the brain. The physicians of the time, including Hip-
pocrates himself, were unable to agree about the soul's exact where-
abouts. They willingly turned the problem over to the philosophers,

who for a while placed the seat of consciousness in the midriff or diaphragm (*phrēn*). To Homer's protagonist Odysseus, the heart is a place of excessive and unruly emotions. "Torn in thought, debating, head and heart," he has to conduct mental dialogues with it: Calm down! Bear up! Remember you've been in a rage before! The heart of Odysseus is no longer the inner sun, the "god-light" of the Egyptians, or the bedrock of his character, good or bad, as the Hebrews understood it; nor is it the inner residence of the holy Self of the Upanishads, or the "fire element" begetter of insight and expression in the Chinese heart. It is the barking bitch in the chest who needs to be reasoned with, admonished, and cajoled into rational behavior.

Plato divided the honors of place: the *immortal* soul was situated in the head; the *mortal* soul was located in the heart. The heart was a guard, a sentinel. In obedience to the head and its higher powers of reason, the heart's job was to fend off the assaults of the "subphrenetic" (sensual) desires boiling up from the liver.

His pupil, Aristotle, rejected the division: the soul was an entity, he said; therefore it could be in only one place, and that place would logically be the central organ (*kentron*) of the body, the heart. The soul, a kind of inner fire giving warmth and light, guided the body from the heart. Aristotle, whose passion was biology, maintained that the brain was cold and therefore could not give life. Whereas the heart, he said, was "the hottest bodily part."

For the Greeks the heart does not play a fundamental part in their systems of ethics or beliefs. They were more philosophical and less "heartful." Little wonder that the God of Aristotle (the "unmoved mover") was scarcely aware of the world it had created, whereas the God of the Hebrews was so intensely involved in the affairs of his people that his heart was often grieved.

In the company of these two major figures of Western philosophy, whose names have become adjectives for major ways we think and perceive, we are off and running into the era of left-brain glories. Propelled by Platonic abstract ideas and ideals and by Aristotelian emphasis on deduction and investigation of the concrete, the big two millennia of "head work" are under way.

In this brand-new millennium, we have some catching up to do if we are to balance "head work" with "heart work," and bring the heart and head back together again at a higher level of consciousness.

SOCRATES (?469–399 B.C.)

Let us look at it together, my dear fellow: and if you can challenge any of my arguments, do so and I will listen to you. . . .

—Plato, *Crito**

Though Socrates wrote nothing about the heart—Socrates left no writings at all; he preferred the give-and-take of dialogue, which came to be known as Socratic dialogue—I can't in good conscience leave the Greeks without an affectionate salute to him. Socrates was another of those nonwriting teachers whose personality keeps eluding and overpowering his gospelers and biographers. We catch lovable glimpses of him between the lines of his reporters and recorders (Aristophanes, Xenophon, Plato, and Aristotle), all of whom had strong personalities themselves—as well as axes to grind. His mis-

---

*Plato's account of Socrates' prison dialogue with his friend Crito, who is trying (unsuccessfully) to persuade him to sneak out of prison and escape his fate.

chievous, warm, intensely *personal* essence bounces up from their
texts like sunshine flirting with a page of homework and disarms
your heart.

Here he is, giving his deposition before an Athenian court of law.
(He has been accused of believing in deities of his own invention—
he claims he has an "inner divine companion" who alerts him whenever he is in error—and of setting a bad example for youth by his
Socratic method of questioning people, a method deemed impertinent by those who are shown up as fools):

"If you put me to death, you will not easily find anyone to take my
place. It is literally true, even if it sounds rather comical, that God
has specially appointed me to this city, as though it were a large thor-
oughbred horse which because of its great size is inclined to be lazy
and needs the stimulation of some stinging fly [the gadfly]. . . . All
day long I never cease to settle, here, there, and everywhere, rousing,
persuading, reproving every one of you."

And here he is, condemned to death, in his final hour in prison,
after having conducted a lively give-and-take discussion with his
friends about the immortality of the soul:

"You, Simmias and Cebes and the rest, will each make this journey someday in the future, but for me the fated hour, as a tragic character might say, calls even now. In other words, it is about time that
I took my bath. I prefer to have a bath before drinking the poison,
rather than give the women the trouble of washing me when I am
dead." (Both translations are by Hugh Tredennick, in *The Collected
Dialogues of Plato*, Princeton University Press, 1978.)

Socrates lived and died embodying heart qualities: humor, propor-
tionality, a steadfast view of the larger picture, which included loyalty
to his inner voice: "human-hearted behavior," as the Confucians
would say. Like Buddha, writhing in the death throes of dysentery

and not wanting his blacksmith host to feel bad about the tainted meat, Socrates in his final moments also is concerned for the feelings of people who will survive him, in this case the women who will lay out his body.

XI. Jesus of Nazareth (? 4 B.C.–A.D. ? 26–36)

Then Peter replied, "Explain the riddle to us."

He said, "Are you still as dim-witted as the rest? Don't you realize that everything that goes into the mouth passes into the stomach and comes out in the outhouse? But the things that come out of the mouth come from the heart, and those things defile a person. For out of the heart emerge evil intentions, murders, adulteries, sexual immorality, thefts, false witnesses, blasphemies. These are the things that defile a person. However, eating with unwashed hands doesn't defile anybody."

–Matthew 15:17–20 (*The Five Gospels*,
new translation and commentary by
Robert W. Funk, Roy W. Hoover,
and The Jesus Seminar)

Only what comes from your heart can make you unclean, Jesus told the Pharisees and scribes from Jerusalem who had traveled to his hometown to question why he and his disciples did not observe the

Jewish purity laws and wash their hands before they ate. In the Judean society of Jesus' day, ritual washing was not just a matter of hygiene. It divided the world into "the clean" and "the unclean." Then he turned back to the crowd gathered around him and continued to teach. "Listen and try to understand: it is not what goes into the mouth that defiles a person but what comes out of the mouth that defiles." The Jerusalem delegation must have departed in high dudgeon, because Jesus' disciples later tell him he has given offense. "Never mind them," he says. "They are blind guides of blind people. If a blind person guides a blind person, both will fall into some ditch." At this point, Peter, who often assumes the role of obtuse spokesman for the others, asks Jesus to explain the riddle again. Exasperated, Jesus proceeds to spell out the purgative function of the alimentary tract from ingestion to elimination, and reiterates that it is only what comes out of the mouth *from the heart* that can defile a human being. He has turned upside down the old religious purity laws of how and what—and *with whom*—one can eat. If there's something bad in my heart, not only am I befouled by its presence inside me, but when it comes out of me it pollutes my surroundings.

The most revolutionary part of Jesus' teaching was that a good inner disposition—a good heart—is more important than following codes for correct external behavior. It's as simple as that, yet the literal-minded and the orthodox sticklers for form keep missing it. Where is this God's kingdom of yours, they keep asking him. What is it like? When is it coming? How should we behave to get in? Give us some rules.

And he keeps telling them, it's here, it's all around you but you haven't recognized it, it's inside you, it's spread all over this earth, and the only rules you need worry about are loving God with your whole heart and loving one another as I have loved you. In *Jesus: A*

Revolutionary Biography, John Dominic Crossan sums up the Nazarene carpenter's essential message thus: "He was neither broker nor mediator but, somewhat paradoxically, the announcer that neither should exist between humanity and divinity or between humanity and itself. Miracle and parable, healing and eating were calculated to force individuals into unmediated physical and spiritual contact with God and unmediated physical and spiritual contact with one another."

Jesus' message was that the Kingdom of God was available to anybody who sought it, male or female, sick or well, rich and powerful, poor and powerless, Roman, Greek, Samaritan, or Jew. And nobody had to go through any political or ecclesiastical hierarchy to qualify for occupancy. There was not just a room but a mansion for anyone who wanted to live in God's house. "Let not your hearts be troubled: you believe in God, believe also in me. In my Father's house are many mansions: if it were not so, I would have told you. I go to prepare a place for you" (John 14:1).

During his intense, short, itinerant ministry, estimated to have been between one to three years, he never traveled more than ninety miles from home, never settled in one place or established "brokerage headquarters" anywhere, never wrote anything except some symbols or letters in the sand when some self-righteous people were castigating a fallen woman. Being of the peasant class, he may have been illiterate, though it is now surmised that, growing up four miles from the Hellenistic city of Sepphoris in Galilee, he might have spoken Greek as well as Aramaic, and quite possibly even attended Greek plays. But in Roman-occupied Palestine, the charisma and verve with which he proclaimed and embodied his message in local gathering places was considered dangerous enough to get him executed. He spoke healing words—and *touched*—anyone who came to

him for help, including lepers. He ate and drank with sinners, out-
casts, tax collectors, women, and gentiles in a world where meal-
taking functioned as a rigorous marker of social boundaries. His language was urgent and provocative. He chose images and figures of
speech that his audiences could relate to: old wine in new skins, lost
sheep and coins, master-servant relationships, good soil versus rocky
ground, leaven (yeast) working its way secretly up through flour,
buried treasure, laborers' wages. He invited listeners to imagine
everyday scenes they were familiar with and see through those
scenes into spiritual realities that their own hearts could attest to.
These truths were often subversive, such as the famous mustard
seed parable.

> And he said, "With what can we compare the kingdom
> of God, or what parable shall we use for it? It is like a
> grain of mustard seed which, when sown upon the
> ground, is the smallest of all seeds on earth; yet when it is
> sown it grows up and becomes the greatest of all shrubs,
> and puts forth large branches, so that the birds of the air
> can make nests in its shade" (Mark 4:30–32).

As Crossan points out, the mustard plant is "a pungent shrub
with dangerous take-over properties" that attracts birds within culti-
vated areas where they are not desired: "Something that you would
want only in carefully controlled doses—if you could control it. It is
a startling metaphor, but it would be interpreted quite differently by
those, on the one hand, concerned about their fields, their crops, and
their harvests, and by those, on the other, for whom fields, crops,
and harvests were always the property of others."

Like Buddha, Jesus directed people to the sacred kingdom within.

Both taught that enlightenment came through the development of an imaginative vision that can transform each of us as individuals and help bring about the enlightenment of others. Jesus also continued the tradition of his own forebears, the Hebrew prophets and psalmists, who held incessant dialogues with the world of the spirit and preached that our supreme good lies in maintaining rightful relations to its unseen order. How did one go about this? Through the heart, the seat of wisdom and understanding. "Commune with your whole heart on your bed and be still. My heart teaches me, night after night. You speak in my heart and say, 'Seek my face.' Thy word I have hidden in my heart."

The heart of the original Jesus movement was a sharing of things material and things spiritual. The first followers were *heart* followers. The first evangelists spoke and corresponded their faith in heart images:

And the multitude of them that believed were of one heart and one soul (Acts 4:32).

And a certain woman named Lydia, a seller of purple, of the city of Thyatira . . . whose heart the Lord opened (Acts 16:14).

And he that searcheth the hearts knoweth what is the mind of the Spirit (Romans 8:27).

Forasmuch as ye are manifestly declared to be the epistle of Christ ministered to us, written not with ink, but with the Spirit of the living God; not in tables of stone, but in fleshy tables of the heart (2 Corinthians 3:3).

That Christ may dwell in your hearts by faith . . . (Ephesians 3:17).

Purify your hearts, ye double-minded (James 4:8).

For if our heart condemn us, God is greater than our heart and knoweth all things; Beloved, if our heart condemn us not, then we have confidence toward God (1 John 5:20).

Only when the Jesus movement became the official religion of Rome under Constantine in A.D. 312 was Christianity codified. The emperor ordered all Christian bishops to gather at Nicea, near Constantinople, and put a unified creed into writing so it could better be imposed on the empire and the world. At that imperial convocation, the Church became head as well as fleshy heart, and one of the most powerful brokerage firms the world has ever known opened for business.

Yet the Nazarene carpenter's revolutionary proclamation of the inner kingdom is still working its subversive leaven inside and outside of churches and inside our hearts and minds. It was H. G. Wells who said either there was something mad about the man, or else our hearts were still too small for his message.

Although some twenty gospels (which mean testimonies of "good news") have survived, either in whole or in part from the first three centuries after Jesus' birth, only four were chosen by the Church Fathers to be included in the New Testament. In the fragmentary *Gospel of Mary*, discovered in Cairo in 1896, which Bible scholars now date between A.D. 90 and 150, Mary Magdalene is speaking with authority to the disciples. They are confused after Jesus' death and she is reminding them of the essence of their teacher's message: he embraced them and told them to "be of one heart." But now they have lost courage and ask Mary, "How shall we go about the nations and preach the gospel of the Human One? If they did not spare him, how will they spare us?" Mary embraces them and says to her brothers, "Do not weep and do not grieve and do not make two hearts, for his grace will be with you all and will protect you . . . because he has prepared us. He has made us Human Being." (In some translations, it is "He has made us Man." But as "Man" is nongeneric in Coptic, "Human Being" would be the more accurate rendering. The important thing is the use of the singular and the startling concept it points to: the possibility of a communal heart. Mary does not say "he has made us men," or "he has made us human beings.") And after Mary has said these things, "she turned their hearts inward, to the Good, and they began to practice the words of the Savior."

What would a communal heart be like? What would have to happen to bring such a thing into being around one conference table or in a single committee meeting—*or in a single church?* What would have to be left outside the door? (Perhaps in a box labeled: Please Deposit All Personal Vendettas, Agendas, and Ambitions Here.) The image of a barn-raising comes to mind when I try to imagine a community of individuals who could "be of one heart" in an endeavor. Let's try to think of some more.

XII. Muhammad (A.D. ?571–632), Prophet of Islam

To those of us whose first introduction to Islam was a sea of angry foreigners shaking their fists at "the American devils" on our television screens during the Iran hostage crisis, it may come as a surprise to discover that Muslims view their religion as the third and final revelation in a Western faith that began with the Hebrew Torah and

continued with the teachings of Jesus. They accept Jews and Chris-
tians as "People of the Book," like themselves. They revere Jesus as a
prophet of the true God and believe that if he had been given a longer
career, like Muhammad, or if the Jews had not been so powerless
under Roman occupation, he might have systematized his teachings.
According to them, his work was completed by their prophet,
Muhammad, to whom the Koran (the Arabic "Quran" means "The
Recital") was revealed in segments over a period of twenty-three years.

As each new segment or chapter (*sura*) was revealed, Muhammad
recited it, the "professional remembrancers" among his followers
memorized it, and the literate ones wrote it down on palm leaves and
stones, or whatever was at hand. The revelations caused him intense
creative labor pains. It felt like having his soul torn away from him,
he later said. It required total submission; *Islam* means "surrender,"
or "submission." He sweated, often had to lower his head between
his knees, and sometimes lost consciousness. Often a revelation was
incoherent: he had to "collect it in his heart" and wait for the meaning to surface in clear wording. (In Chapter 75 of the Koran, God,
speaking through the angel Gabriel, cautions Muhammad not to
move his tongue in haste, rather to let "Us" gather it in his heart and
cause it to be recited as it ought to be recited.)

The Koran is not sequential; it can be browsed in any order.
When it was put into book form, editors arranged it according to the
length of the segments, the longest ones coming first, the shortest
last. Cherished by the Arabic-speaking world as a masterpiece of clas-
sical Arabic prose, its emotional power is said to be untranslatable.
Neither a historical narrative nor an argument, it takes the form of
divine speech: God, or Allah, speaks in the first person, through
Gabriel, to Muhammad. An image that might describe its elliptical,
allusive, unchronological movement is God splashing about in the sea

of his creation, surfacing according to divine whim to remind believers of his infinitely various gifts, mercies, and potencies and command them to honor him and be compassionate to all his creatures. To some Westerners, the Koran is irritatingly abstruse and repetitive. Wasp-tongued Victorian Thomas Carlyle called it "a wearisome, confused jumble" and maintained that nothing but a sense of duty could carry any European through it. But as Karen Armstrong reminds us in *A History of God*, "the Koran was not meant for private perusal but for liturgical recitation. When Muslims hear a sura chanted in the mosque, they are reminded of all the central tenets of their faith." Muslim children learn large portions of the Koran "by heart," thus etching into their neural pathways its maxims and warnings and guarantees for later guidance and assurance.

Having first experienced the Koran for the purposes of exploring its heart aspects for this book, I confess I am smitten by its evocative imagery and sensuous language (as translated into English by the Iraqi scholar and publisher N. J. Dawood). It is unfamiliar enough to be exotic and yet tells fresh stories of familiar figures. ("Jesus, son of Mary, remember the favor I bestowed on you . . . so that you preached to men in your cradle and in the prime of manhood . . . how by My leave you fashioned from clay the likeness of a bird and breathed into it so that, by My leave, it became a living bird" [5:110].) Its chapter titles alone send the imagination skittering down all sorts of paths: "The Cloaked One," "The Night Journey," "The Soul-snatchers," "He Frowned," "She Who Was Tested," "The Overwhelming Event," "Smoke," "The Ant," "The Poets," "The Cave."

In the Koran, the heart is the organ of discernment and therefore the most vulnerable target of corruption. In Chapter 114 the Prophet is enjoined by God to pray for refuge "from the mischief of

the slinking prompter who whispers in the hearts of men." In Chapter 50, God reminds the Prophet of all the mighty generations of
unbelievers he has destroyed, citing Noah's unlucky contemporaries. "They searched the entire land: but could they find a refuge?
Surely in this there is a lesson for every man who has a heart, and
can hear and see." The "intelligence of the heart" is a special kind of
imaginative intelligence, which combines knowing and loving into a
single function. It is a way of seeing "with the heart." The Islamic
mystics, the Sufis, would later elaborate on this "thought of the
heart," and "eye of the heart," and create a range of levels for that
inner sensorium known as the heart. Its outermost level, for a Sufi, is
the breast (sadr), seat of the emotions. Within this are the fleshly
heart (qalb), the pericardium (fu'ad), and the inner heart (lubb).

Only those who possess the inner heart can heed and recall mes-
sages from the divine.

Muslims see God's revelation to humankind as passing through
four great stages. First, God revealed his oneness to Abraham. Second, God gave Moses the Ten Commandments. Third, God gave us
the Golden Rule, do unto others as you would have them do unto
you, through Jesus, and finally, through Muhammad's twenty-three-
year recitation of the Koran, God provided explicit instructions as to
how the believer should live, covering everything from the treatment
of wives and rightful occasions for warfare, to eating and drinking.

The Five Pillars of Islam, the principles that regulate a Muslim's
life are: profess the one and only God; be constant in prayer (five
times daily: just before dawn, just past noon, midafternoon, sunset,
and after nightfall); give charity to the needy (one-fortieth of all you
possess, annually); observe Ramadan, the revolving holy month on
the lunar calendar, by fasting from dawn to dusk (fasting includes
food, drink, and smoke); and make at least one pilgrimage in your

lifetime to Mecca, where God gave his revelation to his messenger Muhammad.

Muhammad's personal story and the lore surrounding it is rich in heart material. Born into Mecca's leading tribe, the Quraysh, who claim to be descended from Abraham's son Ishmael, Muhammad was orphaned very early. At age five, he reported that he had been walking in the fields when two men clothed in white approached him, took out his heart and removed a black clot from it, then replaced it in his breast. His foster brother claimed to have witnessed this incident.

Muhammad spent his early manhood working the caravan routes as far north as Syria, conversing along the way with Jewish mystics, Christian monks, and desert-dwelling anchorites, storing up their scriptures in his highly retentive memory. From all accounts he was a warmhearted, just, and compassionate man, sensitive to human suffering, disgusted by the cynicism and immorality of his contemporaries and by the constant warfare between Arab tribes that kept them from pooling their resources and becoming a united people. At twenty-five, he married the wealthy widow merchant Khadija, whose caravans he managed. Though she was fifteen years older, their friendship and mutual respect had ripened into love, and she was to remain his steadfast supporter and best friend until she died. It was she who got him through the night of his "calling," when an overwhelming presence squeezed the breath out of him three times and commanded him in Arabic "*Iqra!*" ("Recite!"), until Muhammad found these words pouring from his mouth: "*Recite in the name of your Lord who created—created man from clots of blood. Recite! Your Lord is the Most Bountiful One, who by the pen taught man what he did not know*" (Chapter 96).

Muhammad was horrified. He thought he had become demon-possessed and was planning to throw himself off the side of the mountain when a huge man straddled the horizon, announced him-self as the angel Gabriel, and called Muhammad "the apostle of God."

As Karen Armstrong perceptively points out, Muhammad, unlike the Hebrew prophets, had no established tradition of "the terrifying otherness of God" to orient or console him. The only consolation he had was his wife, Khadija. He crawled to her and begged her to shield him from this terrifying presence. She reasoned him out of his fears, reminding him that he was kind and just and *sane*. She sug-gested they consult her Christian cousin, who was learned in the Scriptures. The cousin had no doubts that Muhammad's revelation was from the God of Moses and the prophets and had been appointed to bring the Arabs a scripture in their own language.

Muhammad was eventually convinced, and began to preach to his own tribe, the Quraysh. As few prophets do, he lived to see the fruits of his revelations change the course of his people's history. Not only prophet, but warrior, statesman, and administrator, he articulated a system that transformed a belligerent rabble of tribes into an Arabia unified in government and religion under Islam. His first convert, his beloved Khadija, died when he was approaching fifty. As with Jesus, women were among his earliest converts and the Koran is female-friendly. It strictly forbade killing female babies, or even showing dis-appointment when the baby turned out to be a girl; it gave women legal rights of inheritance and divorce, and addresses believers as "both men and women" (Chapter 33). The Koran does not pre-scribe the veil for all women, only for Muhammad's wives as a mark of respect. After the loss of Khadija, Muhammad exercised the Arab option of taking several wives. He had nine official wives, including two Jewish women. His favorite was the outspoken Aisha, whom he married when she was nine, though they did not consummate the union until she reached womanhood.

Only after the death of its founder, as with Christianity, did Islam get preempted by the men. Muhammad died in Aisha's arms after a short illness in his early sixties. He lived simply and mended his own clothes until the very end and was said to have been cleaning his teeth with a toothpick, a fond habit of his, shortly before he expired.

Two heart qualities of Muhammad the person strike me as vital to his extraordinary achievement. He must have possessed a huge capacity for open-mindedness (and its twin virtue, openheartedness) to have informed himself so thoroughly about the beliefs of other cultures during his youthful years on the caravan routes. How many of us, in our daily business dealings or even our foreign travels, would make a real effort to get under the surface of whatever would be today's equivalent of the Wandering Jew or Christian desert monk that Muhammad took an interest in? There would have been the language barriers, for a start, not to mention all those strange, off-putting customs and habits of a foreign mind-set, but Muhammad's curiosity and sensitivity to others reaped riches out of strangeness for him and the Arab people. He also obviously was able to love another human being deeply and faithfully, thus forging "a marriage of true minds" with his Khadija. She, in turn, could serve as his voice of reason and total supporter, his "other half" who came to his rescue when he doubted the sanity of his visions and might otherwise have hurled himself off the side of a mountain.

XIII. St. Augustine (A.D. 354–430): The Autobiographical Heart

But to whom am I telling this story? Not to you, my God, rather in your presence I am relating these events to my own kin, the human race, however few of them may chance upon these writings of mine. And why? So that whoever reads them may reflect with me on the depths from which we must cry to you. What finds a readier hearing with you than a heart that confesses to you, a life lived from faith?

–Augustine, *The Confessions*, II, 3, 5, translated by Maria Boulding, O.S.B.

It is the heart of Augustine that has most affected psychology, both as a field of thought and as everyday life where heart means feeling, my own interior nature, the secret chamber of my person.

–James Hillman, *The Thought of the Heart and the Soul of the World*

Here it is, the first full-fledged autobiography; the story of a person's life written by that person; a connected, organized narrative, shot through with introspection, telling how "I" became what I am now. The genre of autobiography differs from the memoir in that it is not concerned primarily with the personages and events of the writer's professional life (politics, the theater, etc.) but with the personal journey. It differs from the diary form in that it is meant *from the start* to be read by others.

Augustine began writing *The Confessions* in his forty-third year, one year after he became bishop of Hippo (Annaba in Algeria today). He called it "my confessions in thirteen books." Cynics have suggested he wrote it as a way to win over his less-than-enthusiastic new congregation; its admirers take it as he hoped it would be received, as a retrospective journey through "the immense court" of his memory, tracing his passage from babyhood (he said his memory was helped by observing his own infant son out of wedlock) to a proud, ambitious young professor who very much enjoyed the pleasures of the flesh ("Make me chaste—but not yet" is one of his most famous preconversion prayers) and then into a period of violent floundering into joyful conversion, followed by continued searchings. He wrote that he wanted his testament to be the kind of personal record that would "arouse the human mind" and turn the reader's affections toward the invisible God he himself could never get enough of.

Cast in the form of one long prayer to God, but explicitly meant to be overheard by the world, *The Confessions* is considered to be one of the finest documents in history of a change of heart. Evelyn Underhill attributes its lasting significance to Augustine's remarkable powers of self-analysis and expression and to the fact that he was a "natural mystic," someone who has a rich, personal, and vivid grasp of unseen realities.

Heart is the lode word of *The Confessions*. In his very first paragraph, Augustine announces its central role to his story: "Our heart is restless until it rests in you." This oft-quoted utterance might serve as the plot summary for the entire work. *Inquietus* (restless, unquiet) is Augustine's favorite adjective for describing the unstable condition of the human heart, the yearning imbalance that tilts, or flings, the individual toward God.

A great lover of the Psalms (which are in many ways the forerunners of autobiography), he borrows and builds on their extensive heart imagery and forges vigorous new images out of the raw material of his own passionate experience. His heart is a field owned by God (II, 3, 6). His heart is "our secret dwelling," his and God's; or, in another translation, "our shared bedroom" (VIII, 8, 19). When he is distracted and can't pray, his heart becomes "a bin . . . stuffed with a load of idle rubbish" (X, 35, 57). He reports admiringly that the devout Bishop Ambrose's heart was that holy man's "secret mouth," in which Ambrose chewed the bread of God's word (VI, 3, 3).

Augustine warns his own soul to "take care that the ear of your heart be not deafened by the din of your vanity" (IV, 11, 16). Recalling the turbulence of his conversion at the age of thirty-three, he writes that the argument in his heart "raged between myself and myself" until all his wretchedness was dredged up and heaped together "before the eyes of my heart" (VIII, 12, 28).

In *The Confessions*, the heart is pure protean marvel. It is mouth and ears and eyes. It is a dwelling with a door of its own, on which truth can knock, enter, illumine with the light of certainty, and rain down gentleness within. A heart can be tested, crushed, darkened, broken, hurled hither and thither, taken hold of, pegged down, made to stand still, inebriated, and impregnated by the Spirit. It can pant with anxiety and seethe with feverish, corruptive thoughts, or be the starting place for our climb of the upward paths, singing our songs of ascent.

"A human being is an immense abyss," writes Augustine, "but

you, Lord [paraphrasing Jesus in Matthew 10:30], keep count even
of his hairs. Yet," Augustine adds, "even his hairs are easier to number than the affections and movements of his heart" (IV, 14, 22).

In his provocative essay "The Thought of the Heart," psychotherapist James Hillman calls *The Confessions* "the first book of
psychology developing an idea of person as experiencing subject."
The downside of this, Hillman says, is that we Westerners have
seized eagerly upon Augustine's concept of the "personalized heart,"
the subjective heart that relieves itself through chronicling its feelings and telling its personal story, but we have stopped short of
Augustine's overarching aim. Psychotherapy or autobiography does
not, according to Hillman, free or renew the confessor unless we recognize—as Augustine *did* recognize—that prayer, a devotion to the
divine in the heart, completes the process. ("Confession corrects
personal experience, but does not remove us from it," but "by praying we move out.")

Addressing, questioning, calling on another who is not we, a
being beyond our ken, enables us to move beyond our autobiographical boundaries. We are more than we know, and these exhortations
to the "divine in the heart" become a supreme act of the creative
imagination by which we enlarge those boundaries. (That is what I
hoped to convey at the end of my novel *Father Melancholy's Daughter*,
when twenty-two-year-old Margaret Gower, having chronicled her
personal history to date, addresses she knows not Whom in her
diary. "Oh, You. Who are You? What do You want of me? What will
I be doing on this day next year? . . . Do you know Yourself, or is it
left partly to me? Are You withholding my life from me, or unfolding
it with me? Are You an eternal parent or are we eternal partners?")

Only nine of the thirteen books of *The Confessions* comprise
Augustine's autobiography. Having reconstructed himself through

memory, he steps over the threshold of personal history and, in the final four books, conducts passionate explorations into memory, time, eternity, and the book of Genesis. He breaks into eloquent poetry ("Late have I loved you, Beauty so ancient and so new! Lo, you were within, but I was outside, seeking there for you" [X, 27,38]). He summarizes his discoveries, continues the search for more. With his newfound self, and always addressing God, he achieves every writer's dream: he seems to be able to write anything! He is understanding his life as a model of the very creation that is beyond him and also within him.

As Patricia Hampl points out in her insightful preface to the Vintage edition of the Maria Boulding translation (p. xxiv):

> He makes the central, paradoxical discovery of autobiography: memory is not in the service of the past; it is the future that commands its presence. Yet how bizarre the truncated modern notion of "seeking a self" would seem to Augustine. . . . For Augustine, the memory work of autobiography creates a self as the right instrument to seek meaning.

The self as an instrument for seeking further meaning: yes. But first we have to discover and create that self before we can move on—or out.

St. Augustine's emblem is either a flaming heart, which in religious art stands for the utmost fervor, or a heart pierced by an arrow, which stands for deep repentance under conditions of extreme trial. He is the patron saint of brewers, printers, and theologians: a good all-around mix.

XIV. The Romantic Heart: From Courtly Love to Valentines

THE TROUBADOURS

Everyone has heard of courtly love, and everyone knows that it appeared quite suddenly at the end of the eleventh century in Languedoc. The characteristics of the Troubadour poetry have been repeatedly described. The sentiment [of the poetry] is love . . . of a highly specialized sort, whose characteristics may be enumerated as Humility, Courtesy, Adultery, and the Religion of Love. The lover is always abject. Obedience to his lady's lightest wish, however whimsical, and silent acquiescence in her rebukes, however unjust, are the only virtues he dares to claim. There is a service of love closely modeled on the service which a feudal vassal owes to his lord.

–C. S. Lewis, *The Allegory of Love*

"Never before have I heard of such a thing: you freely place yourself so completely in my power without the slightest instruction from me?"

"My lady," he said, "the power comes from my heart, which commits itself to you; my heart has given me this desire."

–Chrétien de Troyes (circa 1140–circa 1190), "The Knight of the Lion," *Arthurian Romances*, translated by William W. Kibler

Augustine was still alive when Western civilization as he knew it collapsed. Refugees poured out of Rome into Africa, bringing horror tales of its dying throes. As the first autobiographer lay sick and dying, the Vandals were already headed for Hippo, which they would destroy a year later. What we call the Dark Ages (roughly A.D. 476–1000) had begun, and Europeans would be too busy surviving onslaughts from the barbarians for the next five centuries to have much time for art or study or introspection.

Yet Islam, which, only a century after Muhammad's death, had begun its rapid spread, was, by 1000, enjoying the high to late summer of its fabulous culture, and Muslim philosophers and scientists and mathematicians, architects, artists, and poets were keeping the fires of learning stoked and ablaze in all the places Islam had conquered, from Granada to Jerusalem.

Ironically, the major stimulus for the new upthrust of passionate love appearing in the twelfth century seems to have been Western Christendom's determination to trounce these very conservators of human enlightenment and to wrest back the Holy Land from them. Papal authority promised every Crusader against Islam a remission of time spent in purgatory and, in the case of death during an expedition, the status of martyr. Europe embarked on its first Holy Wars. The Crusades supplied an ideal outlet for bored husbands, younger sons of landowners, and adventurers who had nothing to lose and everything to gain.

With husbands going off to fight, and unattached knights passing through, it also provided for those left at home an ideal setup for what came to be known as courtly love. Again ironically, this new kind of love that found its way into castles is thought to have come from Islamic Spain, where women had a good deal of freedom and were often poets themselves. At any rate, courtly love must have been most welcome to the medieval chatelaine, whose marriage was usually a business arrangement and whose husband considered her his property. How refreshing to have a lover who by definition was not a husband, a man who didn't fling himself down on you still smelling of the stable, but got washed up and dressed and kept an abashed distance from you and composed love songs in your honor! However much he idealized you or projected his own fantasies on you, the exchange was at least a first step toward feeling yourself recognized as an individual.

Courtly love developed its own etiquette that stressed restraint, sentimentality, secrecy, pining and inner suffering, and a faithful and constant obsession with the beloved. Eventually there was a rule book, written by a cleric in Eleanor of Aquitaine's famous Court of Love at Poitiers, where courtiers sat around debating the fine points of this new pastime: romance. Andreas Capellanus, in his *Rules of Courtly Love*, sets down the proper conduct for lovemaking between a man and woman who are not married—and cannot be and don't want to be, because marriage kills romance. (However, one rule succinctly states that it's not proper to fall in love with a woman you would be *ashamed* to want to marry.) Another rule cautions that a love easily attained is of little value: the more difficult the pursuit of the lady, the greater the prize.

There is even a rule stipulating that whenever a lover suddenly catches sight of the beloved, *his heart must palpitate.*

The maxim is that *obstruction* is what keeps desire stoked. Eight centuries later, how much have things really changed? "Humanity does not pass through phases as a train passes through stations," C. S. Lewis writes in his essay on courtly love in *The Allegory of Love;* "being alive, it has the privilege of always moving yet never leaving

anything behind. Whatever we have been, in some sort we are still."
And, indeed, as I went down the list of Andrew the Chaplain's rules
from Eleanor's court (*The feeling of love is always increased by true jeal-
ousy*, etc.), I began to feel uncomfortably at home. Then I realized
this advice was right out of my mother's Court of Love tutorials just
before I started going out with boys: "Be hard to get." "No kiss, ever,
under any circumstances, before the third date." "*Keep him jealous.*"
Dating in the 1950s and much of the 1960s still had a lot in common with courtly love, except for the goal. No longer were its pre-
cepts and strategies adhered to in order to prolong a passion *outside
respectable marriage*, but to frustrate the crazed petitioner into making
a proposal of respectable marriage.

However, I would venture to bet that romantic love, whatever
the era and between whomever, will continue to be stoked by
obstructions and kept blazing by poetic restraints. As the American
poet Sara Teasdale wrote, "No one worth possessing can be quite
possessed."

But where, other than the palpitating organ required of the
lover, was the heart in all this? "We may readily admit that [the
troubadours] were often not very perceptive about the human
heart," historian Colin Morris says in *The Discovery of the Individual
1050–1200*. "Indeed one doubts whether troubadour love can really
be regarded as an encounter with other people." The poet-lover
shows little interest in his lady's character, and most often sees himself when he looks into her eyes. Morris even speculates that the
whole phenomenon of courtly love and its poetry was more about
self-analysis and the introspective experience of being in love. The
real center of interest in troubadour lyrics is not so much the lover
or the mistress but one's own very interesting self.

CHRÉTIEN DE TROYES

"Following one's heart" was central to the work of this court poet employed by the daughter of Eleanor of Aquitaine, but he was a subtler and better-trained writer than the average troubadour. In his skills of characterization, symbolism, and inner monologue, he was far ahead of his time. "The space devoted to action that goes forward only in the souls of his characters was probably beyond all medieval precedent," conjectures C. S. Lewis, who goes on to declare him "one of the first explorers of the human heart" and therefore "among the fathers of the novel of sentiment."

Chrétien's literary career extended from about 1165 to 1190. He was one of the first to popularize the Arthurian legends of Britain. The flower of his achievement is his *Lancelot*, in which he tells us in the opening lines that Eleanor's daughter, the countess of Champagne, commanded him to write, providing him with the story of the secret love of Lancelot and Guinevere and even stipulating how she wanted it treated. Chrétien obeyed, as a court troubadour must, and by the time he was done, he had produced a work that not only could have served as a fictional guide to courtly love but was also an eminently readable tale, rising to mystical allegory at times, of the actions inspired by the emotions of a single human heart, that of his protagonist, Lancelot. Chrétien also steps farther than most courtly love chroniclers over the threshold of the bedroom—but all in good taste. Here, at the end of his humiliations and travails on Guinevere's behalf, is Lancelot (and his heart), in his lady's arms at last:

> The queen stretched out her arms towards him,
> embraced him, clasped him to her breast, and drew him
> into the bed beside her, showing him all the love she

could, inspired by her heartfelt love. But if her love for him was strong, he felt a hundred times more for her. Love in the hearts of others was as nothing compared with the love he felt in his. Love had taken root in his heart, and was so entirely there that little was left over for other hearts. Now Lancelot had his every wish: the queen willingly sought his company and affection, as he held her in his arms and she held him in hers. Her love play seemed so gentle and good to him, both her kisses and caresses, that in truth the two of them felt a joy and won- der the equal of which has never been heard or known. But I shall let it remain a secret for ever, since it should not be written of: the most delightful and choicest plea- sure is that which is hinted at, but never told.

—Chrétien de Troyes, *Arthurian Romances*,
translated by William W. Kibler

In the imagery of courtly love, the lover's heart is rarely rewarded as thoroughly as Lancelot's was and allowed to remain whole and rooted in his breast. It is more frequently parted with, either sent fly- ing away on wings to the lady or—as in the famous Musée de Cluny tapestry in Paris—handed over by the knight. In the tapestry, a tiny heart about the size of an engagement ring box is accepted by an abstracted lady who seems more interested in her dog and falcon and hares.

Other works of the time depict the heart as undergoing an imagi- native variety of cruelties. A lover's heart is "stolen" or "wrested from him" by the lady; it is ripped asunder and only her thread can sew it back together again; it is wounded and left as an open, fester- ing sore; it is teased and mocked by her. In a German engraving of the time, hearts are shown being roasted over flames, sawed in half, squashed inside a torture instrument, speared, knifed, and trampled on by a triumphant naked Venus. In a French miniature, a sadistic bunch of well-dressed women in a walled garden gleefully nail the lover's bleeding heart to a cross. In song and story, the lover dies, over and over again, of a broken heart.

Occasionally the lady herself suffers. Several tales, or versions of the same tale, dish up her lover's heart on a dinner plate; unaware, the lady eats it and only afterward does her vengeful husband glee-fully identify the mystery meat. Whereupon the lady declares, "Sir, you have provided me with such a delicious dish that I shall never eat another," and either throws herself out of the window of the castle keep, or dies of a broken heart right there at the table.

THE HEART OF HELOISE (?1101–1164)

When you hurried towards God I followed you, indeed I was the first to take the veil—perhaps you were thinking how Lot's wife turned back when you made me put on the religious habit and take my vows before you gave your-self to God. Your lack of trust in me over this one thing, I confess, overwhelmed me with grief and shame. I would have had no hesitation, God knows, in following you or going ahead at your bidding to the flames of Hell. My heart was not in me but with you, and now, even more, if it is not with you it is nowhere; truly, without you it cannot exist.

– The Letters of Abelard and Heloise,
translated by Betty Raddice

Of all the love letters I have read, the five written by this twelfth-century abbess remain for me the supreme examples of a passionate heart uncompromised.

The exchange of letters between this famous pair could lay claim to being the first great novel of passion-love in Western history, according to Denis de Rougemont in his eccentric but masterful study, *Love in the Western World*. They met in 1118, when the free-lance scholar Abelard, by his own account a man of "exceptional good looks," then in his thirties, came to tutor the brilliant young Heloise at her uncle's house. De Rougemont makes the case that they were the first historical couple who *experienced and recorded themselves* in the context of the new "cult of passion" that was coming into being in their era.

In his *Historia Calamitatum (The Story of My Misfortunes)* Abelard relates the story of their ill-fated love in the form of "a letter to a friend," which was probably a literary device. This letter later reached Heloise in the convent—or Abelard had it sent to her. It initiated their famous correspondence. A small autobiography in itself, *Historia Calamitatum* relates how Abelard heard of the bright young girl in Paris, the niece of one of the canons of Notre Dame, and arranged to get himself invited to tutor her. They had a passionate love affair, she got pregnant, Abelard took her away to his noble family in Brittany, and she bore a son whom they named Astrolabe, after the most advanced astronomical instrument of that time. True to the spirit of courtly love, they had a low opinion of marriage. Being bound only by "love freely given" was their ideal. But to pacify the enraged uncle they married secretly and Heloise continued to live at her uncle's house. Heloise was against committing this hypocrisy, but Abelard didn't want to lose her. The secrecy was to protect

Abelard's career as a philosopher in the church—the higher scholarly offices were not open to married men. However, the uncle broke
his promise and spread the news of the marriage. Abelard took
Heloise away and hid her, disguised as a nun, in a convent, where
they continued to carry on their lovemaking furtively. The uncle,
hearing that his niece was wearing a postulant's habit and thinking
Abelard was trying to get rid of her by making her a real nun, went
into a rage. He sent his servants to break into Abelard's room while
he was sleeping, hold him down, and castrate him. Mortified at being
a eunuch, Abelard sought immediate refuge in the cloister, where he
made a reputation for himself as a great teacher and scholar and
eventually experienced a sincere conversion. He is recognized as one
of the most original minds of the twelfth century.

But Abelard made Heloise take the veil before he took his vows as
a monk. Even in his physically altered state, he was determined not
to lose her. Though she never pretended to love God more than
Abelard, she put her brains and character to good service as a leader
of nuns and educator of young girls. After Abelard's death in 1142,
she arranged to have his body buried at her convent, one that he had
founded, and is recorded to have been buried alongside him. Their
bones now rest together in a single sarcophagus in the Paris cemetery of Père Lachaise.

In their exchange of personal letters, Abelard uses acrobatic
twists of logic to persuade Heloise, whom he calls "my inseparable
companion . . . my partner both in guilt and grace," to stop mourning the treachery performed on his body and accept their fate as
God's way to save them for higher purposes. Heloise writes back
that she will set the bridle of his injunction on the *written* words,
which issue from her unbounded grief, but that she can do nothing
to forestall her own speech, which issues from her heart.

For nothing is less under our control than the heart—
having no power to command it, we are forced to obey.
And so when its impulses move us, none of us can stop
their sudden promptings from easily breaking out. . . . I
will therefore hold my hand from writing words which I
cannot restrain my tongue from speaking; would that a
grieving heart would be as ready to obey as a writer's hand!

The heart of Heloise is the apotheosis of the courtly ideal: it is the
heart that is to be followed throughout all obstructions, the heart
that suffers itself to be tormented, the heart that, throughout everything, remains steadfast in its undefiled intention. It is the heart that
rises to Shakespeare's definition of true love in Sonnet 116: "Love is
not love / Which alters when it alteration finds, / Or bends with the
remover to remove. . . ."

It continues to throb resonantly in the poems, songs, novels,
operas, and plays based on its story. In the heart of the very Age of
Reason itself, the eighteenth century, Alexander Pope was moved by
the stubborn outpourings of Heloise's committed heart to commit a
sublimely romantic poem to paper. Here are the opening lines of his
"Eloisa to Abelard," even more sublime when read aloud slowly:

> *In these deep solitudes and awful cells,*
> *Where heavenly-pensive contemplation dwells*
> *And ever-musing melancholy reigns;*
> *What means this tumult in a Vestal's veins?*
> *Why rove my thoughts beyond this last retreat?*
> *Why feels my heart its long-forgotten heat?*
> *Yet, yet I love!—From Abelard it came,*
> *And Eloisa yet must kiss the name.*

THE VALENTINE

The first recorded instance of someone calling a lover or herself a "valentine" appears in a February 1477 letter from an anxious young Englishwoman to her fiancé: "Unto my ryght welebelovyd Voluntyn John Paston Squyer, be this bill delivered. . . ."

Margery Brews has become engaged to John Paston, but her father is refusing to come up with the dowry John expects. John has written to tell his fiancée that he will be arriving soon to conclude the matter with her father. In Margery's letter, in which she addresses John as her "right well-beloved Valentine," she reports that her father will part with no more than 100 pounds and 50 marks, "which is right far from the accomplishment of your desire," but she dares to hope that John will be satisfied with that amount.

> If that ye could be content with that Good, and my poor Person, I would be the merriest maiden on ground; and if ye think not yourself so satisfied, or that ye might have much more Good, as I have understood by you afore; good, true, and loving Valentine, that ye take no such labor upon you, as to come more for that matter, but let [what] is pass, and never more to be spoken of, as I may be your true Lover and Beadwoman during my life.
>
> No more unto you at this time, but Almighty Jesu preserve you both body and soul &c.
>
> By your Valentine, Margery Brews

John did persist in further haggling and Margery's mother intervened and belabored the matter with the father. After more negotiations and setbacks, the wedding finally took place later in the same year. And though poor Margery's heart was in anguish for a while ("for there wots no creature, what pain I endure," she writes in a late February poem to John), we are in possession of the first extant English valentine in the hit-or-miss spellings of the time, when English was changing faster than orthography could keep up with it.

Because of this evidence in the Paston letters, which chronicle three generations (1422–1509) of that family in Norfolk, England, social historians conjecture that the practice of sending "valentines" on the Feast of St. Valentine came into fashion in England sometime between 1400 and 1450. Very often it is just a simple personal utterance of a long-ago diarist or correspondent that provides the piquant detail missing from the official records.

The origin of Valentine's Day appears to have evolved out of the ancient Roman feast of Lupercalia (after the fertility god, Lupercus, or Faunus, the Roman Pan) on the fifteenth of February. Various sorts of fertility games got people in the mood for mating. Young men girdled themselves in the skins of sacrificed goats and ran about the town striking all the women they met with little strips of goat flesh to propitiate the wolf god and evoke fertility. Young men and women would also choose partners for erotic games by exchanging love notes, or "billets," with names on them.

The festival continued to be popular into Christian times, though it was denounced by the Church Fathers as being lewd and heathenish. They tried to substitute pious sermons on the "billets," but you can imagine how well that went over with the young. Finally, in the fifth century, the Church succeeded in banishing the festival altogether. Meanwhile it had taken advantage of the convenient February 14 death of a "St. Valentine," which could have been one of two clergymen by that name, both of whom were supposedly martyred in Rome in 269–270. By instituting St. Valentine's Day on the four-teenth, the day birds were supposed to begin mating, the Church hoped to upstage the pagan festival the following day. On the eve of St. Valentine's Day, people were allowed to draw lots to determine their sweethearts. The tradition of drawing lots on Valentine's Eve to forecast marriage partners lasted into the eighteenth century in England, a custom that clergyman Henry Bourne in his book *Antiq-uitas Vulgaris* pronounced "altogether diabolical."

Two St. Valentines are listed in the old Roman Martyrology for February 14. The first was a Christian priest and physician, mar-tyred in 270 under Claudius the Goth and buried on the Flaminian Way. In 350, the Church of St. Valentine was built over his tomb.

The other St. Valentine was a bishop of Terni, the one John Donne chose to use for his poem for the king's daughter's valentine wedding in 1613.

> *Haile Bishop Valentine, whose day this is,*
> *All the Aire is thy Diocis,*
> *And all the chirping Choristers*
> *And other birds are thy Parishioners . . .*
> —"An Epithalamion, or Marriage Song,
>   on the Lady Elizabeth and Count Palatine I
>   Being Married on St. Valentine's Day"

This Bishop Valentine was said to have been martyred about 269, also under Claudius the Goth. But the Bollandists, a group of Jesuits who have been separating legend from biography in the lives of the saints since the middle 1700s, have concluded that the bishop was simply another version of the priest-physician.

In 1969, the Roman Catholic Church removed St. Valentine from its official calendar of saints, though he continues to be listed in local calendars. This was also the fate of certain other popular saints who were researched out of their literal existences, such as Catherine of Alexandria and Margaret of Antioch and St. Christopher, the patron saint of travelers and a particular favorite of motorists. The largest protest on the desanctified Christopher's behalf was led by popular film stars in Italy, that country of wild drivers. However, St. Christopher medals and dashboard ornaments continue to sell well, as do valentines. The first commercial valentines were created in the 1840s by an American lady named Esther A. Howland and have been a major source of income, in that slow period between Christmas and Easter, for the greeting card industry ever since.

XV. The Great Heart Split of the Seventeenth Century

Early in the seventeenth century something new is already apparent in science. The changes which then manifested themselves meant that an intellectual barrier was crossed and the nature of civilization was altered forever. There appeared in Europe a new attitude, deeply utilitarian, encouraging men to invest time, energy and resources to master nature by systematic experiment.

–J. M. Roberts, *History of the World*

The dead heart was born into Western consciousness . . .
at that moment when Harvey conceived the heart to be
divided. . . . Thought lost its heart, heart its thought.
—James Hillman, "Harvey's Heart,"
  The Thought of the Heart and the Soul of the World

Most of us, whether we admit it or not, still live our lives under the
influence of the great rift between heart and head that fractured seventeenth-century thought. This rift, concurrent with the Industrial
Revolution of the next two centuries, utterly changed the landscape
of human relations, splitting us into divided kingdoms of intellect
versus feeling, provables versus intangibles, and a host of other
"either/or" dualities. Wholeness, and *wholeheartedness*, are concepts
to be achieved all over again, but this time on a sturdier level of
consciousness.

We are image-making creatures, and we form our images out of
the materials of our experience. The science of a given time will not
only provide metaphors for its intangibles, but also images of how
we see ourselves. In Dante's *Divine Comedy*, the "lake of the heart"
was still believed to be a physiological concavity in the heart where
blood gathered as water gathers, and remains, in a lake; thus it was
also thought to be the location of fear in the human body.

WILLIAM HARVEY (1578–1657)

And so, when a seventeenth-century English doctor who gave popular dissection lectures in the anatomical theater at the Royal College
of Physicians presented his audiences with a visible, tangible heart, a
hard, tense muscle that you could hold in your hands, a "pumping
machine" that measures "six fingers in length, four in width," whose

beat "produces a perpetual circular motion of the blood," this new materialized, mechanized image was bound to have an enormous impact on the way we imagined ourselves and our hearts. At the moment the anatomist held up the excised heart of some hanged felon, a sort of Eucharistic celebration of the literal heart could be said to have occurred. In the church of the anatomical theater, the heart became demythologized.

This Harveyan heart, raised up for viewing during the opening throes of our love affair with "scientific proof" and material values, relegated the heart of older cultures to the status of myth. The new demonstrable material heart (Harvey would inhale and exhale into a glove to show people how systole and diastole looked) became the "real" heart and took pride of place over the symbolic heart: the "seat of wisdom," and "wellspring of qualitative feeling" known to the Hebrews and Egyptians; the Chinese "thinking heart"; the Islamic "throne of God"; the abode of Brahma; the true home of the Nazarene teacher's "Kingdom of God." From now on, when people spoke of the heart, they were more likely to specify which heart they meant: the muscle in the breast or the sentient organ described by poets and lovers. We were entering the period where heart was one or the other, but never both. "Thought lost its heart, heart its thought," writes Hillman in his essay on Harvey's heart. "A wall had now been set between the world out there and subjective feelings in here, because even in the center of the breast there was division."

It is apparent from his lecture notes that William Harvey must have been quite a performer as well as a metaphorist. He used sensational images to keep the attention of his large, and largely uneducated, audiences. He compares the dissection of the corpse on the table before them to a meal that he will serve to them in three courses in three different parts of a house, starting in the "kitchen

shop" with the least savory, that of the lower abdomen ("nasty yett
[sic] recompensed by admirable variety"), then on to "the parlor" of
the thorax, and finally to the "divine Banquet of the brayne (sic)."
(Dr. Hannibal Lecter surely must have been familiar with Harvey's
lecture notes!)

In 1628, when Harvey was fifty, he published the treatise that
scientifically established that the blood circulates through the four
chambers of the heart: *An Anatomical Dissertation Concerning the
Motion of the Heart and Blood in Animals.* It described the motions of
the heart in the mechanistic terms of a pump. When the heart-
muscle contracts (systole, from the Greek *systolē*, "a drawing up"),
the blood in the right lower chamber is propelled via the pulmonary
artery to the lungs for fresh oxygenation, and the blood from the left
lower chamber, which has been oxygenated during a previous beat,
is sent out via the aorta into the rest of the body. When the heart
muscle relaxes (from the Greek *diastolē*, "expansion," "dilatation"),
its upper chambers refill with blood, the newly oxygenated blood
returning from the lungs into the right upper chamber, and the blood
returning from its travels through the body into the left upper chamber. At the next systole, or contraction, the whole process begins
again. Harvey was also the first to confirm that *there was no passage
between the right and left chambers of the heart.* (A thirteenth-century
Arab doctor, Ibn an-Nafis, living in Damascus, had described pulmonary circulation and also had stated that there was no communication between the left and right chambers, but medical historians
think it improbable that Harvey could have known of this.)

Now we're beginning to see that Harvey's "pump in the chest" isn't
the whole medical heart, either. Findings in the relatively new fields

of neurocardiology and cardioenergetics show that the central role of the heart in our consciousness is much more than mere metaphor. Transmitters, which play such a critical role in neural behavior, have now been found in the heart and are somehow connected with the brain. Already we know that the heart is controlled by hormones and responds to our thoughts and feelings; stress can injure or stop a heart, and people can, quite literally, die of heartbreak.

Before we go on to two prominent mystical hearts of the seventeenth century, I have two further anecdotes pertaining to the medical heart. I found these in *The Heart: Its History, Its Symbolism, Its Iconography and Its Diseases*, by Belgian cardiologist Noubar Boyadjian (1985, English translation by Agnes Hall). It is a gorgeously produced book, made for complimentary distribution at cardiology conventions, featuring in full color the author's extensive collection of heart objects, ranging from holy water stoups and convent art to jewels, boxes, valentines, and romantic postcards, and interlaced with the doctor's engaging commentary.

THE FIRST STETHOSCOPE

The first medical story has to do with the invention of the stethoscope in the early nineteenth century by a Breton doctor, René Laennec (1781–1826). In Laennec's time, doctors sounded the chest by percussion, but one day Laennec was trying to sound the chest of an obese young woman in her chemise, and could hear nothing. Let Dr. Boyadjian finish the story:

> He was extremely upset and thought that if he put his ear
> up against the patient's chest, he might be able to dis-
> cover what was wrong with her. But in those days, to put

your ear up against a lady's chest was quite unthinkable. Then he had what turned out to be an inspiration. He picked up an exercise book which was on his desk, rolled it up, held it tightly and made a cylinder of it. He applied one end of this cylinder under the patient's left breast and put his ear to the other end. He was surprised to find that he could distinctly hear sounds coming from the heart.

Laennec had invented auscultation. He replaced the roll of paper with a hollow wooden cylinder, which he named the stethoscope (Greek for "the spy of the chest") and has since become the identifying emblem of the physician rushing through the halls of the hospital.

ST. TERESA'S HEART PRESERVED IN ALCOHOL

The second story is of Dr. Boyadjian visiting the convent in Alba de Tormes to see the heart of St. Teresa of Avila, preserved since 1582 in a jeweled rock-crystal urn—heart-shaped, of course—and having a little epiphany of his own:

> The eye of the cardiologist, looking closely at this heart . . . was overwhelmingly surprised to notice a split, a tear in the myocardium of the left ventricle, and after four centuries pronounced this audacious diagnosis: Teresa d'Avila could perhaps have died from a coronary thrombosis with rupture of the heart; the arrow [of the angel] which pierced her heart during her illness was probably the manifestation of an attack of angina.

THE NUN WHO POPULARIZED
THE SACRED HEART OF JESUS

Once more, let all this remain secret in his Sacred Heart. Be so good not to mention my name nor disclose my identity to anyone. . . . I almost gave in to the temptation to send you a little manuscript version of the Sacred Heart in verse, but then I thought the postage would be too high and you might find it useless anyway. I eagerly anticipate seeing the picture of this holy Heart in the other books you have printed. You may rest assured that I will do all I can to make them known. I am sending you one of the booklets printed when the devotion began. And since you say that we must pray to the Blessed Aloysius Gonzaga to get what we want, please be so good as to send us a copper plate picture of him. . . . It is for our chapel dedicated to the Sacred Heart.

    —Letter from Sister Marguerite-Marie Alacoque,
       Order of the Visitation at Paray-le-Monial,
       to Father Jean Croiset of the Society
       of Jesus at Lyons, August 10, 1689
       (*The Letters of St. Margaret Mary Alacoque,*
       Apostle of the Sacred Heart,
       translated by Fr. Clarence A. Herbst)

Marguerite-Marie Alacoque (1647–90), born nineteen years after the publication of Harvey's treatise on the heart, probably knew nothing of that work, but was well acquainted with the life of St. Teresa of Avila and therefore must have been familiar with Teresa's experience, in the previous century, of having her heart speared by an angel with an arrow of burning gold. She also was likely to have known about Catherine of Siena (1347–80), who left prolific testimonies about her visions. During one of Catherine's ecstasies, Jesus opened her left side, took her heart out, kept it for several days, and then replaced his own in her body while she was praying in chapel one night. "You see, dearest girl," He said, "as I once took your heart, now I give you mine to live with."

Marguerite-Marie took the habit at the age of twenty-four and had the first of her series of visions two years later. The visions ended when she was twenty-seven and, until her death at forty-three, she devoted herself to carrying out their injunctions, trying to keep her unworthy self out of the picture. In the latter she was not successful: in her final eighteen months a young Jesuit, not yet ordained, encouraged her to relate these visions as explicitly as possible to him in a series of letters. A year after her death, he published his book based on her visions, *The Devotion to the Sacred Heart of Our Lord Jesus Christ;* he had deliberately withheld publication until her death so that he could preface it with a sketch of her life.

Marguerite-Marie's visions came in the triple-sensory form of sight, hearing, and touch. She saw Christ's heart surrounded with rays brighter than the sun. Though transparent as crystal, the heart bore the wound given to him on the cross when the soldiers pierced his side with a spear and drew blood and water. There was a crown of thorns around this heart and a cross above it. Simultaneously with the image came his voice telling Marguerite-Marie that as he was no longer able to contain the flames of his love for humankind he had chosen her to spread the knowledge of them. He thereupon took out her heart, placed it inside his own, and set it on fire, then replaced it in her breast with the words: "Hitherto thou hast taken the name of my slave, hereafter thou shalt be called the well-beloved disciple of my Sacred Heart."

In a later vision, Christ revealed to her in detail the exact devotion he wanted her to set in place for him. Every first Friday after the week of the Holy Sacrament was to be made into a special holy day in honor of his heart. There was to be a general communion and ser- vices to make amends for the indignities his heart had received. He promised her that his Sacred Heart would dilate to shed with abun- dance the influences of its love on all who participated in the service as well as those who encouraged others to do the same.

She got it done—the spreading of public and liturgical devotion to the Sacred Heart, thanks to the disseminating skills of the Jesuits who recognized that the heart—*Christ's* heart—could be a power- ful proselytizing emblem. It took them seventy-five years, because there was vigorous resistance, especially from the Jansenists, a sect of seventeenth-century Catholics who believed Christ did not die for everybody, just the elect. But in 1765, Pope Clement XIII advocated the institution of the Feast of the Sacred Heart, which was made a general practice in 1856, and proclaimed universally in 1928 by Pius XI.

As a disciple of the Sacred Heart, Marguerite-Marie was certainly effective. Her visions have influenced the devotional life and habits of Roman Catholics ever since the Feast of the Sacred Heart was made general in 1856. She herself was declared Venerable in 1824, Blessed in 1864, and officially became St. Marguerite-Marie in 1920.

However, according to her French biographer, Monseigneur Bou- gaud, Marguerite-Marie the nun became increasingly useless around the convent, and much resented by some. Her superiors tried her in the infirmary, but without much success, though "her charity rose to acts of such a heroism that our readers would not bear the recital of them." They tried her in the kitchen, but she dropped everything. They put her in the school, where the little girls loved her and cut pieces out of her habit for relics as if she were already a saint, but she was too inwardly absorbed to give them the necessary attention. She seemed to have done somewhat better as novice mistress. Five years before her death, the novices, to entertain her on her own feast day, put up a little altar with a drawing of the Sacred Heart. The original is preserved in the Convent of the Visitation in Tours, but Dr. Boyadjian, the Belgian cardiologist, has a copy of the little drawing in his vast collection of hearts, and there's a color reproduction of it in his book. It resembles an old-fashioned valentine, with a yellow heart inside a lace-edged oblong. The heart oozes little drops of blood from a gash in its center. Printed across the gash is CARITAS. Perched in the heart's cleft is a cross. The heart is surrounded by two painstakingly intricate circlets of hearts and curlicues, which must have taken the novices hours to draw.

In her chapter on "Voices and Visions," Evelyn Underhill, in her classic work *Mysticism*, deplores that Marguerite-Marie's vision of the Sacred Heart, "a pictured expression of one of the deepest intuitions of the human soul caught up in the contemplation of God's love," should have been "impaired by the grossly material interpretation which it has been forced to bear." But that is the fate of all transcendent experiences when they get popularized. Yet some ineffable heartbeat continues to pulse through even the worst of *kitsch* when the original intention was intuitively sound. Every convent-educated child of certain generations, including myself, has had the experience, years later, of coming across a garish holy card in an old book and wincing at the bad taste of the art. But then you turn over the card of that smarmy Jesus in regal robes that he never would have worn in life, holding out his red heart to you like a thorn-bound cas-

ket of jewels, and there on the back is a message from a long-ago
admired and beloved teacher in the exquisite handwriting you tried
and pretty much succeeded in trying to copy, and your heart is kin-
dled with its old ardor. *Something* is very much alive here, something
of great value has been transmitted via the *kitsch*, and I think the
canny Jesuits knew exactly what they had found in Marguerite-
Marie's "assignment" from her Lord.

As the Romanian hagiographer E. M. Cioran wrote in *Tears and
Saints* (translated by Ilinca Zarifopol-Johnston, University of
Chicago Press, 1995): "No one truly understands sainthood if he
does not feel that the heart is its world. *The heart as universe*—this is
the deepest meaning of sainthood. *Everything happens in the heart*:
that's mysticism and saintliness. But this doesn't mean people's
hearts, only saints' hearts."

BLAISE PASCAL (1623–62)

The heart has its reasons of which reason knows nothing:
we know this in countless ways. (Fragment 277)

It is the heart which perceives God and not the reason.
That is what faith is: God perceived by the heart, not by
the reason. (Fragment 278)

—Pascal, "The Wager," *Pensées*,
translated by A. J. Krailsheimer

We know the truth not only through our reason but also
through our heart. It is through the latter that we know
first principles, and reason, which has nothing to do with
it, tries in vain to refute them. . . . For knowledge of

first principles, like space, time, motion, number, is as solid as any derived through reason, and it is on such knowledge, coming from the heart and instinct, that reason has to depend and base all its argument. The heart feels that there are three spatial dimensions and that there is an infinite series of numbers, and reason goes on to demonstrate that there are no two square numbers of which one is double of the other. Principles are felt, propositions proved, and both with certainty though by different means. *It is just as pointless and absurd for reason to demand proof of first principles from the heart before agreeing to accept them as it would be absurd for the heart to demand an intuition of all the propositions demonstrated by reason before agreeing to accept them.* (Fragment 110, italics added)

—"Greatness," *Pensées*

Pascal's life overlapped with Harvey's and Marguerite-Marie Alacoque's, Pascal being the "middle child" in this trio of seventeenth-century heart figures. He was a rare combination, both a mathematical genius and a mystic. Contrary to his older contemporary René Descartes (1596–1650), the father of Rationalism who formulated the Cartesian mind-body split, and unlike Jean-Jacques Rousseau (1712–78), who would a century later side rhapsodically with heart and throw reason overboard, Pascal saw the two as complementary. Each had its function and both were meant to work together, each in its own way (as described in Fragment 110, above). Rational thought was accompanied by an equally valuable logic of the heart.

Though he died before he was forty, he lived long enough to

incarnate his own maxims; he balanced the two intelligences of head and heart. Pascal lost his mother when he was three, and he and his two sisters, one older, one younger, were raised by their father, a legal officer and mathematics enthusiast, who took over Blaise's education. Before Pascal turned twelve he had worked out for himself the first thirty-two principles of Euclid. When he was seventeen, he published a paper in solid geometry, on conic sections, that Descartes refused to believe had been written by someone so young. Two years later, at nineteen, he built the first metal-toothed-wheeled calculating machine, later developed by Leibniz. With his father, Pascal confirmed the theory that nature does *not* abhor a vacuum. The two carried mercury barometers up a mountain and showed that the column of mercury varied in length, thus disposing of the Greeks' notions of pneuma and the void. Pascal was the cofounder of differential and integral calculus and devised the first public transport service in Paris, which was inaugurated shortly before his death, from either tuberculosis or cancer, or a combination of both. Pascal's law in physics, Pascal's theorem in geometry, and Pascal's triangle in mathematics are all named after him. It was as a man of all-around distinction that the Bank of France chose his portrait for the 500-franc note, though later he was supplanted by Marie and Pierre Curie.

The Pascals were observant but nonfervent Roman Catholics, until father Pascal fell and met some bonesetters who in turn introduced him to a priest who had been converted to Jansenism (the Jansenists, remember, were the Catholic sect who fought Marguerite-Marie's Jesuit-spread devotion to the Sacred Heart and its promises of "reparation"; incidentally, their theology was based on that of our old friend St. Augustine, who maintained grace could not be earned by good works). As a result of the father's friendship with the Jansenist priest, Pascal and his sisters underwent a sort of family conversion. His favorite sister, Jacqueline, subsequently entered a Jansenist-influenced convent, and, at age thirty-one, Pascal had an overwhelming personal conversion. Of the manifestations of this awakening we have no details, other than the famous "Memorial," which he inscribed on parchment and carried on his body, sewn up in a leather pouch, like an amulet, until his death. Dated Monday, November 23, 1654, "From about half-past ten in the evening until half-past midnight," there is a single word, "Fire," followed by a series of scriptural phrases and rapturous utterances. ("Certainty, certainty, heartfelt joy, peace . . . sweet and total renunciation. . . .")

There is no record of voices and visions or touch in Pascal's ecstatic perception, as in the experience of Marguerite-Marie Alacoque. Underhill, in her chapter "Ecstasy and Rapture," speculates that Pascal underwent "a violent uprush of subliminal intuitions," resulting in "a final and unforgettable knowledge—which is characteristic of all ecstatic perception."

Comparing these "broken phrases" and "childlike stammering speech" of the "Memorial" with the irony and glitter of his *Provincial Letters* (in which he attacked the Jesuits and supported the Jansenists) and the sharp and lucid definitions of the unfinished *Pensées*, Underhill professes: "I know few things in the history of mysticism at once more convincing, more poignant than this hidden talisman upon which the brilliant scholar and stylist, the merciless disputant, has jotted down in hard, crude words—charged with passion—the inarticulate language of love."

Pascal composed his *Pensées* in the last decade of his short life, and, though much of it remains in fragmentary form, it is the reason his reputation is still growing. For modern skeptics trying to square their "head" rationalism with the spiritual intuitions of their hearts, he is the ideal place to begin. (I have a young friend, now a professor and a priest, who was able, as he puts it, "to acknowledge that I had a religious nature in spite of my intellectual qualms," by accepting Pascal's "Wager," Kierkegaard's image of the "leap of faith," and William James's philosophy of pragmatism.)

According to Pascal's English translator Dr. Krailsheimer, much more has been learned in the last thirty or forty years about Pascal's working methods. He worked on large sheets of paper, writing his thoughts down fast, with many erasures and transpositions, some-times arranging the words like a poem.

And listen to this: "For whatever reason, Pascal did not compose in linear, logical style, but by 'noyaux,' that is, by centres, nuclei, *in the order of heart rather than mind*" (italics added). Judging from the more finished sections of the *Pensées*, Pascal scholars see that all the fragments relating to specific subjects would later have been sub-sumed into their proper centers.

Provocative thought: is this what "heart-writing" would be like? Utterances written down without left-brain censorship, in "shapes" rather than lines, as they pulsate out from the intuitive thrusts of heart-knowledge? And later, gone back to and harvested (if you live long enough) into *noyaux* of compatible fragments to make a com-bined effort of heart and head? After I learned this about Pascal, it occurred to me that when I jot down images and phrases in a rush of inspiration, I never end up with a page of lines, but with *clusters*— like bunches of flowers thrown down at random, later sorted out and connected by means of circles, squares, and arrows.

Pascal was the superb balance of head and heart in his time. Philosophers in the next century's Age of Enlightenment often came down hard in favor of one or the other or teetered with reservations in the middle. Jean-Jacques Rousseau preached the absolute superiority of the heart over reason and even went so far as to declare that the state of thinking was contrary to nature! Immanuel Kant (1724–1804) in his *Critique of Pure Reason* attempted to define precisely the domain of rational understanding. He challenged the Enlightenment's faith in reason's unlimited scope, allowing that in matters concerning feeling and faith, the heart must prescribe to reason. However, he warned of the human heart's proclivity to evil: there were frail hearts, impure hearts, and vicious and corrupt hearts. A frail heart lacks the strength to practice the good that it recognizes, the impure heart confuses moral and immoral impulses, and the vicious heart has an affinity for evil. In *Faust*, the highly intellectual Johann Wolfgang von Goethe (1749–1832), who claimed his heart was his own chief guide, has nevertheless given us the brilliant portrait of an obsessively intellectual man who has let his heart atrophy.

And the impassioned Friedrich Nietzsche (1844–1900) was a Faust story in himself, though one without a redemptive ending. Proclaiming the highest intellect of the superman to be the future mission of humankind, he nonetheless wistfully looks forward to a future epoch "when heart and head have learned to live as closely together as they are now far apart" (*Human, All Too Human*). His work grew more and more contradictory as his syphilitic descent into madness progressed. Poignantly, one of the last things written by this man—who in *Antichrist* calls himself "Dionysus versus the Crucified" as well as "the Antichrist"—was a description of the kingdom of heaven as a "state of the heart."

> The kingdom of God is like nothing we expect; it has no
> yesterday and no day after tomorrow; it does not come in

"a thousand years"—it is something experienced in the
heart; it is everywhere and nowhere . . .
>   —Quoted from "Friedrich Nietzsche—a Heart
>   Full of Contradictions," in Frank Nager,
>   *The Mythology of the Heart*

In a sense, we who are living now remain the children of the Great
Heart Split. We're not orphans; both our parents, mind and heart,
are still alive, we visit them regularly, but they don't live together
anymore. They subscribe to their different values, and we have to be
careful to respect the realities of the parent we're currently staying
with. The one who admires anatomical lecturers and dissected
hearts isn't impressed with crackpot nuns who switch hearts with
Christ, and thinks Pascal's mad midnight jottings were the aberra-
tion of an otherwise splendid mind. Whereas the one who likes to
read us to sleep with metaphysical poetry tends to go glassy-eyed
when we speculate about the possibilities of neurotransmitters and
bioenergetics. But like all children from divided homes, we continue
to dream, like the tragic Nietzsche, of a future epoch when all of us
can be together under one roof.

XVI. Hard Times and Where Is the Heart?

The Industrial Revolution to the Present

We are to admit no more causes of natural things than such as are both true and sufficient to explain their appearance.

—Sir Isaac Newton (1642–1727)

May God us Keep
From Single vision & Newton's sleep
—William Blake, letter to Thomas Butts,
November 22, 1802

Coketown, to which Messrs Bounderby and Gradgrind now walked, was a triumph of fact. . . . It was a town of red brick, or brick that would have been red if the smoke and the ashes had allowed it. . . . It was a town of machinery and tall chimneys, out of which interminable serpents of smoke trailed themselves for ever and ever and never got uncoiled. It had a black canal in it, and a river that ran purple with ill-smelling dye, and vast piles of buildings full of windows where there was a rattling and a trembling all day long, and where the piston of the steam engine worked monotonously up and down, like the head of an elephant in a state of melancholy madness. It contained several large streets all very like one another,

and many small streets still more like one another, inhab-
ited by people equally like one another, who all went in
and out at the same hours, with the same sound upon the
same pavements, to do the same work.

                    —Charles Dickens, *Hard Times*

Mind was apotheosized, and Heart—with all its troublesome imma-
terial loose ends—was devalued as we plunged headlong into the age
of scientific enlightenment. Together with the Industrial Revolution,
it was a time that provided new metaphors of the universe as Newton's "clockwork machine" and of the human being as a "cog" in the
almighty economic machine.

   Now, as we all know, Newton's worldview has been supplanted
by the fluid dance of quantum physics, and globalization and the
microchip are our latest economic models, whose argots we have
downloaded as brand-new metaphors for describing ourselves.
We're quantum selves living in a quantum society, my relationship
with you has its wave aspect as well as its particle aspect, if only you
would see it, etc. Yet how much of the old "single vision" premise
that "what you can measure is all there is" continues to order our
priorities? How often in a single day does the utilitarian model of
"human being as machine"—or machine *part*—still raise its ugly
head in our dealings with industries and institutions?

> [People] are grown mechanical in head and in heart as
> well as in hand. They have lost faith in individual
> endeavor, and in natural force, of any kind. Not for inter-
> nal perfection, but for external combinations and arrange-
> ments, for institutions, constitutions—for Mechanism of
> one sort or other, do they hope and struggle. . . . This, we

take it, is the grand characteristic of our age. By our skill in Mechanism, it has come to pass that, in the management of external things, we excel all other ages; while in whatever respects the pure moral nature, in true dignity of soul and character, we are perhaps inferior to most civilized ages.

In fact, if we look deeper, we shall find this faith in Mechanism has now struck its roots deep into men's most intimate, private sources of conviction; and is thence sending up, over his whole life and activity, innu- merable stems—fruit-bearing and poison-bearing. The truth is, men have lost their belief in the Invisible, and believe, and hope, and work only in the Visible. . . .

That was Thomas Carlyle, writing on "Signs of the Times," in the *Edinburgh Review* in 1829. How many of those same "signs" are still with us 172 years later? Note, though, that he does grant "fruit- bearing" as well as "poison-bearing" properties to the great epoch of management of material things. How can we preserve the fruits and get rid of the poison? How can we restore heart to our management of external things?

Charles Dickens dealt with these questions in his 1854 novel *Hard Times*, a rousing moral fable that speaks to our own era as freshly as it did to his. (Dickens's complete title was *Hard Times for These Times*, and he dedicated it to Carlyle, whose chastening social criticism in "Signs of the Times" may have served as inspirational prod for the novelist's art.) The shortest of Dickens's novels, except for *The Mystery of Edwin Drood*, which he didn't live to finish, *Hard Times* is both a brilliant send-up of the worst qualities of mechanism and a passionate plea for the return of heart. With his personal blend of the macabre, the hilarious, and the heartrending, Dickens shows us what happens to a family when heart is banished from life's necessities. If I were ever to teach a course on "Heart: The History of an Idea," it would be *Hard Times* I would use for its spirited and entertaining demonstration of how we lost our cultural heart and what is needed for us to reinstate it again.

The novel's opening takes us into a classroom of Victorian children having imagination and heart educated out of them in the fashionable utilitarian style of the day. Mr. Thomas Gradgrind expounds on his teaching method:

> "Now, what I want is, Facts. Teach these boys and girls nothing but Facts. Facts alone are wanted in life. Plant nothing else, and root out everything else. You can only form the minds of reasoning animals upon Facts; nothing else will be of any service to them. This is the principle on which I bring up my own children, and this is the principle on which I bring up these children. Stick to Facts, sir!"

Gradgrind, who presents the effect of "a kind of cannon loaded to the muzzle with facts, and prepared to blow them clean out of the regions of childhood at one discharge," proceeds to demonstrate his method by calling on a new girl who has been brought up in a traveling horse-riding circus to "define a horse." Having lived with horses all her life, and among people whose livelihood depends on the intimate understanding of horses, Sissy Jupe understandably falters. "Girl number twenty unable to define a horse! . . . Girl number twenty possessed of no facts, in reference to the commonest of animals!"

Gradgrind then calls on the boy Bitzer, who responds correctly: "Quadruped. Graminivorous. Forty teeth, namely twenty-four grinders, four eye-teeth, and twelve incisive. Sheds coat in the spring; in marshy countries sheds hoofs, too. Hoofs hard, but requiring to be shod with iron. Age known by marks in mouth."

But it will be "Girl number twenty" whom Gradgrind adopts when Sissy's father abandons her, who will subtly, but with increasing results as the novel progresses, restore heart to its needful place within the family. Gradgrind's children, Louisa and Tom, suffer in different ways from their utilitarian upbringing (no fairy tales allowed, no "fancies," no "wondering"): Louisa, whose heart has partly atrophied, allows herself to be married off by her father to a much older bullying banker-manufacturer, mainly to further the interests of her brother, who works for the bank; Tom grows up to be petulant and without scruples. It is only when Louisa's feelings are awakened by a worthless, contriving playboy and she flees in despair to her father, and when Tom robs his employer's bank and tries to frame an honest millhand, that Gradgrind is forced to realize the shortcomings of his method. Here is Louisa, giving voice in her anguish to what it is like to be raised without heart-values:

> "How could you give me life, and take from me all the inappreciable things that raise it from the state of conscious death? Where are the graces of my soul? Where are the sentiments of my heart? What have you done, O Father, what have you done, with the garden that should have bloomed once, in this great wilderness here! . . . Would you have robbed me—for no one's enrichment— only for the greater desolation of this world—of the immaterial part of my life, the spring and summer of my belief, my refuge from what is sordid and bad in the real things around me . . . ?"

And here is Tom, mouthing back his father's laws of statistics, after Gradgrind has professed himself lightning-struck by his son's crime:

> "I don't see why," grumbled the son. "So many people are employed in situations of trust; so many people, out of so many, will be dishonest. I have heard you talk, a hundred times, of its being a law. How can I help laws? You have comforted others with such things, Father. Comfort yourself!"

And here is Bitzer, the model student, the triumph of Gradgrind's system, when his old teacher begs him to show mercy and let Tom escape the country rather than turn him over to the police:

> "Bitzer," said Mr. Gradgrind, broken down, and miserably submissive to him, "have you a heart?"
>
> "The circulation, sir," returned Bitzer, smiling at the oddity of the question, "couldn't be carried on without one. No man, sir, acquainted with the facts established by Harvey relating to the circulation of the blood, can doubt that I have a heart."
>
> "Is it accessible," cried Mr. Gradgrind, "to any compassionate influence?"
>
> "It is accessible to Reason, sir," returned the excellent young man. "And to nothing else."

And finally we have Sissy, the subversive good heart at work in the blighted Gradgrind family, as she undertakes her successful mission to convince the elegant trifler with Louisa's affections that it is his duty to leave town forever.

Remember, back with Buddha, when we were wondering what having a cool mind and a warm heart would be like? Well, here is how it looks in the person of Sissy Jupe, as experienced by her adversary, the elegant trifler. Because the following passages so succinctly present the combination of cool mind and warm heart in action, I will boldface some of the outstanding characteristics.

Her face was innocent and youthful, and its expression remarkably pleasant. She was not afraid of him, or in any way disconcerted; **she seemed to have her mind entirely preoccupied with the occasion of her visit, and to have substituted that consideration for herself.** [They have their interview. Then:]

. . . If ever man found himself in the position of not knowing what to say, [he] made the discovery beyond all question that he was so circumstanced. . . . Her **modest fearlessness, her truthfulness which put all artifice aside, her entire forgetfulness of herself in her earnest quiet holding to the object with which she had come** . . . presented something in which he was so inexperienced, and against which he knew any of his usual weapons would fall so powerless; that not a word could he rally to his relief.

If she had asserted any influence over him beyond her plain faith in the truth and right of what she said; if she had concealed the least doubt or irresolution, or had harbored for the best purpose any reserve or pretense; if she had shown, or felt, the lightest trace of any sensitiveness to his ridicule or his astonishment, or any remonstrance

he might offer; he would have carried it against her at this
point.

   . . . He was touched in the cavity where his heart
should have been.

And so, in our survey of the heart through time, we've come all the
way from the cave to the factory: from the appealing life drawing of
the extinct woolly elephant with its heart in exactly the right place by
a prehistoric artist who wanted to capture that animal's singular
essence, to Dickens's detached elephant-head piston on the factory
steam engine stuck in its monotonous mad and melancholy industrial age rhythm. It's been a long time between elephants, so to
speak, and we've covered a lot of ground.

   Back home in the third millennium, after we have recovered from
detail overload, and have a chance to sit back and digest our impressions, what heart-wisdom from those other times and cultures can
we find use for in our present world? What have we brought back
with us that might be of service to the revaluation of the heart?

A RECAPITULATION

We have been bowling along through time, hitting the heart-spots,
cavalierly skipping whole millennia and centuries, allowing ourselves
to overstay when the company is interesting, and undoubtedly
slighting many worthies.

   Keeping in mind C. S. Lewis's dictum that humanity does not
pass through phases "as a train passes through stations," and that
whatever we have been, to some degree we remain, we have held the

dripping sacrificial heart of a brave enemy in our Aztec hands, we have sketched the woolly mammoth and its red heart on our cave wall, we have wept with the brokenhearted Gilgamesh when he touched his friend Enkidu's unbeating heart and realized that he, too, must die, and what did that new knowledge mean? We have prepared ourselves as all good ancient Egyptians should, to make our negative confession of the sins we have not committed before our heart is weighed on Anubis's scale, and with some twentieth-century paleopathologists we have shared a curious affection for an Egyptian teenager through his well-preserved 3,200-year-old heart.

With the ancient Hebrews, we entered into a personal relationship with the invisible God, wounding his heart over and over again until he wondered why he bothered, but occasionally letting him transform our hearts; with the Hindus we become conscious that the divine being already resides in the secret cave of our heart and that we are more than we know. We meet cool-minded, warm-hearted Buddha, and set out to clear our hearts of delusion, craving, and hostility through the Four Noble Truths and the Eightfold Path. We learn from practical Confucius that the tradition of "human-hearted behavior" at its best is also good politics, and from Lao-tzu that a heart in alignment with the way the universe works will lead to the right action even if we never leave the house. With the Japanese, we greeted Buddhism when it reached our island, and then set to work blending it with aspects of earthly beauty and awe from our ancient Shinto, with its "bright heart," "pure heart," "correct heart," and "strong heart," and made our very own Flower Garden Sutra, the object of which is to make a garland of harmonious beings out of the Buddha nature of each person. (Another echo of Jesus' "be of one heart.")

We have seen baby Dionysus torn apart and put back together in

Greek mythology, thanks to Zeus' quick-thinking gesture of swallowing his son's heart for safekeeping until he could find someone else to provide a womb for the boy-god's rebirth. And we located the point in Greek history where the fathers of philosophy left behind the "whole heart" concepts of the ancient world and began to differentiate the mind from the heart, a separation process that has continued into our present day. We have lingered with the disarming Socrates right up until he takes his bath before drinking the hemlock, and we have compared his Confucian "human-hearted behavior" with that of the Buddha in his last hour.

We have heard Jesus tell his critics that codes of behavior and ritual washing are not as important as the condition of a person's heart; and have entertained the possibility that we may still be capable of fulfilling his injunction to "be of one heart" in endeavors that can put heartfulness back into the world—if our individual hearts are not too small.

With Muhammad we worked the trade routes in the service of our dear employer, Khadija, later to become wife, and listened with ardent interest to the tales and beliefs of strangers, until one terrifying night they all blossomed into a revelation powerful and poetic enough to unify our people and change the course of their history.

With Augustine we wrote our autobiography, though we didn't know the term. We thought we were simply addressing God one-on-one like the ancient Israelites, pouring our heart out.

Our hearts were refreshed and stimulated, in our Crusading husbands' absence, by the secret love poems and self-abasements of our courtly lovers, and if we happened to be the suffering lovers, we writhed ecstatically as our unattainable ladies devised new ways to trample on our hearts. With Heloise, our heart remained steadfast to Abelard throughout our life as lover, wife, nun, and abbess; we made the best of a bad situation, but we never pretended we loved God more than Abelard.

We exchanged "billets" during the Roman feast of Lupercalia, and went off into the woods with the person whose name we drew; and even though the saint has now been declared nonexistent, our hearts still skip a beat when we open a modern commercial valentine and find the right signature inside.

In the anatomical theater, we watched with our hearts in our mouths as the popular doctor dissected a corpse and held up a dripping human heart, and heard him declare it was just a pump and we felt enlightened and ever so modern, but also a little sick at heart. Still, there was so much to learn and put to use! You couldn't lay your ear against the obese lady's chest, but you could make a cylinder out of an exercise book, and become the father of cardiology.

With Sister Marguerite-Marie, we had our hearts removed, cleansed by fire, and returned to our breasts. With Pascal we devised calculus, the calculating machine, and public transit, successfully balanced reason with heart, and, during a single mystical evening, were granted two whole hours of heartfelt certainty: enough to last a lifetime.

And now, though we've graduated from the industrial age and consider ourselves ever so global, and post-post-modern, there are still plenty of polluted rivers and abundant factory sites that Dickens could excoriate with his potent combination of humor and outrage if he were writing today. The worst ones have been shunted to other hemispheres where the sight of them doesn't have to bother our consciences, but there are still plenty of sweatshops with people laboring too long and too young and for not enough recompense and in not enough air or light. The heartlessness of industry and commerce still wreaks its damage.

And now, though we've been apprised about waves and particles and quarks and quanta, and notified that space and time are not the independent absolutes we once thought they were, and that things behave differently when you're observing them, and that a single butterfly riding the air currents over the Pacific sets all kinds of things in motion vast distances away, and that atoms are neither solid nor separate as we'd once been assured, and that—to sum it up with scary simplicity—*everything may be connected to everything else*, we're still scrabbling around and around on our single-vision squirrel-wheel much of the time. The fragmenting, depersonalizing, compartmentalizing mind-set still goes on dominating our lives, breaking up wholeness—the element in which heart breathes best.

"In our modern world we have achieved sexual freedom," Marie Louise von Franz wrote in 1988 in *The Way of the Dream*. "Now comes the much bigger problem, the liberation of the heart. That is the program of the next fifty years."

Notice she didn't say we would *achieve* its liberation in the next fifty years, but I think most of us would agree it's marked "urgent" on the agenda.

XVII. Heart Signs in These Times?

Just as my old reptilian brain still coils at the base of my cerebral cortex, the old Cartesian and Newtonian worldviews still influence my judgments. And though I have evolved far enough to know that I admire Sissy Jupe and Buddha and aspire to their rare combinations of "cool mind, warm heart," I also recognize that Bitzer is still very much alive inside me, sending up Gradgrind rebukes every chance he gets to shoot me down from my flights.

Yet I see signs every day that make me hope a revaluation of heart is in progress, though Bitzer is not convinced. Those aren't statistical examples, he scoffs, they're just isolated instances. They're just . . . *personal.*

Well, yes, Bitzer, but if isolated and personal are, like that solitary member of the Lepidoptera species aviating the Pacific air currents, somehow connected to everything else, maybe they're . . . *useful.* You understand that word quite well, I think.

BOOKS WITH HEART

Titles bearing the word "heart" proliferate on the display tables and shelves of our local bookstore. "Heart" (and "Soul") has eclipsed yesterday's hot title words of "Self," "Power," "Success," and "The End of," and day-before-yesterday's stylish themes of "Alienation," "Lonely," and "Existential." Naturally, over the course of my project, I have brought lots of these heart books home, and ordered others from heart searches on the Internet, and many of them have gone into the making of this book. I get as many as I can carry from my shelves, stack them on the table here beside my computer, and record their titles and something of what's inside.

There's Dr. John Stone's *In the Country of Hearts: Journeys in the Art of Medicine,* a love of a book by a cardiologist-poet who reminds us in his introduction: "The literal heart is at the very center of our lives: without it, we would all be dead. But the metaphorical heart tempers the literal one and adds an extra dimension." There's *A Change of Heart* by psychologist Lawrence A. Decker, his account of how he set out to change his metaphorical heart after undergoing quadruple coronary bypass surgery and realizing the two hearts were vitally connected. There's psychotherapist James Hillman's *The Thought of the Heart and the Soul of the World*, in which he maintains that Western culture has dire need of "a philosophy of the heart," and attempts to build one based on the Sufi concept of *himma*, "the intelligence of the heart." There's Buddhist monk Thich Nhat Hanh's *The Heart of Understanding*, commentaries on the Heart Sutra (which inspired my journey to the local Tibetan Buddhist monastery described in the epilogue). There's psychoneuroimmunologist (my alarmed spell check underlines this in red, but can't produce an alternative) Paul Pearsall's provocative *The Heart's Code*, in which he makes the case that the physical heart thinks, remembers, communicates with other hearts, helps regulate immunity, and contains stored information that continually pulsates through the body.

There's Puran Bair's *Living from the Heart*, an introduction to Sufi-based Heart Rhythm Meditation for improving daily life; the Dalai Lama's Buddhist perspectives on the teachings of Jesus in *The Good Heart*; American Buddhist nun Thubten Chodron's *Open Heart, Clear Mind*, a straightforward and readable application of Buddha's "cool mind, warm heart" principles to modern life; and Cistercian priest and abbot Father Thomas Keating's *Open Mind, Open Heart*, a guide to internal transformation through the practice of contemplation and centering prayer.

And there's Swiss cardiologist Frank Nager's congenial, wide-ranging, and lavishly illustrated treasure, *The Mythology of the Heart*, in which he says one of the great future tasks of medicine will be to combine cardiology with what he terms *cordiology*, "the symbolic language of the heart":

The *cardiological* heart pumps, fails, depolarizes and repolarizes, fibrillates, is palpated, auscultated, electrocardiographed and echocardiographed, catheterized, biopsied, digitalized, computer tomographed, fibrinolysed, compensated and transplanted.

The *cordiological* heart sings, laughs, rejoices, cries, awakes, flourishes, complains, trembles, shatters, bleeds, languishes, breaks. . . .

Making room for myth and symbol can enable us to see how one thing depends on another. . . . Cordiology could show us that cardiology is part of a network of correspondences, analogies and deeper relationships of which, up to now, too little account has been taken.

What unites all these books? Their call for a coherent culture in which mind and heart are partners, not competitors, in perception.

OPEN-HEART OCCUPATIONS

While I was traveling a few weeks ago, some long-made plans for a boring institutional dinner went awry, and instead I found myself spending the evening with a lively, attractive young woman, recently out of college, who knew exactly what she wanted to do: create a "really nice" shelter and resource center in her city to help poor women of all ages and women in trouble. To this end she had spent half a year in Mexico and Central and South America acquiring fluency in Spanish, and now she was describing to me, with an interestingly mature mix of humor and anger, her first training session at a rape crisis center. "Our teacher walks in and she goes, 'Okay, now the first thing everybody needs to know is how to recognize a false accusation of rape.' I mean, hello, what are we here for, anyway? To help someone up, or pick their story apart before they even *get* up?"

What have we here? I asked myself, drinking in this fiery young idealist who was at the same time inviting me to laugh with her at the preposterousness of the situation. I remembered myself at her age, intently boarding the train on the day of my graduation and heading in a straight line to my job on *The Miami Herald* to become a star reporter. Had I been simply another personality type than this girl, or had I been at a less-developed stage of our evolving species? Had something essential changed in human values over the last forty years, and if so, what? When I graduated from college, I had never heard of a rape crisis center (were there any in 1959?), and if you had said "shelter," I would have assumed you were talking about a roof or a portico. Women who embarked on careers went into some institution that was *already there*: a newspaper, the public school system, nursing or graduate studies, an advertising or accounting firm. The idea of a career was that of imposing yourself on the world in the way you were most likely to make a dent. True, one of my class-mates became a missionary, but missionary work also fell under the rubric of imposing yourself on your surroundings: she packed her Wycliffe Bible, I packed my spiral notebook, and off we went to make our preconceived dents.

Whereas this girl seemed to have *concave* ambitions. Contain the world rather than impress it; make an attractive hospitality and resource center to help it to its feet. She wanted to build something out of the needs she saw around her rather than enter a ready-made institution, but was prepared to go about it coolly and practically, becoming fluent in another language, putting up with self-righteous bullies in the system. Was she a brand-new wave of humanity or were we each just being the children of our respective times? Am I right, or merely wishful, in seeing her as a harbinger of more imaginative openhearted occupations today?

I can answer your question, says Bitzer. If you'll flutter down from your "concave, new wave" sky-riding for a minute. You both wanted jobs to improve your livelihood and show yourselves off in the bargain. In your day, there were more newspapers to do it on. (By the way, at the *Herald* now they wouldn't let you in the door without fluent Spanish.) In her day, there are more poor people who know they can get something for nothing, and more women who have nothing to lose by saying they've been raped. She serves their need; they serve hers. It's as simple as that. Open-heart jobs, closed-heart jobs, take your pick. But at bottom it's still supply and demand.

Ah, well, but Bitzer. Just as I'm keeping you alive by troubling to imagine your side of the dialogue, you're extending the range of my listening heart simply by putting me through the exercise.

PART TWO

Heart Themes in Life and Art

I. Heartbreak

Heartbreak is an invisible affliction. No limp comes with it, no evident scar. No sticker is issued that guarantees good parking or easy access. The heart is broken all the same. The soul festers. The wound, untreated, can be terminal.

—Thomas Lynch, *The Undertaking:*
Life Studies from the Dismal Trade

TERMINAL: MY BROTHER'S STORY

Though the official cause of death was gunshot wounds to the head, I believe my brother Tommy died of a broken heart. Half brother, actually, but why quibble about the half when he and I kicked and floated, eighteen years apart, in the same watery womb and grew to the rhythms of the same mother's heart?

It was October 2, 1983. October 1 was our mother's birthday, and that was why I was in North Carolina; she liked all her children to be there for her birthday. I flew down from New York, my half sister, Franchelle, and her family drove up from South Carolina, my half brother Rebel, still in college, drove across the state from Chapel Hill.

I wrote about this in *A Southern Family*. Tommy became Theo, a name that would have suited him well. Rebel became Rafe. I chose the name Clare for myself because I hoped for more clarity. There is no other sister in *A Southern Family*, because my younger sister— once again, why quibble about the half?—who is an attorney, told me after the publication of *The Odd Woman* that she would rather be excused from serving for any characters in my future novels.

What happened, what we *know* happened, as opposed to all that we can never know, was that on Sunday afternoon, October 2, Tommy, who had just turned twenty-eight, ironed a shirt. When he left his parents' house, where he had been living with his three-year-old son since his separation from his young wife, he told Mother he was going over to see J., the woman he was in love with. J., a nurse, was also separated with a three-year-old son. There had been serious talk of marriage, they had even made out a budget, until J. suddenly broke it off. Tommy told Mother he was going over to J.'s to ask her to reconsider. "I'm going to settle it one way or another before the afternoon is out," he said, and drove off in the bright October sunshine, leaving his son behind.

In the late afternoon of the same day, I was sitting in the kitchen, talking on the phone to a classmate from childhood, when the operator broke in and asked if I would "give up the call." I did. The voice of my mother, strangely fey and faraway, came on the line.

"Where *are* you?" I said.

She was at the hospital, she said.

"Oh God, are you all right?" She had a tricky heart.

"*I'm* fine, it's Tommy."

"Oh, no, what has he done now?" A frequent response to Tommy's turbulent life.

Mother replied in the same faraway voice: "Tommy's gone. And so is J."

Afterward, we would go over and over it. My stepfather would hire a detective. The police report would be taken out of the files, again and again, and scanned, as though the family believed that if we stayed faithfully on the case some magical number of times the *real* truth would suddenly float up from beneath the official text. The real truth being something everybody could bear.

This much we know. Tommy, J., and J.'s three-year-old son were in J.'s car. The little boy was in the backseat. The car suddenly pulled over on a shady residential street. A ten-year-old boy riding his bicycle in front of his house saw two people arguing inside the car. Shots were fired. A neighbor called the police. When the police arrived, the woman lay on the street on the passenger's side of the car. She was already dead. The man was unconscious and writhing on the ground on the driver's side. A .25-caliber Belgian semiautomatic lay on the front seat of the car. J.'s son was found uninjured in the backseat.

COUPLE FOUND SHOT was the headline in the newspaper next morning. The nuns from our old school told me the local TV channel reported it on the evening news, but they hadn't dreamed it was *their* Tommy.

Tommy had his own pistols; he belonged to the National Rifle Association; he had won prizes for marksmanship; but this particular pistol belonged to his father, Frank. He and Frank had lent it to J. several weeks before, to keep in her glove compartment, because she said a man had been stalking her. J. had been in the army and knew how to shoot, too.

J.'s three-year-old son was unable to tell anyone what had happened.

The day before, on Mother's birthday, I knew Tommy was unhappy. We all knew he was unhappy. Tommy was often unhappy. He "felt things more than most" was the family euphemism for his troubled nature. He was the person who took most to heart the family's fractures and troubles as well as the world's. When he was unhappy he would gladly tell you all about it, if you showed interest. Drawing you in with his sly closemouthed smile, he would then embark on his latest tale of woe, keeping his story line taut and considerably embellishing details for you. But always, always before, there had been a quality of *entertainment* about his stories, as if he were narrating the latest in a series of episodes starring a knight errant with a penchant for pratfalls and setbacks, but also a knight errant with missions to complete, a knight errant with a future.

Tommy was one of those modern Samaritans who carried a first-aid kit and a blue flasher light in his car in case he came across an accident; he had dreamed of becoming a state trooper, but even the state troopers he hung around with urged him to get a college education first and "then see." So he went to college and became an accountant. Just before he died, he had applied for a job with the IRS. He was sick and tired of helping boring businesspeople keep more of their money, he said; he wanted the high drama of catching the cheaters.

On the afternoon of my mother's birthday, the day before his death, Tommy had been telling me the story of his latest disappointment, in the kitchen, but something was different from the other times. After he had gone on for a few minutes about J. and his bafflement and pain over her sudden jettisoning of him and their plans, I began to realize that I was *not*, as usual, deriving the usual listening satisfaction from my brother's narrative of woe. I thought it was because I had noticed signs of aging and defeat on him for the first time, and it made me depressed and angry. Why didn't he pull back his shoulders and forget this woman? He was handsome and good and sensitive. He had a child he adored. The fallen world needed more people like him, people who carried first-aid kits in their cars and felt the world's suffering as their own. He would find another woman to suit his heart.

Now, seventeen years later, as I recall that kitchen scene, I realize what spooked me about it. Not only was there no sly, closemouthed smile, there was no longer any knight errant starring in my brother's story. There was no feeling of progression, no sense of any more missions.

I believe that I was sitting across from a broken heart and that the soul had begun to fester. And as the undertaker-poet Thomas Lynch put it, the wound was terminal.

In *The Art of Loving*, a book on love in all its aspects, from romantic love to family love to self-love to love of God, the psychoanalyst Erich Fromm wrote: "[The] desire for interpersonal fusion is the most powerful striving in man. It is the most fundamental passion, it is the force which keeps the human race together, the clan, the family, society. The failure to achieve it means insanity or destruction—self-destruction or destruction of others."

When he was younger, Tommy's son, Justin, would say: "When I grow up, I am going to go find J.'s son. By then maybe he'll remember what he saw from the backseat and I will know at last."

Justin is in his second year of college now. He hasn't mentioned going to find J.'s son for several years. While he was still in high school, Justin had his own show on a country music station. Once I stayed up until midnight so I could hear him. At midnight a man's voice said to stay tuned for Justin Cole on Kiss Country. The man's voice, smooth and playful and enjoying the sound of itself, continued talking after each song. Get off, why don't you, I snarled at the radio voice, so I can hear my nephew before I conk out. Then I realized two things: the man's voice *was* Justin's, and the voice sounded like Tommy's voice—only infinitely more at home with the world than my brother's had ever been.

Would Tommy's voice have become more at home with the world if his keen sensitivity had been allowed to grow into its full maturity? He would be forty-five now. If, at that unbearable moment on that October afternoon, there had not been a pistol available in the glove compartment of J.'s car, would Tommy have remarried, either J. or somebody else, and raised his son, and reconciled himself to a world full of pain and disappointments as long as he had a blue light and a first-aid kit in his car and a progressive series of missions that could foster his sense of drama and assuage other people's pains?

But, now, here I *do* hear his voice, the old Tommy voice, just as it was in life, chiding me as he posthumously defends the position of his beloved National Rifle Association with its perverse singsong refrain: "Gail, *guns* don't kill people; people do."

A year after Tommy's death, my mother met a woman whose daughter, berserk with heartbreak, had recently gone to the house of the man who had broken up with her, shot him dead in the shower, and then blasted herself to smithereens. The two mothers became friends, and continued to visit and write letters until my mother's death.

During the winter following Tommy's death, I had an awful dream. I awakened with my heart thudding and it took a few moments to remember who I was, and then some more time for the rage and hopelessness to drain out of me.

It was unlike any dream I'd ever had. There was no action in it, there were no visuals. I didn't see anything or hear anything. I was in the black box of myself and felt only stark, pure emotion. I wanted to die—or kill somebody—or both, because this person didn't, or couldn't, love me. The person didn't have a gender. I didn't have a gender. The whole thing was just the overwhelming agony of knowing myself not loved and wanting to kill/die to avenge myself and put an end to the pain.

I have had repeats of that *genre* of dream, but in the later dreams I am always at least myself—myself at an earlier age or myself now, trapped in a longing for someone I have outgrown in real life. The person doesn't, or cannot, love me, and I rage in anguish and wake flailing in a morass of hopelessness and shame. But never again, except for that single dream, have I been that boxed soul floating in its final heartburst of pain.

We are always being told we can never really experience what it means to be someone else. Erich Fromm says we will never get back to our original oneness with things. Our harmony with all around us was lost irretrievably when we ate of the Tree of Knowledge and became aware of ourselves as separate entities, each of whom must be born without willing it and die without willing it. But we can assuage our separateness, he says, by teaching ourselves the practice of the art of loving. This is accomplished through discipline, concentration, patience, and a *supreme concern* with the mastery of the art. Just as with any other art, you have to want to do it more than anything else. It isn't easy, but it can be done. With lots of practice.

Was my heartbreak dream a gift from my supersensitive brother while his spirit was still hovering in consolatory reach of his mourners? It would be just like Tommy to have found a posthumous way to share his pain.

Because of that dream, I now know the feeling of terminal heart-break. And because I have felt it, I am that much closer to the sorrows and heartbreaks of others.

This is what it was like, I can hear Tommy saying. Maybe it will help you to feel it, too. And hands it over like an awful package, the big red throbbing heart soon to die. Hands it over the way Jesus, in those classroom pictures at the convent school, with his inscrutable gaze, was always offering you his thorn-encased heart.

Here, feel my pain.

I felt it. I feel it.

Last month, I found myself struggling to write a letter to a young man in town whose father had just taken his own life. The father was someone Robert and I knew well. It was easy to write about the father's charm, his talents, the enjoyment and pride we had seen him take in this son, but then, when it came to the place in the letter where one is supposed to write something hopeful for the future, I balked. What could I say? Certainly not "you'll get over it in time." I'll never get over Tommy. I don't want to get over Tommy. Maybe that in itself is the hopeful part, and that is what I tried to convey in my letter. How you never get over it, and how as time goes on you realize you are *glad* you'll never get over it because the lost one remains alive in your heart as you continue to engage with the who and the why of him.

Why, for example, did Tommy go under, but we, his siblings, didn't, or so far haven't, during our heart-threatening times? Each of us has failed miserably at things, lost faith, lost face, lost heart. Each of us has been dropped, or left, or been hurt by somebody we wanted to love us. Like Tommy, at the end of my twenties I also found myself back home with Mother and Frank, a second marriage col-lapsed, without having published anything at all, looking in the mirror and glimpsing the outlines of a person who might not be going to get what she wanted.

I say, well, the gun, the gun made the difference. But there were pistols in that house available for me, too, as well as for my sister and remaining brother, and we all knew where they were kept. We weren't marksmen like Tommy, but all of us had been taught to shoot.

I ask, was it our *work* that made the difference? That all of us but Tommy, by age twenty-eight, had found pursuits we knew we could give our hearts to? Rebel has always loved to take numbers and fool around with them and create models for what might happen, what could happen, and how to prevent what shouldn't happen from happening. Franchelle's early appreciation for the conducts and codes of fairness and justice has blossomed, after two decades of law practice, into the particular heart-specialty of elder law, for which she wrote the South Carolina handbook. I discovered early that I could write my way out of misery and boredom, I was blessed with the facility to describe or make up something when things threatened to overwhelm, and finally, at thirty-three, I saw my first book in print and felt vocationally rescued. Just five more years from the age Tommy died. Would five more years have made a difference for him if—if *what*? If J. had been somewhere else that afternoon? If he had driven instead to the state trooper headquarters and said to whatever friend was on duty that Sunday, "I'm sick to death with my job, I've been to college, damn it, like you told me, and now I want to get out there with you guys and be a Knight of the Road"? If he had known more about paramedical training, which was just coming into its own? If he had come home and worked some more on his poem about his broken heart, and then, rather pleased with his revisions, taken his little boy out for pizza?

Are some of us born with strong hearts, others with fragile ones?

My delivery into this world, back in the days when mothers were routinely sedated, went without trauma (Mother's first cousin wrote a bubbly on-the-scene account of my birth to my grandparents, a letter I still have); Franchelle, fifteen years later, was a textbook model of the new "natural childbirth"; Rebel, a late-in-life child, Mother's last, arrived before the doctor could get there to deliver him. Tommy alone, both a breech and placenta previa baby, had a lengthy and harrowing delivery. His was a difficult story from the beginning, and he grew up hearing, and later telling, the blow-by-blow details of how he almost didn't make it. If you had a harrowing birth the first time around, are rebirths more difficult later? According to a modern Chinese medical model, prolonged delivery involving the cord can result in the condition of "Heart Small," in which the person throughout his life experiences "a frequent, unexpressed, and always unexplained fear, which creates a lifelong tension" (Leon Hammer, M.D., *Dragon Rises, Red Bird Flies, Psychology and Chinese Medicine*). Since the Heart is especially sensitive to the shocks that accompany all trauma, Dr. Hammer writes, the damage is particularly severe when the shock occurs at birth, especially when forceps, drugs, surgery, or artificial induction are used. In another part of the book Hammer cites a Cornell University Medical College study (1984) that found a link between respiratory distress for more than one hour at birth and youthful suicide.

Can heartbreak "accumulate" until it reaches a point where "the wound, untreated" becomes "terminal"? When Tommy's marriage was breaking up, he became so distressed one night that he tore his Bible to pieces in a fit of rage. Afterward he was shocked by his act and spiraled into remorse. He told Mother he felt he had killed something. But the death of the marriage and the dismemberment of his Bible didn't kill him. Then he met J., who was in many ways a more compatible partner than his wife had been. She was nearer his age; he took pride in her profession as a nurse. Each had the custody of a child; the two little boys enjoyed each other. And best of all, he told his mother, he could *talk* to J., *reveal himself to her*. A better life than ever seemed about to become his; he could build on his mistakes. Was the loss of that possibility like being told to go back to square one and he just didn't have the energy—the heart? Having revealed his heart at last to someone, who then decided to reject it: was that the killing blow? (Would Muhammad have thrown himself off the mountain that night if he hadn't had his beloved Khadija to crawl home to and reveal his heart to?)

Can heartbreak be treated before it is terminal? Many say it has been and will continue to be: by prayer and its sometime companion, grace; by psychotherapy, counseling, spiritual direction; by the various arts through which anguish can be given form. Turn to your nearest country music station and listen to the lyrics; somebody's heart is breaking every three minutes and somebody lived to make the stories singable.

> But, for the unquiet heart and brain
> A use in measured language lies,
> The sad mechanic exercise,
> Like dull narcotics, numbing pain . . .

That's how Tennyson, heartbroken by the sudden death of his best friend, described the inadequacy, yet the necessity, for him, of using poetry as an instrument for creative heart repair in his great long poem, "In Memoriam."

Tommy wrote to me when he was eighteen that he was "gathering a whole lot of material for a best selling novel called *Teenage Rookie* with the main character as a young man who learns more about life in his eighteenth year than he has ever learned or could hope to learn in the future." I never saw any of the material. But I know he tried to apply the medicine of measured language to his heartbreak, because he left behind a typed poem in two drafts. One is titled "Why Not Just Leave It Alone?"; the other, "Why Change the World?"

I'm never going to sum him up, track him down, figure him out. He's the family mystery, never to be solved; all I can do now is cultivate the enigma of Tommy in my heart. Nevertheless, I pore over the legacy of those two poems, his entire literary output, comparing the rhyme schemes, both basically of the aa/bb/cc type (unknown, condone; evoke, choke; gone, on; world, unfurled). I try to guess which draft he wrote first and how long the whole effort took him: two hours, three, six? I like to picture him sitting downstairs at the basement typewriter, screwing up his handsome face as he tries to balance his iambic and anapestic feet so they won't jolt against each other and sound amateurish, and *as long as he's doing that, he's still safe.* Only one line is exactly the same in both drafts: "My pride is broken since my lover's gone." And both drafts end with the same image: the poet being laid in his wooden home, "with my trooper hat on my chest bone."

In that place in myself where I keep people alive, I speak to his still-living heart: "Now, write a *third* draft, Tommy. A fourth, a fifth. Okay, it still hurts. Write a sequence of dirges for fallen lovers with trooper hats; go for a thousand-line elegy on what you have lost. But stay with us and keep revising!"

AVENGED THROUGH ART:
GEORGE BERNARD SHAW'S *HEARTBREAK*
HOUSE AND ELIZABETH BOWEN'S *THE DEATH*
OF THE HEART

Ellie: I have a horrible fear that my heart is broken, but
that heartbreak is not like what I thought it must be.
—Heartbreak House

Shaw's Play

Irish playwright George Bernard Shaw (1856–1950) and Anglo-
Irish novelist Elizabeth Bowen (1899–1973) both fell in love with
people who could not, or would not, love them back. Shaw was fifty-
six at the time of his unrequited love; Bowen was thirty-seven at the
time of hers. Yet both lived to survive the experience—and to use the
heartbreakers as cold, unsympathetic, rather foolish characters in
their most memorable creative works, both about heartbreak.

Shaw's *Heartbreak House* was completed four years after the
actress Mrs. Patrick Campbell bolted from their planned tryst at
Sandwich Bay, leaving him in a wretched rage. Elizabeth Bowen's
Death of the Heart was published within two years of the summer that
Goronwy Rees came to stay with Bowen at Bowen's Court in Ireland
and ended up neglecting Elizabeth and sleeping with her friend, the
beautiful novelist Rosamond Lehmann.

The heroines of both works are innocent, candid young women
who have their hearts broken by the duplicitous and unfeeling society into which they are just coming of age.

In Shaw's play, Ellie Dunn, eighteen, arrives at Heartbreak House at
the invitation of Hesione Hushabye, a seductive older woman who has

taken her up as a protégée. Within a single day, Ellie loses her romantic illusions and chooses to give "my broken heart and my strong
sound soul to its natural captain." Ellie realizes that the man she loves
is Hesione's philandering husband, and that the rich man she was
going to marry out of loyalty to her father is too gross for her soul
(which she still has, despite her broken heart—the play makes a
strong point of that). Ultimately she makes a spiritual marriage with
Hesione's old father, Captain Shotover, a misanthropic retired sea captain who represents what is left of the life force and of integrity. The
play is an allegory in which Shaw indicts the enervated, futile drawing-
room atmosphere of England and Europe just before World War I;
bombs are exploding around Heartbreak House in the last scene.

All characters bear symbolic names and each represents a particular evil in a world shortly to be smashed to bits by war. Hesione, the
chatelaine of Heartbreak House, is a false enchantress of romance
and sexual infatuation who lures people into her net and then leaves
them stranded. She is based on Stella Campbell.

"I . . . got two stage characters out of you (Hesione and Orinthia)
and will perhaps get six more out of your manifold nature," the seventy-
five-year-old Nobel laureate Shaw wrote from England to Mrs. Patrick
Campbell, by then an actress in decline, living in the Barclay Hotel in
New York, "but except for a little harmless waving of my scalp at first
you could get nothing out of me, could not believe in me, shrank from
letting me touch anything you were doing, made it impossible for us to
work together in the theatre, and now finally, when you want to publish
our letters, are mortally afraid lest I should write the preface or see a line
of the story instead of thanking God that you have expert help at hand
to save you from making a dozen *gaffes* in every chapter."

But Stella Campbell kept badgering Shaw by Western Union
cablegram: would he have her go on another cruel American lecture

tour at her age, packing and unpacking and ironing her own crumpled gowns, catching trains alone at unearthly hours? Or instead, would he let her publish his letters, and send back her own letters to him, so she could settle down in Mrs. Gerald Murphy's lovely house in Cap d'Antibes and write "something vital but artistically true" around the love letters, supporting herself with the advance from the publishers?

Shaw wrote back that he knew how exhausting the lecturing road was in America ("in fact I know everything better than you do"). Then after assuring her he hadn't "a scrap of unkind feeling about her," he concluded: "But as to the letters: NO. The fates, not I, decree it. G.B.S."

Three years pass. Mrs. Campbell persists. Writing from Sunset Boulevard, she encloses her photograph ("you will see I still hold together") and confides that though his veto on the publication of the letters lost her a fortune, she sometimes reads one particular letter when she wants to set her heart aglow. "I showed it to a brilliant lady the other day—her words were: 'It is more beautiful than anything he has ever written, what a crime the world doesn't know this man.' "

That did it. Almost by return mail comes, "My dear Stella, My antiquity, now extreme at eighty-one, has obliged me to make a clearance among my papers and take measures . . . for my probably imminent decease. I find that I have done a very wicked thing: I have kept all your letters in spite of my rule never to keep anything but necessary business memoranda. I kept Ellen Terry's because her handwriting made pictures of them which I could not burn: it would have been like burning a mediaeval psalter or a XV Century French Book of Hours, I have no such excuse in your case."

Ouch. Touché.

Three days later Shaw wrote again: "I have now, with infinite labor and a little heartbreak packed all the letters, from the polite one to dear Mr. Shaw in 1901 when you wouldn't be Cleopatra, to your last cablegram, into six compact envelopes."

Warning her that there can be no question of publication of the letters until his and his wife's ashes are scattered, Shaw at last turns over the correspondence to his old love, which "will be a valuable literary property," and concludes with: "And so, blessed be your days, dear Stella."

Stella Campbell died at Pau, in the South of France, in 1940. She was seventy-five.

Mrs. Shaw died in 1943, at the age of eighty-six.

When George Bernard Shaw died in 1950, at the age of ninety-four, he was at work on a comedy.

The letters, *Bernard Shaw and Mrs. Patrick Campbell: Their Correspondence*, were published in 1952. Mrs. Campbell's daughter, Stella M. Beech, writes in a foreword that Mr. Shaw had expressed to her the desire that any proceeds arising from the publication should be used for the secondary education of Mrs. Campbell's great-grandchildren, who at the time of publication, however, were already sixteen and thirteen years old.

Bowen's Novel

"Darling, I don't want you; I've got no place for you; I only want what you give. I don't want the whole of anyone. . . . What you want is the whole of me—isn't it, *isn't it?*—and the whole of me isn't there for anybody. In that full sense you want me I don't exist."

—Eddie to Portia, *The Death of the Heart*

When *The Death of the Heart* came out in 1938, two years after Elizabeth Bowen's unhappy (for Elizabeth) house party at Bowen's

Court, Goronwy Rees immediately recognized himself in the character of Eddie. Flattered at first, he told Rosamond Lehmann, with
whom he had betrayed Elizabeth, that the novel was brilliant. Then
he reversed himself, wrote Bowen an emotional, bitter letter, and
was making plans to sue her for libel until E. M. Forster and other
friends talked him out of it.

I find myself rereading *The Death of the Heart* every three or four
years and, like all great books, it becomes a new book each time.
Young women of Portia's age, honorary daughters and goddaughters
that I have given it to, love it passionately, though I expect they skip
over some of the weather-as-metaphor passages as well as the autho-
rial voice-over musings about the workings of the heart. But they
will read it again, when they are the age of their mothers, and then
their grandmothers, and find that, like well-invested savings, it has
compounded in value.

After reading about the Goronwy Rees affair in Victoria Glendin-
ning's biography of Bowen, I must say I was downright glad that
Elizabeth had suffered so during that house party of 1936. I think
she eventually came to be glad herself, because, as she often said, she
was a writer before she was a woman and thus could chalk up these
heartbreaks to valuable experience. She was to remark of another
man with whom she was later (briefly) in love that he was "one of
those people who do not understand that affairs have their natural
termination." "One wants to say," she reflected on another occasion,
"break my heart if you must, but don't waste my time."

Being a novelist myself, I derived satisfaction from learning how a
master of the form turned personal pain into art. I also found myself
wondering if her early exorcism of Goronwy in *The Death of the Heart*
had helped to transform her into that "writer first, woman second,"
who counted a broken heart less of an inconvenience than having

her time wasted. And I also ask myself, having performed a few fictional exorcisms of my own, whether the practice might not eventually form calluses on the heart, making you more invulnerable to betrayal, but less open to new opportunities to love.

The Death of the Heart is set in a house in "Windsor Terrace" shortly after World War I, whose opening volleys were heard at the end of *Heartbreak House*. According to Bowen's biographer, the Windsor Terrace house was the author's own in Regent's Park, London, with the same upstairs drawing room where Elizabeth Bowen, like the childless and charming Anna Quayne in *The Death of the Heart*, entertained her visitors, and the same downstairs study where Anna's husband, Thomas, like Elizabeth's husband, Allan Cameron, waits grudgingly until the visitors are gone. Bowen's husband called Elizabeth's male friends the Black Hats because of their hats hanging in the hall when he came home from work. Goronwy Rees, ten years younger than Elizabeth, was a Black Hat with whom Elizabeth had formed an attachment.

Into this fictional house, where "the rooms were set for strangers' intimacy, or else for exhausted solitary retreat," a house in which there is "no point where feeling could thicken," comes orphaned Portia Quayne, sixteen, Thomas Quayne's half sister from his father's embarrassing late marriage. Portia, still mourning her mother, the "not quite-quite" Irene (who knew that "nine out of ten things you do direct from the heart are the wrong thing, and that she was not capable of doing anything better"), watches Anna and Thomas; she judges them, she keeps a diary that Anna, threatened by Portia's "perfectly open face," reads on the sly.

Into this setup comes Eddie, one of the most fickle neurotics in modern fiction.

He had been the brilliant child of an obscure home, and
came up to Oxford ready to have his head turned. There
he was taken up, played up, played about with, taken
down, let down, finally sent down for one idiotic act. His
appearance was charming: he had a proletarian, animal,
quick grace. His manner . . . had become bold, vivid, and
intimate. . . . The one thing no one, so far, knew about
Eddie was quite how he felt about selling himself.

Eddie, twenty-three, becomes Anna's "troubadour" at Windsor
Terrace until he ruins things by trying to kiss her. He digs himself in
further by explaining he only did it because he thought she expected
it. Later, when he is about to break young Portia's heart, he explains
that it's because he "can't get on with people" that he has to "get off
with them." Perhaps the most deadly thing about his match with
Portia is that he, too, is an innocent in his way. He tells Portia that
people like her "have a lunatic instinct for picking on another person
who doesn't even know where he is." Turning the knife, he justifies
his betrayal of Portia with Daphne at the movies:

"How can I keep on feeling something I once felt when
there are so many things one can feel? People who always
say they feel as they did simply fake themselves up. I may
be a crook but I'm not a fake—that's an entirely different
thing."

In *The Death of the Heart*, the only person who comes off
unscathed at the end, neither betrayer or betrayed, is Matchett, the
maid, who could be said to represent the heart of the house on
Windsor Terrace. It is Matchett who keeps the rhythms that count

pulsing along beneath whatever genteel dissimulations and "unnatu-
ral living" (Matchett's phrase) are taking place in the elegant rooms
with closed doors. Season after season, at Windsor Terrace, it is
Matchett who keeps the steady *tempo giusto*.

If, coming into Portia's room to say good night, Matchett lowers
her voice,

> ... This seemed to be in awe of approaching sleep. She
> awaited the silent tide coming in. About now, she served
> the idea of sleep with a series of little ceremonials—laying
> out night clothes, leveling fallen pillows, hospitably open-
> ing up the beds. Kneeling to turn on bedroom fires, stoop-
> ing to slip bottles between sheets, she seemed to abase
> herself to the overcoming night. The impassive solemnity
> of her preparations made a sort of an altar of each bed.

It is Matchett who is sent by Anna and Thomas to fetch Portia
"home" to Windsor Terrace after the girl, betrayed twice over, first
by Eddie, then by Anna's reading her diary, has run away to Major
Brutt, a lonely war veteran who has sent her two picture puzzles,
and whom Anna and Thomas make fun of behind his back.

In a strange echo of young Ellie Dunn in *Heartbreak House*, who
makes a spiritual marriage with old Captain Shotover, Portia shows
up at Major Brutt's seedy residence hotel and proposes marriage to
him. "Had nothing in Major Brutt responded to it he would have
gone on being gentle, purely sorry for her," but as it is, he has too
much to lose, Thomas and Anna are his only remaining social life.
He gets up briskly, almost to the point of being callous, and leaves
the hotel room to telephone the Quaynes that Portia is safe. We last
see Portia through his eyes, as she waits to be retrieved by her right-

ful owners: a young girl lying on his bed, her arms locking his eiderdown, "her last shelter," tightly to her chest.

> Her detachment made her seem to abandon being a
> woman—she was like one of those children in an Eliza-
> bethan play who are led on, led off . . . and are known to be
> bound for some tragic fate which will be told in a line. . . .
> At the same time, her body looked like some drifting object
> that has been lodged for a moment, by some trick of the
> current, under a bank, but must be dislodged again and go
> on twirling down the implacable stream.

Elizabeth Bowen the writer has been able to divide herself into
the character of the ironic Anna of the "shut-in rooms," whose
unhappy love experience of her own youth, an affair before she was
married to Thomas ("who dreaded . . . to be loved with any great
gush of the heart. There was some nerve in his feeling he did not
want touched"), has given her a "turned-in heart," and the character
of young Portia, whose impressions are still fresh and open, whose
heart can still innocently give itself and be betrayed and broken.
Elizabeth the disappointed lover has made the bygone summer
heartbreak of 1936 into a story that still speaks to the hearts of the
Portias and Annas of today.

Shaw, the disappointed lover at fifty-six, has, through his play, created a spiritual marriage between a wise, tough, cantankerous old
survivor (as he himself would become) and a young woman who
pledges her broken heart and her strong, sound soul to "its natural
captain." Their union is Shaw's alchemical marriage between the
writer's tough ego and his intact soul, or anima, that together can
navigate through the detritus of broken hearts and collapsed worlds.

Both Bowen and Shaw were exceptional writers who could avenge themselves through their art and present us with bouquets of insights plucked from their disappointments. But what kinds of exorcism can a *nonwriter* practice? someone asks. I ask, where does one draw the line between writer and nonwriter? Is there such a human creature as "a nonwriter"? My brother Tommy would have been the last person to call himself a writer, yet he left evidence that he turned to poem-making in his last days to sort out and give utterance to his anguish, and, who knows, it may have prolonged his life for a short time. Words are the most available material for creative repair work, even if you're illiterate, like Muhammad, or can't hear words or speak them, as Helen Keller couldn't. Words don't cost anything, you don't have to acquire canvas or pigments at the art supply store before you can express your vision. You don't need to learn scales first, or how to play with both hands at once, or count rhythms, or own any instrument other than a pencil in order to give voice to your plight.

At this point, providentially (synchronistically?) I had to interrupt my writing about writing as creative repair work in order to keep a noon phone date with a book club chat room on the iVillage.com site. The topic was my novel *Evensong*, and by the last quarter of the hour, I felt so at home with the people in the "room," whether they were in Brooklyn or Alaska or Australia, that I asked them if they would be willing to answer a question for me to help me with something I was writing in my heartbreak chapter. Let's get started, let's get going! they replied eagerly. My question to them was, Has writing ever saved you from despair, and if so, how?

The answers came pouring in quicker than my chat room mediator could relay them to me over the phone. I scribbled as fast as I could. Here are the results (minus some that got buried in the overload before the hour was up and someone typed, "Go grab lunch, Gail!"):

Yes oh yes! Journaling through recovery from incest kept me sane.

Writing has helped me see that my problems are not as bad as I thought, and that my problems, hopes, and dreams are the same as everyone else's.

Writing has been my way to deal with despair. I'm in despair right now because I should be writing not chatting.

Writing is how we share those darknesses we've dealt with and present them to others in a form that everyone can relate to.

I don't cry nearly as much since I have been releasing my emotions with my pen.

Fictionalization of things that have happened to me releases me from childhood and demons.

I can't tell you how many times Harrison Ford has kissed me in my stories!

We dream of doing things through our characters; we also use them to test out things we're afraid of doing.

I'm a writer who can benefit from my writing, not just a sufferer of my fate waiting for someone to help me recover.

Whether speaking aloud in the dark or writing in a room by yourself, you have crossed the line from inchoate animal suffering into the privilege of being human. Whether, like Tommy, your lover has broken your heart or, like Muhammad, a terrifying angel has commanded you to open your heart and "give voice" to strange things, or, like Job, you had everything taken away from you at one blow and refuse to stop asking God why, the putting into syllables of your predicament is your unique human accomplishment.

The moment you begin to shape words and images into an utterance, you have summoned an interlocutor. Now you can be the one who asks and then listens in the silence for the kind of answer that might never speak for itself out of your own lonely void.

HEARTBREAK OBSERVED: C. S. LEWIS

The most precious gift that marriage gave me was this constant impact of something very close and intimate yet all the time unmistakably other, resistant—in a word, real. Is all that work to be undone? Is what I shall still call H. to sink back horribly into being not much more than one of my old bachelor pipe-dreams? Oh my dear, my dear, come back for one moment and drive that miserable phantom away. Oh God, God, why did you take such trouble to force this creature out of its shell if it is now doomed to crawl back—to be sucked back—into it?

—*A Grief Observed*

Observe does not only mean watching from an uncommitted distance, such as in "[Cassius] reads much; he is a great observer," in

Shakespeare's *Julius Caesar*, or as in "UN observer," or "She observed the pedestrians on the street below."

The Latin verb derives from *ob–* (to, toward, before) + *servare* (to keep, to hold) and, in the case of C. S. Lewis's memoir of the "mad midnight moments" after his wife's death, describes the very antithesis of distance. *A Grief Observed* is heartbreak adhered to, *heeded*: observed with the same attention with which Lewis, the Christian apologist and former confirmed bachelor, always observed Easter.

The marriage of the divorced American writer and mother of two boys, Helen Joy Gresham, dying of cancer, to Oxford don and misogynist C. S. (Jack) Lewis, entering the sixth decade of his life, is a compelling and moving love story. You can rent the excellent movie *Shadowlands* and watch Debra Winger and Anthony Hopkins as Joy and Jack go through the whole thing again, and if your heart is anywhere in the vicinity you will probably find yourself in tears by the end.

The story of the Gresham-Lewis marriage has a powerful allegorical quality to it; it is a miraculous tale with a moral, an adult version of the sort Lewis wrote so successfully for children.

The bare bones might go something like this: There was a little boy of nine whose beloved and devoutly religious mother died of cancer. His heart shut down. No more pain like *that*, thank you very much. He became a confirmed atheist and remained one during his teens and most of his twenties. He was wounded in the Great War. Earned firsts in classics and philosophy and English at Oxford, then became a Fellow at a college there. At age twenty-eight, during a whiskey-splashing talk with a tough, cynical philosophy don who admitted he believed in the Trinity, the atheist felt the magnetic pull of the divine despite himself. From then on, everything he read and wrote was, in one way or another, a quest for God. He became a famous apologist for Christianity and used his learning and facility with words to convince many people of its truths. He and his brother, a retired soldier, lived with a housekeeper, the mother of a friend killed in the Great War. He had many correspondents and friends, but steered clear of love and of women. At age forty-five, he wrote to a Benedictine monk friend: "The decay of *friendship*, owing to the endless presence of women everywhere, is a thing I'm rather afraid of."

When he was fifty-three, the foreshadows began. First the housekeeper died. Lewis's brother wrote in his diary that the late housekeeper had enslaved his brother, raped his life, robbed him of his holidays, and "rescued him from the twin evils of bachelordom and matrimony at one fell swoop!" But now she was gone.

The following year, two more foreshadowings:

1. Lewis went on an Easter walking holiday with a male friend and found something significant missing. He afterward wrote a poem which began with the lines,

> By now I should be entering on the supreme stage
> Of the whole walk, reserved for the late afternoon . . .

But something hadn't happened. What was it? The landscape was not as expected. Where were the "light drops of silver temperance, and clover earth sending up mists of chastity"? Why was not his rest secure? "Was the map wrong?" the fifty-four-year-old religious bachelor-poet inquires at the end of the poem.

2. A month later, Lewis gets a phone call. "When are you going to pay Mrs. Hooker's bill?" Who was Mrs. Hooker, and why should he pay her bill? "She's your wife!" came the reply. For the past year

Mrs. Hooker, advertising herself as the wife of the great man, had been running up bills at resort towns and borrowing money on the strength of his name. He went down to London to make the acquaintance of "his wife" at the police court. Justice did its work swiftly on the larcenist, but the experience was peculiar in that he admitted to friends *he had been curious to meet her.*

Four months later, he went to a hotel to have lunch with two married women, one of whom was Helen Joy Gresham, an American writer who had been corresponding with him about religious matters.

Friendship began that day. He asked her to lunch again. He asked her and her young sons to spend Christmas with him and his brother. Afterward, she returned to America, found that her husband wanted a divorce in order to marry her cousin, fled back to England and put her sons in school. When school money ran out, Lewis gladly supplied it from his "Agape Fund," set up for friends down on their luck and the deserving needy. When her temporary visa ran out, Lewis gladly made a secret civil marriage with her, "in name only," so she could become a British citizen. She was limping badly on the day of the April ceremony from something diagnosed as fibrositis, but in October she was hospitalized with runaway cancer. She would probably need round-the-clock care until the end came. Lewis went to his bishop to get permission to marry his stricken friend in the church so he could care for her in his house without scandal. The bishop refused: she was a divorced woman. Five months later, death was imminent and Lewis found a priest who agreed to marry them "properly" before God. The marriage, Lewis explained, would last a day, perhaps a week, maybe as long as a month.

And the fifty-nine-year-old groom took his wife home to die.

But the unexpected happened. Radiation, testosterone, and remission kept Helen Joy Lewis alive for two and a half more years, during which time, as her son Douglas was later to write, the love between her and Lewis grew until it was "almost a visible incandescence."

> What was H. not to me? She was my daughter and my mother, my pupil and my teacher, my subject and my sovereign; and always, holding all these in solution, my trusty comrade, friend, shipmate, fellow soldier. My mistress; but at the same time all that any man friend (and I have good ones) has ever been to me. Perhaps more. If we had never fallen in love we should have nonetheless been always together and created a scandal.

Before it was over, "no cranny of heart or body remained unsatisfied." The man who had shut down his heart at the age of nine slowly opened it again until, as the blurb on the back of the *Shadowlands* video proclaims, "their romance shatters the walls of his cloistered world." But a heart open to great love is equally open to great pain when that love is lost.

And how does the fable end? With the smooth, eloquent apologist besieging God, in short bursts of agony, for an explanation: Why did you take the trouble to force me out of my shell if I am now doomed to crawl back—or be sucked back—into it? But what Lewis lived to see was that he had outgrown that doom. When his heart got broken, so did the shell.

What makes *A Grief Observed* so much more than a "grief book," even a grief book by a man of spirit and intellect accustomed to making words do his bidding, is its fully *alive* quality. The short, agonized endearments and entreaties, the sharp arguments with God, the achingly detailed catalog of just how much has been lost for good, all exemplify the unsettling paradox that one must be completely alive to completely experience heartbreak. Heartbreak, in *A Grief Observed*, is an amalgam of despair and elation, of realizing that one is awake enough to experience it fully. Though heartbreak permeates his life in every line, *it has a vitality of its own.*

Toward the end of the book, the widowed Lewis describes coming face-to-face in the night with "an extreme and cheerful intimacy," almost businesslike, an intimacy that did not seem to pass through the senses and emotions at all but was just the impression of her mind momentarily facing his own. There was no message from the dead, just intelligence and attention. ("I'm almost scared at the adjectives I'd have to use. Brisk? cheerful? keen? alert? intense? wide awake? Above all, solid. Utterly reliable. Firm. There is no nonsense about the dead.")

This unusual testament from a man who answered the call of the heart to transcend himself, and who lived to tell about it, is also a tribute to how much he could allow himself to love—at last. It was first published a year after his wife's death under the pseudonym N. W. Clerk.

Back in 1954, the complacent bachelor wrote these unwittingly presageful lines to his friend the monk: "Has any theologian allegorized St. Mary Magdalene's act in the following way, which came to me like a flash of lightning the other day! The precious alabaster box which we have to break over the holy feet is our heart. It seems so obvious, once one has thought of it."

II. Absence of Heart/Heartlessness

"I wish very much you were not so heartless," said Madame Merle, quietly. "It has always been against you, and it will be against you now."

"I'm not so heartless as you think. Every now and then something touches me—as for instance your saying just now that your ambitions are for me. I don't understand it; I don't see how or why they should be. But it touches me, all the same."

—Henry James, *The Portrait of a Lady*

INVALIDS OF EROS: GILBERT OSMOND IN *THE PORTRAIT OF A LADY*

"I don't understand it," he says, and that's the nature of his deficiency. Gilbert Osmond just cannot imagine why his old friend Madame Merle should want to do something for him, in this case put a lovely, intelligent, charming, *rich* young woman in his path. He can't feel what it's like to want to give someone else something without getting something for it yourself. Nonetheless, he admits himself "touched" by it. He's not as heartless as she thinks, it's just that there's something missing in him. What is missing? The ability himself to have such feelings *on behalf of* another. He is aware of his deficiency, and because he is clever and subtle he will be able to impersonate a man with heart and thus win the heart of Isabel Archer.

All of us have known someone with an absent heart. You knock on this person's organ of response and get no reply. The first few times, you make excuses for the lack of resonance. He's preoccupied with something else; maybe she didn't hear me. But after the dozenth—or hundredth time, if you're the hopeful type—your knock begins to echo the terrible truth. There's no response. Something basic seems missing, but you still can't believe it's the heart.

Such people are fascinating in their way, especially to those of us with lively imaginations. Once I tried to make one of them the model for the protagonist for a novel but soon foundered in the attempt. I could present her from the outside, from the point of view of others who met her or were affected by her, but when I looked for her inmost sanctuary, the door was nowhere to be found. Then I started doing what Isabel did: creating a heart for my character out of my own thoughts and feelings. In my case, the transplant was rejected, and the novel died. In Isabel's case, she fell in love with her creation and married Gilbert Osmond and became acquainted with true suffering.

As author, Henry James keeps a prudent distance between himself and Gilbert Osmond, who of all the characters in novels I have read remains for me the best-drawn embodiment of absence of heart. Dowell, the obtuse unreliable narrator of *The Good Soldier*, by Ford Maddox Ford, runs a close second, but Osmond is far more interesting because he is so subtle and intelligent and attractive. My fascination with Osmond in rereadings of *The Portrait of a Lady* has made me better at recognizing signs of the absent heart when I come across them in a person.

Yes, the Master keeps his distance, except for two incursions into Osmond's interior workings. The first, which reveals Osmond's hidden drive for power, James completely excised in his 1909 edition of the novel, possibly because the sixty-six-year-old author, now in his ultradiscreet phase, felt he had been too heavy-handed at thirty-eight. It's also possible that James recoiled at certain aspects of his own shadow side. James's biographer Leon Edel has suggested that Osmond is what Henry James *without his artistic gift* might have become. "In creating [Osmond] Henry put into him his highest ambition and drive to power . . . while at the same time recognizing in his villain the dangers to which such inner absolutism might expose him. In the hands of a limited being, like Osmond, the drive to power ended in dilettantism and petty rages. In Henry's hands the same drive had given him unbounded creativity."

I was delighted when the Library of America made the earlier version of the novel available again, so I could finish my jigsaw puzzle of Gilbert Osmond's absent heart. Here is a sampling of the material the older, "discreet," James excised:

> Certain it is that Osmond's desire to marry had been deep and distinct. It had not been notorious; he had not gone about asking people whether they knew a nice girl with a little money. Money was an object; but this was not his manner of proceeding, and no one knew—or even greatly cared—whether he wished to marry or not. . . . He was a failure, of course; that was an old story. . . . Success for Gilbert Osmond would be to make himself felt; that was the only success to which he could now pretend. . . . Osmond's line would be to impress himself not largely but deeply . . . the clear and sensitive nature of a generous girl would make space for the record. . . . He had waited so long in vain that he finally almost lost his interest in the subject. . . . When at last the best did present itself Osmond recognized it like a gentleman . . . it was his own idea of success.

Henry James's other ingress into Osmond's mind comes midway through both versions of the novel, when Gilbert Osmond, through the machinations of Madame Merle, has just become engaged to the heiress Isabel. (I'm still quoting from the 1881 edition; I like it better because it's more unguarded.)

> Gilbert Osmond was not demonstrative. . . . Content-
> ment, on his part, never took a vulgar form; excitement in
> the most self-conscious of men, was a kind of ecstasy of
> self-control. This disposition, however, made him an
> admirable lover; it gave him a constant view of the
> amorous character. He never forgot himself, as I say; and
> so he never forgot to be graceful and tender, to wear the
> appearance of devoted intention. He was immensely
> pleased with his young lady; Madame Merle had made
> him a present of incalculable value. . . . His egotism, if
> egotism it was, had never taken the crude form of wishing
> for a dull wife; this lady's intelligence was to be a silver
> plate, not an earthen one—a plate that he might heap up
> with ripe fruits . . . so that conversation might become a
> sort of perpetual dessert. He found the silver quality in
> this perfection in Isabel; he could tap her imagination
> with his knuckle and make it ring.

Even in this foray into Osmond's interior, James holds on to the safety rope of his own omniscient voice. ("He never forgot himself, *as I say*.")

A person with an absent heart makes an ideal villain, but why would anyone want to make a person with an absent heart the protagonist of a novel? The simplest answer might be that a mystifying person is always challenging because she rouses our curiosity; we want to look inside her and observe the workings of her secret springs. Our love of gossip probably has its source in this same fiction-making instinct: What do you think her past is? What is his real motive?

And people with absent hearts are *very* mystifying. The more imagination we have, the more mystery we can project onto them. Maybe one reason for wanting to make a main character out of them is to see how far we can penetrate mysterious, shadowy aspects of ourselves. On the other hand, if we have an idealistic nature like Isabel's, we fill in their empty spaces with the qualities that attract us, qualities that we ourselves would like to have, and that can be dangerous.

Some idealistic people just can't accept that someone's heart can be totally absent. And perhaps they secretly believe they will succeed where others have failed to locate that absent organ. Isabel's dying cousin Ralph calls Osmond a sterile middle-aged dilettante with no fortune; but Isabel, in love, sees her fiancé as admirable because he has borne his poverty with dignity and indifference; he has "never scrambled for worldly prizes." Until recently, she herself has been poor, and she admires this in Osmond. Defending her lover to Ralph, Isabel tells her cousin she rejoices that her money has put it in her power to marry a man who has no title, no position, no brilliant belongings of any sort. "It is the total absence of all these things that pleases me," she concludes in passionate, idealistic high dudgeon. (The terrible irony, unknown by Isabel, is that Ralph asked his late father to leave Isabel part of his own fortune so she could satisfy the demands of her high ideals!)

The rest of the novel takes us behind the scenes of her marriage and shows how she lives with these "absences," including the biggest absence of all.

Adolf Guggenbuhl-Craig, in *Eros on Crutches: On the Nature of the Psychopath*, describes absent-hearted people as "invalids of eros," yet cautions that we all bear traces of this deficiency in varying degrees. One good reason for studying them, he suggests, is to be better able to spot the absent places in ourselves.

> I find myself compelled . . . to remind the reader constantly that I am not speaking of "us" and of "them," of us as integrated, balanced or whole and of the others who are missing something, the psychopaths. Admittedly, it is important to be able to recognize psychopathic individuals when we are confronted by them. It seems to me far more important that . . . we strive to realize in what way we are psychopaths.

The word *psychopath*, from the Greek *psyche* (soul) and *pathos* (suffering), is still used by European psychiatric professionals to describe a person with a lack of feeling and morality. In the American *Diagnostic and Statistical Manual of Mental Disorders IV*, the term *sociopath* is preferred, the term *psychopath* having shrunk to mean social maladjustment or criminality: thus the need to find a fresh description for the dark paradigm that can reveal similar shadings in those of us who haven't committed criminal acts.

How, then, *do* we recognize "an invalid of eros," someone whose heart seems not just "cold," or "hard," or "lost," but simply absent?

Guggenbuhl-Craig uses the word *eros* in its widest sense, to cover the entire range of human emotional engagement, from sexual attraction to friendship, to love of one's work, to love of God. Though by no means a guarantee of happiness or security, eros manifests itself in us through our loving and creative involvement with other beings and things, just as, say, a musical awareness in us might manifest itself through the desire to attend concerts, play or compose music, or even through a musical sensitivity to sounds: the pitch of an animal cry, the tempo of a dripping faucet.

But whereas a nonmusical person will readily admit to you she never makes up tunes or goes to chamber music concerts and can't identify the pitch of an owl cry in the night, the eros-deficient person is likely to be incapable of perceiving her deficiency. It wouldn't occur to her that she has no "thou" pitch, or to say: "I really don't see you as a person in your own right, I see you only as something that can be of use to me—or of no use, in which case I will turn away from you at a party and not answer your phone calls. On the other hand, if it suits me, I can carry on an animated, even intimate, conversation with you, but when my back is turned you will cease to exist again. I will lie if it suits my needs or my mood, I will make false promises to get something I want, either personally or profession-ally, and I will feel no remorse about my tactics afterward nor even necessarily be aware of them as such. Though I can impersonate a person of loving feelings if there is something to be gained by it—a rich or famous husband or business partner, for instance—I don't feel a loving identification with anyone. I can hurt you, betray you, forget you. It's just the way I am."

Guggenbuhl-Craig lists and elucidates five primary symptoms of eros-invalids: inability to love, a missing or deficient sense of moral-ity, absence of any psychic development, background depression (a lifelong lack of meaning, lack of hopefulness or a sense of growth), and chronic background fear (they do *not* trust the world).

Invalids of eros can be charming and intelligent and relate easily to others on a superficial level; they can exhibit feelings or, like Gilbert Osmond wooing Isabel Archer, *act as if they have the proper feelings.* They can carry on an amiable conversation with you one minute and forget you as soon as their backs are turned. Describing two patients of this ilk, Guggenbuhl-Craig writes that relationships for them were passing things that could be taken up as the situation demanded. "They never seemed to have the need to spend time with others on a frequent basis. They seldom wrote to acquaintances—if they were gone they were gone. . . . Relationships did not seem to be something to be developed and enjoyed, but were simply temporal necessities."

He then goes on to cite secondary symptoms, which may or may not be present in a particular eros-invalid, and are frequently found among our own "absentee" tendencies and traits. One secondary symptom is lack of guilt feelings; another is the absence of any real understanding or insight; invalids of eros don't see into themselves. They rarely seek counseling, unless they are forced into it by a spouse or an employer—or a court of law. Another tendency is the ability to evoke pity, to manipulate our protective instincts and call forth our savior fantasies. ("I have only one ambition," the newly affianced Isabel tells her cousin, "—to be free to follow out a good feeling. . . . There have been moments when I should like to go and kneel by your father's grave [because] he put it in my power to marry a poor man— a man who has borne his poverty with such dignity.")

Another secondary symptom in the eros-invalid is boredom, due to lack of inner reserves; sometimes eros will put in a redeeming appearance in the form of painting or gardening or collecting

(Patricia Highsmith's psychopath character Tom Ripley paints in watercolors, plays the harpsichord, collects antiques, and buys and sells forged paintings when he's not looking for risks or thrills out of boredom); but if eros is altogether absent, the vacuum is filled with meaningless or destructive activity, such as restless travel, or driving at high speeds on the thruway (or, in Tom's case, trying his hand at garroting a mafioso in the lavatory of a moving train).

A frequent trait of eros-invalids is, as mentioned already, charm: "Because eros does not clutter their relationships, they can dig into their bag of tricks without any inhibitions or scruples," writes Guggenbuhl-Craig. They know how to please and flatter their objects and often succeed in utterly bewitching them.

Many eros-invalids are social climbers. Social recognition assuages their depression and gives them a sense of power. Poor Isabel, after she has been Mrs. Osmond for four years, realizes that her husband, far from being serenely detached and independent from base, ignoble society, has kept his eye on it from morning to night, indeed has always lived for it, "not to enlighten, or convert, or redeem it, but to extract from it some recognition of [his] own superiority."

> Her notion of the aristocratic life was simply the union of great knowledge with great liberty; the knowledge would give one a sense of duty, and the liberty a sense of enjoyment. But for Osmond it was altogether a thing of forms, a conscious, calculated attitude. . . . There were certain things they must do, a certain posture they must take, certain people they must know and not know.

Guggenbuhl-Craig also makes the interesting observation that eros-invalids can be quite restful to be with on occasion. Why?

Because they *make no demands of relationship!* Real relationships are *tiring.* As we all know, being in true relationship to anyone, even an acquaintance we run into at the drugstore, requires a certain effort of empathy and imagination: one has to be present for the other person in order to have any true exchange. In a sense, one has to *be* that other person, to feel from that person's point of view. In the company of the eros-invalid, we can pass a pleasant interlude in chitchat and gossip, even though in retrospect the experience feels insubstantial and ephemeral. Nothing has been built or changed between the two of us.

The sex act, with or for the person deficient in eros, can be uncomplicated and quite physically enjoyable, but it retains an impersonal and unloving element; the symbolic potential for expressing an intimate, even a sacred, relationship to another is simply not there.

I have often speculated, as I'm sure many readers have, on how it must have been between Isabel and Mr. Osmond in the bedroom. We know they did have sex, because the novel tells us she had a baby boy who died. Henry James, in the tradition of novelists of his time (though George Eliot implied more about the unsatisfactory Roman honeymoon of Dorothea and Mr. Casaubon, who were the fictional forerunners of Isabel and Osmond), remains mum on the subject. But I think I have satisfied myself that at the beginning Isabel was still so under the spell of the ideal man she believed she had married that Osmond's mere touch—and, from what we know of Osmond, it would have been a subtle, practiced, and properly loverlike touch—would have sent her, a creature of finely vibrating feelings and expectations, over the edge. And even after Isabel has realized the extent of her mistake, she admits to herself that his charm for her has not passed away.

She still knew perfectly what it was that made Osmond delightful when he chose to be. He had wished to be when he made love to her, and as she had wished to be charmed it was not wonderful that he succeeded.

AM I ONE?

This morning, just as I'm swallowing the last of my coffee and preparing to take my morning stroll with Ambrose, the phone rings.

It's someone who's been reading this heart book as I write it.

"Listen, Gail," he says worriedly, "do you think I'm one of these people?" He begins quoting from "Absence of Heart": " ' . . . never seemed to have the need to spend time with others on a frequent basis . . . seldom wrote to acquaintances—if they were gone they were gone. . . . ' Does that sound like me?"

"It sounds like me, too," I tell him. "But at least we worry about it sometimes. Can you imagine X or Y reading this? Would they say, Oh, my God, am I like that? No! It would never cross their minds. And if it did, they wouldn't feel worried about it."

"You're right," he says, laughing. "I feel better."

X and Y are major-league examples of eros-invalids. Both, in their quite different styles, could be described as "charming," "ambitious," "successful," and "enigmatic"; and, with equal accuracy, as "callous," "cruel," "manipulative," and "heartless." In several of the overlapping milieus I inhabit, X and Y are often alluded to as paradigms of absent-heartedness, though they have been on the scene long enough now to have been edged from center stage by ferocious new and younger models of contemporary heartlessness. However, anecdotes of X's and Y's latest acts of personal ruthlessness or profes-

sional brutality, related with gusto by incredulous observers—
and/or victims—continue to provide entertainment. We still get
excited when telling or hearing the latest X or Y story. The energy
level goes up. Why? Are they carrying something for all of us?

It was my acquaintance with X that prompted me, some years
ago, to try to capture the essence of someone like her, from her own
point of view, in a novel.

Inscrutable was the first adjective I chose for X after our first meeting. Then it got confusing. I knew she had reasons to court me
because she wanted something I could give her, and I knew what it
was. I had been warned of her egregious ruthlessness by others. But
then it seemed she also wanted to befriend me just for myself, and I
was frankly touched and flattered. In her girl-to-girl evening phone
calls and her letters to me, she came across as artless, almost childlike, in her candor, hoping she hadn't sounded too banal in our last
conversation, pointing out the things we had in common. We were
both youngish single women then, supporting ourselves by our art.
We had to be on our guard in the dog-eat-dog professional world, or
we might get eaten ourselves. She could be funny in a flat-toned way,
relating her latest setback. Why, underneath, X is just a sweetly
struggling pilgrim like me, I thought. She needs an empathetic friend
to understand her nature and defend her from her detractors. I *like* X!

Then she got what she wanted from me, and phone calls and letters abruptly stopped. Twenty years passed before she phoned again.
She gave me a late-night update of her wins and losses, just as if we
had spoken the previous night: it was still dog-eat-dog out there and
she was still slogging. She wanted me to do something I didn't feel at
all like doing, but since, as she pointed out, it would benefit both of
us, I reluctantly agreed. I asked for one favor in return. She gave me

to understand it was no problem for her, but when I reminded her of it later, after I had fulfilled my part of the deal, she curtly replied it was out of the question.

In the novel I tried to write, the pages flowed as long as I described my protagonist—I named her Violet—from the points of view of professional acquaintances or those personally drawn to her or injured by her. But whenever I got Violet alone and tried to climb inside her head and feel how she felt, track where she was coming from, the flow thickened to the consistency of sludge until I found myself totally blocked.

All I salvaged from that abandoned piece of work was the name, Violet, because it still evoked the struggling-pilgrim aspect I felt I shared with X, maybe neither of us so sweet in reality, fighting for our patch of sunny turf in the dog-eat-dog garden. I made the new Violet a painter—not a saint but very far from an eros-invalid; she was a person on the cusp of bringing forth, or failing to bring forth, her creative gifts. This time I was able to follow my protagonist all the way through the novel that bears her name, but she is nothing like X. (I did, however, manage to capture a mere sliver of X in the cameo role of the woman who fires Violet from her illustrator's job.)

Yet you go on imagining that hour of judgment in the lives of the absent-hearted ones who have crossed your path or turned your head, whether in real life or fiction. "Do you think that when X is old and maybe lonely, she might suddenly turn to the mirror and ask herself, as Madame Merle did, 'Have I been so vile, all for nothing?'" I recently asked a friend. "I don't think I have the mental energy to go there today," he replied with a baleful laugh, and we got off that topic.

And I often think about Osmond—more, lately, than about his wife. What does that mean? That I am coming closer to my own

inner Osmond and wondering what to do with him? As we aficiona-
dos of *The Portrait* know, Isabel went back to him after she had gone
to England against his wishes, though James gave us every reason to
believe Osmond was going to make her return hell for her, in his elegant dry-ice manner, while calling her "Mrs. Osmond," and saying
he cares about "the honor" of their marriage vows. I haven't got to
the place where they're in the same room together, but I'm watching
him copying a drawing of an antique coin in watercolors, as he was
doing when she left him in Rome: he's spent all afternoon on his fastidious little reproduction, and I'm watching his fine-featured concentration as he examines his effort through a magnifying glass, and
I'm trying to get inside that well-shaped grizzled head. What do I
want him to be thinking? "Why have I been so vile?" What do I
wish he would do next? I guess I'm still hoping he will surprise me
with some heart, but that, as they say, may be *my* problem.

POCKETS OF HEART-ABSENCE

They're all around us: sinkholes of heart-absence. They blight the
landscape wherever the heavy traffic of *getting there* has undermined
the value for us of simply *being there*—for ourselves, or for someone
or something else.

They proliferate between the lines in our go-getter schedules
where there's an hour penciled in for everything but reflection, or a
transcendent moment of well-being, or an uncompensated grace
note, or a show of affection or appreciation for someone. They pock-
mark the culture that respects and rewards nonheart values, a culture that regards "having a heart" as a potential detour from the road
to success and maybe even a downright foolish waste of time. ("I've
got this job to finish, I don't have time to hear your tale of happiness

or woe. I'm on my way to an important appointment, you'll have to haul yourself out of that ditch. Yes, I know I promised I'd come to work for you, but an hour ago someone offered me a better deal. Yes, I know I offered you the job, but an hour ago someone showed up who asked for less money.")

Pockets of heart-absence are in every situation where a person is valued primarily as a commodity, or a function, or a number to be ticked off on a list, or a means to an end, or a roadblock—or a stepping-stone—to a goal.

They dehumanize our daily speech. "But I've invested a lot in this relationship," a disgruntled lover hedges, as though relationship is played by the same rules as the stock market. "She's about halfway through her grieving process," we say, as though grief can be charted like a night course in psychology at the community college. "We're going to fly in a team of counselors so the relatives of the victims can get some closure on this," as though shock and outrage and numbness can be decently wrapped up by a deadline and stuffed out of sight. They lurk and breed in the interstices between the words *managed* and *care* every time the prospect of a fully healed or fully developed person becomes secondary to "cost containment" or "workplace efficiency."

They infect our charities and poison our good intentions. We read about the emaciated two-year-old who almost starved to death on a urine-soaked mattress in an airless room because his foster mother neglected to feed him, and his caseworker "forgot" to visit him.

How could this happen? we ask. Where were their *hearts*?

Fallen into a sinkhole somewhere between my place and yours. Lost somewhere in the heartless mazes of bureaucracy. Lost in casework overload at that point where a boy becomes just another number on a list too long to finish, or even to remember. Lost somewhere in the absent heart places of the foster mother's or the caseworker's own neglected childhood. When—if—that boy grows up, what absent spaces will he carry in his own heart and inflict on others?

It's little wonder, living as we do among so many sinkholes of heart-absence, that stressed places in ourselves should suddenly cave in to become depressed areas where waste and drainage and pollution collect. We mirror and affect each other, my society and I. Its sinkholes can become the sinkholes in my own heart; I, in turn, can depress it with my own absences of heart.

Yes, but here I am, *living* in the pockmarked landscape, facing my own worst potential in the latest tale of heartlessness in today's news. If my circumstances had been the same as that foster mother's, that caseworker's, how would I have measured up? Better not to think about it too much. If I took to heart every tormented child I had ever met or heard about, every cowardly act or every brutality I witness or commit every day, I would soon be a quivering mass of ineffectual protoplasm.

How do I strike a balance between ivory tower and basket case?

Balance is the sane approach, most heart wisdom tells us. "Be in the world but not *of* the world." "Joyfully participate in the sorrows of life." "Be wise as serpents and harmless as doves." Learn what in your life threatens to cave in your thin spots. Learn to recognize the places of stress or cynicism in your life that muffle the fire in your own heart. Accept the heart-absences in yourself that you can't change, and modify your behavior accordingly. If you can't feel love or sympathy or courage in certain areas of life, lay down a firm bridge of courtesy and decent behavior over those places to cover the gaping void. We should be grateful for morality's crutch, says Guggenbuhl-Craig: "Decrying good manners and morality as hypocritical is like saying that someone who is missing a leg is hypocritical for wearing a prosthesis."

In terms of guaranteed success, it would probably be easier for me to string a tightrope between two poles in my backyard and learn to walk across it than it is to attempt, every single day of my life, to strike a successful balance between a healthy self-regard (and its attendant, self-protection) and an active, loving involvement with the maddeningly imperfect world in which I comprise a single unit of consciousness.

This is a balancing act that can never be mastered by practice or rules or rote. Can never be mastered, period. Every fresh encounter has to be confronted as the singular event it is; yet I must have some sort of rule of life. Maybe a rule as simple as, love when possible; when not possible, settle for empathy; when empathy fails, fall back on courtesy; when courtesy fails, stay true to purpose and don't hang back from the necessary toughness!

Example: I'm visiting a cardiac patient in the hospital. The woman who collects the money for the TV and telephone bustles in with a menacing frown and demands the patient's daily fee.

"I don't want the TV," he says from the hospital bed, hooked up to his heart monitors, "but could you please tell me what I have to do to call out on the phone?"

She turns her back on us. "First I have to unplug your TV if you're not going to use it," she says accusingly. She takes her time fiddling with the underside of the set, takes some more time writing something on a pad. "I'm two hours behind schedule," she scolds as she scribbles. "I've never been two hours behind schedule before and I have three jobs and this means I'll be late for the next one. I've never been late for the next one."

"If you could just tell us what he has to do to call out on his telephone," I say. Why am I intimidated by rude people? I'm wondering.

"He hasn't *paid* me for the telephone yet," she snaps, and goes back to her robotic litany. "And I'm two hours behind, and—"

"Here's the three dollars," I say, holding it out to her.

"I'm not ready to take it yet," she shoots back triumphantly. "I'm two hours behind my schedule and I've never—"

The patient, who is not very patient even when he is well, says in a menacing tone that goes right past her, "I—am—very—sorry—you—are—having—a—bad—day."

"We are very sorry you are having a bad day," I echo, my courtesy worn down to its mock version.

No response other than the stock litany. "I've never been two hours late and I have three jobs and—"

Time to shift into mode four: "Take this money, please, and give us the information before the patient gets stressed and we call your supervisor and you have one less job to worry about."

Every day I am challenged by at least one instance of heart-absence, and every day I perpetrate at least one of them on somebody else. Some days I'm so beset by the absences of heart around me that I spitefully choose to become a besetter myself. I remember once snatching a taxi away from some people in New York after what X would have called a dog-eat-dog day—a day when I'd run up against just one too many meannesses.

"But that was our taxi, that's not fair," protested the people who had flagged it down.

"I know," I shot back, hurling myself in front of them. "But I'm tired of being fair today."

I wince when I think of how I must have looked and sounded as I clopped past them in my high-heeled boots and shoved myself into their taxi. Quite likely I was *their* last straw of the day and, following my example, they hardened their hearts and turned around and ruined someone else's.

It is as if heartlessness were a communicable disease.

III. The Heart of Darkness

> Hadn't I been told in all the tones of jealousy and admiration that [Kurtz] had collected, bartered, swindled, or stolen more ivory than all the other agents together. That was not the point. The point was in his being a gifted creature and that of all his gifts the one that stood out preeminently, that carried with it a sense of real presence, was his ability to talk, his words—the gift of expression, the bewildering, the illuminating, the most exalted and the most contemptible, the pulsating stream of light or the deceitful flow from the heart of impenetrable darkness.
>
> —Joseph Conrad, *Heart of Darkness*,
> Robert Kimbrough, editor

WHAT AND WHERE IS IT?

In the late nineteenth century, "the heart of darkness" was a stock metaphor among travelers for the innermost reaches of the Congo River in Africa. After Conrad in 1899 chose it as the title of his profound tale of a man's descent into his darkest possibilities, the phrase merged with early-twentieth-century depth psychology. More and more, the term began to be used to refer to the dark place in you or me where the light of consciousness has yet to shine.

If *heart* is the symbol of the inmost sanctuary of personal being, and *darkness* a symbol for the unconscious, the unknown, evil, ignorance, death, and the underworld, *as well as for the dark of germination and potential new life*, you get an astonishing range of meaning when you put the two images together. After his novella *The Heart of Darkness* had appeared in serial form, Conrad altered its title to *Heart of Darkness*, which may well have indicated that he wanted to emphasize the dark heart of a man as well as the dark doings going on in King Leopold's Belgian Congo, the Zaire of today, where European "pilgrims," under the banner of "civilization and improving the lot of the natives," plundered ivory, wrecked a culture, and killed the natives. Ian Watt, in his classic study, *Conrad in the Nineteenth Century*, muses suggestively on potential meanings of the "heart of darkness" phrase:

> Both of Conrad's nouns are densely charged with physical and moral suggestions; freed from the restrictions of the article, they combine to generate a sense of puzzlement which prepares us for something beyond our usual expectation: if the words do not name what we know, they must be asking us to know what has, as yet, no name. The more concrete of the two terms, "heart," is attributed a strategic centrality within a formless and infinite abstraction, "darkness"; the combination defies both visualisation and logic. How can something inorganic like darkness have an organic centre of life and feeling? How

can a shapeless absence of light compact itself into a shaped and pulsing presence? And what are we to make of a "good" entity like a heart becoming, of all things, a controlling part of a "bad" one like darkness? *Heart of Darkness* was a fateful event in the history of fiction; and to announce it Conrad hit upon as haunting, though not as obtrusive, an oxymoron as Baudelaire had for poetry with *Les Fleurs du Mal*.

The phrase *heart of darkness* also brings to mind images of a *dark human heart*. Dark in what way? Unfathomably dark? Barbarically dark? Cruelly dark? An unlit-as-yet human heart? Does the phrase mean the dark potential slumbering in the depths of every human heart? "What other dungeon is so dark as one's own heart!" wrote Hawthorne in his "Custom House" introduction to *The Scarlet Letter*. Did Hawthorne mean dark-obscure, or dark-evil, as in that exordium from the old weekly radio program "The Shadow": "Who knows what evil lurks in the hearts of men?" "Heart," as we remember from our Old Testament heart studies, is not *always* a "good entity": "Now Yahweh saw that . . . every form of their heart's planning was only evil all the day" (Genesis 6:5).

And darkness does not always equal "bad," just as dark-as-a-dungeon does not necessarily indicate the end of hope for release. "Within my heart I made closets, and in them many a chest," writes the seventeenth-century religious poet George Herbert in "Confession." Closets are dark, and chests within closets even darker; but then the poet goes on to describe the afflictions God sends (such as grief) as being able to make closets into halls and hearts into highways.

One thing, however, is for sure: "heart of darkness" immediately arouses our attention and activates our imaginations. It is not a restful, end-of-the-struggle phrase, whether it evokes for you the innermost core of a journey into darkness, or the darkness of a particular human heart. The interest it generates in us points in addition to something as yet unconceived by us, "what as yet has no name," in Ian Watt's suggestive phrase. "Heart of darkness" prefigures something that remains to be known and, if endured, articulated by the knower.

"Above all else guard your heart," warns Proverbs 4:23, "for it is the wellspring of life." What would it be like for you and your heart to journey into a darkness that might poison or dry up this treasured wellspring—or deepen and enlarge it, if you come through? Why does it strike a richer emotional chord when someone says, "let me tell you about my heart of darkness" rather than my "core" of darkness, or my "utmost experience of darkness"? Why does the word *heart* leap to your tongue in these matters? What does the human heart have to do with the heart of darkness?

Could it be that our utmost experiences of darkness *always engage the heart*? If my heart, if the inmost sanctuary of my being, the taproot of its love and will, the very source of its energy and life—to borrow from Evelyn Underhill's definition—has not been touched, or broken, or altered, or shaken to the core by the darkness, hasn't it been just another head trip, a barren intellectual undertaking that bears no fruit?

Have you known anyone who has been to the heart of darkness? How did they describe it? Have you been there yourself? If you came

back from it, how did you get back and how were you changed? That
story is always worth hearing. Some would say it's your duty to go
public: like Rilke, after having descended from his realm of ideal
images into an agonizing confrontation with his own emptiness,
which became the foundation for his final Orpheus poems. "This
seems to me more than just a private event," he wrote to a friend,
after having experienced years of "horrible obstructions," during
which he was "split to the very depths of his soul" and then providentially discovered beneath this "torn-open split" the rebirth of his
spirit that led to the continuity of his work (letter to Arthur Fischer-
Colbrie, December 18, 1925, quoted in the notes to *The Selected
Poetry of Rainer Maria Rilke*, edited and translated by Stephen
Mitchell).

Since I began wandering (with all of wandering's attendant meanings: rove, digress, deviate, err) in this "Heart of Darkness" chapter
several months ago, I have asked some people what "heart of darkness" means to them. Most of them are surprisingly direct about
"their" heart of darkness experiences: ordeals they despaired of
emerging from, rampant cruelty in wartime (or in the warm family
kitchen), a loss of faith in humankind, betrayal by a parent or spouse
or close friend, a child's suffering, some fateful experience that
brought them face-to-face with their own damnable propensities—or
their utter powerlessness. They generously told their stories, a few of
which I will relate. Most seemed to know, better than I did from all
my generic digressions and hoard of literary examples, what they
personally meant by the term, although the meanings were as different as their individualities and circumstances. What all of the stories
had in common was that *their hearts were afflicted, tested, or changed.*

Yet even if the person undergoing his heart of darkness is a character in a myth or a poem or a work of fiction, his story can provide

guidance to us. Mythical and fictional people are, after all, constructed out of the materials of human experience, and a heart of darkness looms somewhere in the course of every human journey. Odysseus was sent by Circe to the land of the dead to consult Tiresias the Seer before she would allow him to continue his voyage home. In Virgil's *Aeneid*, the Sibyl ("who hides truth in darkness") agrees to guide Aeneas to the underworld so his dead father can instruct him on how to make the transition from Troy to Rome and endure all the future hardships he is going to face as a leader. Dante, midpoint in the wandering wood of his life, makes himself into a character and descends into the Inferno, taking as his guide the poet Virgil, who got Aeneas through the underworld. In the epic stories, the hero must explore the lower dark world in order to probe the depths of his/her own— and the nation's, and the era's—conscience. The descent always has a fateful shading to it: this is where the protagonist *has* to go next.

In the Katha Upanishad, the boy Naciketas annoys his father, who is preparing to sacrifice some cows, by asking three times, "Father, to whom will you give me?" The father, exasperated, cries, "I'll give you to Death!" and then realizes he cannot take back his words. So he prepares the boy the best he can. "When you go down there, Yama (Death) will be away for three days. Do not eat anything, and then Yama will be under obligation to you when he returns because it is a discourtesy to have left you in his house without food." The boy goes to the kingdom of Death and obeys his father's orders. When Death returns, he grants Naciketas three wishes to make up for his lack of hospitality. Naciketas asks Death to restore him to his father and to let his father greet him with joy. He then pleases Death (who is also called, interestingly enough, "the large-hearted one") by asking how to construct a proper fire altar for sacrifices. Death explains to him that the fire altar that leads to heaven ("to the attainment of an endless world") is hidden in "the cave of the heart." The boy then asks for his final wish, which Death, shocked, begs to be released from. But the boy insists. He wants Death to tell him this: When a man is dead, does he exist or has he ceased to exist? Death honors his promise and instructs the boy in the entire set of yogic rules, culminating in this teaching: "When the knots are all cut that bind one's heart on earth; then a mortal becomes immortal."

> *A person the size of a thumb in the body (*atman*)*
> *always resides within the hearts of men;*
> *One should draw him out of the body with determination,*
> *like a reed from the grass sheath;*
> *One should know him*
> *as immortal and bright.*
> *One should know him*
> *as immortal and bright.*
> —*Upanishads*, translated by Patrick Olivelle

At the end of this Upanishad we are told that Naciketas, after receiving the body of knowledge taught by Death, attained *brahman*. "He became free from aging and death; so will others who know this teaching about the self."

You journey into darkness in order to find *someone who knows the truth*—or to confront the truths hidden in your own heart. Heart is the integral part of all the stories: hearts that need to grow in darkness, hearts that need to be cleaned in darkness, hearts that need to be emboldened and instructed in darkness, hearts that need to be comforted and rebuilt in darkness. Heart is the indwelling companion on our dark journeys and it may be that heart is the goal at the end of them. If an individual *doesn't* make it out of the darkness, as Kurtz didn't, is it because that heart was hard or hollow?

> The wilderness had found him out early, and had taken on him a terrible vengeance for this fantastic invasion. I think it had whispered to [Kurtz] things about himself which he did not know, things of which he had no conception til he took counsel with this great solitude—and the whisper had proved irresistibly fascinating. It echoed loudly within him because he was hollow at the core.
>
> —*Heart of Darkness*

Does a full heart withstand the ordeal better because there is more woundable, absorbable substance to it? Could it be that the very vulnerability of a heart can serve as its talisman?

WITNESS-EXPLORERS OF THE HEART OF DARKNESS

> "I don't want to bother you much with what happened to me personally," [Marlow] began . . . "yet to understand the effect of it on me you ought to know how I got there, what I saw, how I went up that river to the place where I first met the poor chap. It was the farthest point of navigation and the culminating point of my experience."
>
> –*Heart of Darkness*

The story begins with a whim, a sudden desire of Inanna for the netherworld, a desire that comes to rule her to the exclusion of everything else:

She set her heart from highest heaven
on earth's deepest ground
the goddess set her heart from highest heaven
on earth's deepest ground.
        —Thorkild Jacobsen,
        The Treasures of Darkness:
        A History of Mesopotamian Religion

Ah, what better beginning? The promise of a good tale enjoyed in safety, a journey into some dark place "at the farthest point of navigation" that we can sit back and experience vicariously, like Marlow's group of mariners on a pleasure yacht at anchor on the mouth of the Thames, waiting for the tide to turn, listening to his story of journeying up the Congo and meeting the fascinating Mr. Kurtz.

Even Inanna, the heroine of the four-thousand-year-old Sumerian story cycle, announces her descent into the heart of darkness as that of an onlooker. She tells the gatekeeper of the underworld that she has come to *witness* the funeral of Ereshkigal's husband. Ereshkigal is her terrible sister, queen of the underworld as Inanna is queen of heaven and earth. Inanna has made her descent deliberately into the Great Below, because her heart (also translated as her "ear to the ground," an interesting variation on the meaning of heart) has told her that she needs something from down there.

However, like most of us who venture willingly into hearts of darkness, or the dark places in our hearts, Inanna hopes to get a good look around and escape wiser and richer—and unscathed. I knew a writer who wasn't able to make such a safe escape. He took a year off to research a planned book on the subject of evil in the human heart; halfway through the year he had a nervous breakdown and abandoned his project. My scholar-character Magda Danvers in

The Good Husband had a similar experience when she set out boldly to impress her professors by writing a groundbreaking survey of all the types of evil in literature.

Inanna has no idea when she uses her brother-in-law's funeral to get admitted to the underworld that she will soon be transformed from witness into funeral fodder herself. Marlow (as did Conrad) also uses "family influence" to get assigned as master on a steamer going up the Congo River because it is a place that has fascinated him "as a snake would a bird" ever since he was a boy with a passion for maps. ("I felt somehow I must get there by hook or by crook.") Marlow's determined curiosity, like Inanna's, will lead him straight into the heart of darkness to meet his shadow in Kurtz, as Inanna will meet hers in Ereshkigal. Both Marlow and Inanna will undergo a dying experience and both will return changed. Kurtz, however, will not survive his heart of darkness, and, having pondered his journey in comparison with Inanna's and Marlow's, I think I am closer to knowing why.

I came to Inanna late in life—she was not in the mythology books of my childhood. Yet I know of nothing else like her cycle of stories, deciphered from broken and separated shards of clay tablets by twentieth-century Sumerologists. It is the growing-up saga of a goddess, her exultant puberty, her courtship and marriage, and then her sudden decision to descend to the underworld, and what it cost her to return.

I first read *Heart of Darkness* in high school (missing most of it, of course, except for " 'The horror! The horror!' "). Subsequent readings have pulled me deeper into its paradoxes. It remains one of the most haunting, and most critiqued, journeys in modern literature. Francis Ford Coppola spent five years of his life trying to capture its essence in *Apocalypse Now*, transplanting the story from the Congo to Vietnam, and underwent his own heart of darkness in the process. Brando's idea of what Kurtz should be like was not Coppola's

(Brando arrived on the set without having read *Heart of Darkness*), and the director kept giving in to the actor's improvisations to keep Brando happy and to satisfy creditors. After the film was made, Coppola told *Rolling Stone* that he considered its ending "a lie." His capitulation was a striking example of life imitating art. Marlow, asked by Kurtz's fiancée back in Belgium what her beloved's last words were, compromises himself with a lie.

The experiences of these two "witness-explorers," one the chief goddess of Mesopotamia, four thousand years ago, the other a storytelling sailor in late-Victorian England, play off of each other in ways that bring new insights into heart of darkness journeys.

INANNA'S DESCENT

nin-mu an mu-un-sub ki mu-un-sub kur-ra ba-e-a-e
My mistress has abandoned heaven, abandoned earth
and is descending to the netherworld.
　　—Transcription and translation from the cuneiform
　　　of the fourth line of "Inanna's Descent to the
　　　Netherworld," by William Sladek, Ph.D.
　　　thesis, Johns Hopkins University, 1974

Neti [the gatekeeper of the underworld] said:
"If you are truly Inanna, Queen of Heaven,
On your way to the East
Why has your heart led you on the road
From which no traveler returns?"
　　—Diane Wolkstein and Samuel Noah
　　　Kramer, *Inanna, Queen of Heaven and*
　　　Earth, Her Stories and Hymns from Sumer

Yes, why, Inanna? You're top of the heap in the Great Above, you're the best-loved goddess of your people: you are Goddess of the Storehouse, that most important place. You are Queen of Heaven and Earth, Holy Shepherdess, Light of the World, Forgiver of Sins, Opener of the Womb, Framer of all Decrees, Loud-Thundering Storm, Goddess of War, the Amazement of the Land. That pretty much covers the gamut of power epithets on earth and in heaven. Why would you wish to leave your upper kingdom, abandon your temples and your office of holy priestess, and your attractive consort, Dumuzi, and your loyal and capable female emissary, Ninshubur? Why would you abandon all these things and descend into the Great Below to see a sister so dreaded that the gods send her food down to her so she won't show up at their banquets?

Why indeed, Queen Inanna, has your heart led you on this road from which no traveler returns?

All I knew of Inanna when I began this book was that she was later called Ishtar and that her temple rituals in ancient Sumer included a great deal of sexual activity. The only women in my reading acquaintance who had descended into the underworld were Persephone and Eurydice from Greek mythology, and Psyche, in the Cupid and Psyche story from *The Golden Ass* by Apuleius, the second-century Roman writer.

Persephone, daughter of the agriculture goddess, Demeter, strayed off by herself to pick narcissi in a meadow, when Hades drove his chariot up through a crack in the earth and abducted her, making her his queen of the underworld. After her mother refused in protest to let anything grow on earth, Persephone was allowed to rise from the dead each spring, but she remained "the goddess who died" each year, "the maiden whose name must not be spoken."

Eurydice, a mortal, had just married Orpheus, part god on his mother's side. Immediately following the wedding, while walking in a meadow (again!) with her bridesmaids, she was stung by a viper and died. The heartbroken Orpheus, who could charm anyone with his lyre, managed to get her released from the underworld, but lost her forever just short of the light because he disobeyed the gods and looked back into the gloom to be sure she was following him.

Psyche was sent to the underworld by her spiteful mother-in-law, Venus (the Greek Aphrodite), to bring back to Venus a box of beauty ointments from Proserpine (the Greek Persephone). It was the final of the four "impossible tasks" assigned to Psyche in order to regain her lost husband, Cupid.

But unlike Inanna, none of them went of their own decision to the underworld. Eurydice never came back. Persephone returned as less than her former self, and only for half of each year. Psyche made it out of the underworld but then couldn't resist looking into the forbidden beauty box, and it was Cupid who had to rescue her from the subsequent punishment of deathlike sleep.

Only Inanna, the first goddess of recorded history, whose legend was inscribed in cuneiform on clay tablets twelve hundred years before theirs, chose to go to the underworld. Though her written story cycle dates back to 2000 B.C., the tablets were excavated only in 1899–1900 (at the very same time that Conrad was writing *Heart of Darkness*) from the ruins of Sumer's spiritual and cultural center, Nippur, Iraq.

Not only did Inanna descend to the Great Below of her own volition, but she came back with more of herself than ever—after, of course, going through hell and making some choices and sacrifices on her return. She came back fully conscious of her powers and how she wanted to use them, and also with the compassion and largerheartedness that suffering brings. As queen of heaven and earth she had been responsible for the fertility of plants, animals, and humans; after her journey to the underworld, like Naciketas, she took on the additional powers and mysteries of death. Truly the goddess in all aspects now, she was subsequently celebrated in hymns by the title "Lady of Largest Heart." Her trip to the Great Below, into the heart of darkness, with its knowledge of death and rebirth, life and stasis, also made her "An Honored Counselor." She has been there; she *knows*.

Why did Inanna undertake the journey and what can her experience tell us about our own descents? For, just as we've known someone with heartbreak or been heartbroken ourselves, just as we've encountered absent-hearted people or had to face up to pockets of heart-absence in ourselves, it's likely that most of us will enter the heart of darkness sooner or later—if we haven't already. The stories of others who have gone down into the hells of their own hearts can give us a better understanding of the descent—whether we *choose*, like Inanna, to go, or whether the Great Below opens up and snatches us unwilling into its maw.

Why at this point in her life does the goddess set her heart on the Great Below? Why do any of us feel compelled to venture into the fearful unknown, unless we are pushed from behind? What are the circumstances that confront Inanna?

In earlier stories of her cycle, the girl goddess delights in her puberty, sings praises to her emerging pubic triangle, wonders who will be the plowman for her fertile fields. Eagerly preparing herself to come into power, she sets off to visit her grandfather Enki, god of waters and wisdom, to see what she can get from him. He welcomes her with butter cake and "cold water to refresh her heart," and then they sit down together and drink beer, toasting and challenging each other. Soon he is swaying with drink and proceeds to offer her lavish gifts, including high priesthood, queenship, godship, truth, *descent into the underworld, ascent from the underworld* (remember those gifts later!), the art of lovemaking, the setting up of lamentations, the rejoicing of the heart, the giving of judgments, the dagger and the sword, the art of song, the art of the hero, treachery and straightforwardness; in other words, all the skills and wiles civilization has so far developed in order to survive chaos.

The last gift he bestows on her is the gift of decision, and Inanna promptly *decides* to load all the gifts in her boat and make off with them before her grandfather has second thoughts. When Enki sobers up, he feels he has been overgenerous and sends his sea monsters to bring the gifts back to his shrine. But Inanna angrily accuses Enki of breaking his pledge, and she and her faithful servant Ninshubur ward off the monsters and float triumphantly up the Persian Gulf into Uruk. As Inanna unloads Enki's gifts and presents them to the people of Sumer, more gifts appear from her own bounty: the gift of allure, "the art of women," the placing of the cloth on the ground, the drums and the tambourines: these are the grace notes of civilization. Inanna founds her shrine on the spot.

Enki himself is impressed and relents and gives his blessing: Let Inanna keep the gifts in her shrine rather than his if she's so determined. One can imagine a modern grandfather, in his cups, overgenerously signing over all his property, then asking for it back when he has sobered up. But she's as tough as the old man, and he ends up being proud of her. ("That's my estate. It belongs to my granddaughter now. Notice the improvements she's made by adding her own touches.")

Her queenship fully established, Inanna is ready to choose a husband. In one version of her courtship story, her brother chooses for her; in another, she chooses for herself, but both result in the same husband, Dumuzi. Their courtship is passionate, the songs they sing to each other erotically explicit, filled with images of abundance and fertility. ("My honey-man sweetens me always." "Great Lady . . . I will plow your vulva.") The marriage is consummated and Dumuzi becomes king. One story relates that after Dumuzi is sated with lovemaking he begs Inanna to release him from the bed so he can go to the palace and take up his duties. He calls her "sister" and says from now on she will be "a little daughter" to his "father." The "honeymoon" is over.

And now we come to the part of the cycle that concerns us, "The Descent of Inanna." Inanna seems to be alone, as we usually are when our hearts first vibrate with the rumblings of the Great Below. We don't know how much time has gone by—time probably isn't all that important to goddesses. We can only speculate about what sparks Inanna's decision to journey into the fearful unknown. Is she fed up with something in the upper world, has she had some trial or sorrow, has her daily round of being priestess, queen, and wife lost its savor and challenge? Does the goddess of the storehouse feel depleted in some way? Does she covet her sister's realm of death and decay in addition to her own? Does her desire to "witness" the funeral of Ereshkigal's husband, the bull king, indicate that she senses it is time to bury some "bullish" aspect of her own behavior (like making off with her grandfather's gifts before he could change his mind)? Or has she simply felt a curious desire to know her awful sister better?

Whatever has called her to "go deeper," she makes up her mind on the spot, abandons her seven cities and seven temples, decks herself in all her regalia: crown, jewelry, royal robe, breastplate, ring, lapis measuring rod and line. She daubs her eyes with a wedding salve called "Let him come, Let him come" (because she knows she is going to her death-wedding?), and off she goes wearing the symbols of her status, which we assume will also serve as talismans. Before she disappears into the underworld, however, she instructs her faithful female vizier Ninshubur to set up a howl and a protest and go to the sky gods first and then to Enki for help if Inanna doesn't return in three days.

When Inanna arrives at the outer gates of the underworld, she knocks "loudly," and calls out in a fierce, imperious tone to Neti, the gatekeeper, to open the door. When Neti asks why her heart has led her on the road from which no traveler returns, she gives her funeral excuse and Neti withdraws to convey Inanna's message to the queen of the underworld. After he has described Inanna's attractions and enumerated her impressive articles of dress, Ereshkigal slaps her thigh and bites her lip. After "taking the matter to her heart and dwelling on it," she instructs Neti to bolt the seven gates of the underworld and remove one of Inanna's royal garments as she passes through each gate. Ereshkigal declares she wants the holy priestess of heaven to enter her territory "naked and bowed low."

At each gate Inanna enters, she asks indignantly, "What is this?" when Neti takes away another article of clothing. And each time the gatekeeper tells her to be quiet, the ways of the underworld must not be questioned. Yet she keeps going, asking the same question at each gate, always receiving the same rebuke. When she at last enters Ereshkigal's throne room, she is stripped and bowed low (curled), as the dead were then buried in ancient Sumer. However, she still retains enough of her old bullish acquisitiveness to rush in and try to seize her sister's throne the minute Ereshkigal stands up to greet her. This time Inanna has gone too far. The judges of the under-world pronounce Inanna guilty, Ereshkigal fastens the eye of death on her sister, and Inanna's corpse is hung from a hook on the wall, "like a piece of rotting green meat."

You can't get much lower than that—a piece of rotting green meat hung from a hook in the underworld. Inanna's present state is beyond wanting, beyond hope of recovery. She is humbled, stripped of all her earthly powers, gone back to earth. *Humble* comes from the word *humus*—rotted organic material, good only for use as fertilizer. Who among us has been beyond wanting or hope of recovery? Some have: the severely depressed, those who have died to life; those who, because of some literal journey through hell imposed on them by outside influences, must be brought back to wanting to live again. For Inanna, nothing remains except her will—left behind in her foresightful instructions to her faithful servant—to be brought back to the land of the living if she cannot bring herself back.

Let's leave her dead self hanging and rotting there, like an icon for meditation, and return for a moment to the upper world. When Inanna does not return, Ninshubur does as ordered: she sets up a howl, she mourns and tears her clothes, then she goes to the sky gods, one of whom is Inanna's father, the other her paternal grandfa-ther. Both refuse to help. Inanna has gone too far this time, they say; she who goes to the underworld must stay there. Ninshubur then goes to Enki, the maternal grandfather, who gave her all the gifts. Sympathetic to her plight, Enki takes the nearest material at hand, some red dirt under his fingernail, and fashions two cunning little creatures perfectly suited for his delicate mission to the underworld. Being the god of flowing waters *and* wisdom, he knows what the moment calls for. His creatures slip through the cracks in the under-world like flies and proceed to win over its queen with their empathy and their harmlessness (they are sexless, therefore not a threat to the underworld, which abhors procreation).

When they arrive, Ereshkigal is going through some lonely suffering of her own, and every time she moans, "Oh, my inside! Oh, my outside! Oh, my belly! Oh, my heart! Oh, my liver!" they moan back feelingly, "Oh, your inside! Oh, your outside! Oh, your belly! Oh, your heart! Oh, your liver!" It is probably the first time anyone has empathized with poor dreadful Ereshkigal and she is touched. She promises them a blessing if they are gods, any gift if they are mortal. They ask for Inanna's corpse hanging on the wall. She doesn't like it—as Death didn't like it when his young guest Naciketas asks for the answer to the mystery of death—but, like that other host in the Upanishads, Ereshkigal honors her word. The creatures then sprinkle it with the water and food of life Enki has given them, and Inanna revives and leaves the kingdom of the dead.

But the judges rule that she must send back someone to take her place, because the rule is that no one leaves the underworld without paying a price. That someone will be Dumuzi, who has not been relating to Inanna from the heart: he has been enjoying his powers of kingship in her absence and not mourning her at all. He, in turn, in a later chapter, will be redeemed for half of each year by his loving sister, who offers to time-share with him in the underworld.

But our meditation has to do with Inanna's descent, death, and rebirth and what it can reveal to us four thousand years later. Though we are a different society from the Sumerians, this story still touches and explicates something alive and deep down about human motivations. Why do some explorers, like Inanna, like Dante and Aeneas, like Marlow, survive their heart of darkness and others, like Kurtz, do not? How do their journeys compare and what can we learn from the differences?

INANNA, MARLOW, AND KURTZ

Motives

What initiated the descent of each? Inanna, we are told, "set her heart," or, in other translations, her mind/ear (the same word in Sumerian) to the ground, or "great below." Something has turned her heart/mind/ear to the soil and away from the sun. She desires something from below and straightaway goes for it. Whatever "it" is, it is announced by an instinctive, heartfelt, gut reaction whose energetic summons cannot be denied.

As is Marlow's: what sets him on his journey is the resurgence of "the little chap" in him "with a passion for maps," his fascination for a coiling river into the unknown. Marlow also sets his heart: he has to get there "by hook or crook," and see for himself.

Whereas, for Kurtz, the call seems less heart-set and more premeditated. We are never allowed into Kurtz's head, but all the evidence points to a murky mixture of motives: desire for plunder and reputation and the resultant ego gratifications, but disguised (maybe even to Kurtz) behind eloquent verbiage about humanizing, improving, and instructing the savages. He has even drafted a pamphlet in the Congo (later read by Marlow) arguing that "we whites" had developed so far that we seemed like supernatural beings to them and "by the simple exercise of our will can exert a power for good practically unbounded." But at the end of these seventeen closely written pages of "burning noble words," Marlow finds scrawled in an unsteady hand, "Exterminate the brutes!"

Precautions and Safeguards

Inanna leaves behind her loyal vizier and executor, Ninshubur; she gives her precise instructions on what to do if she isn't back in three days and three nights. Psychologically speaking, Inanna takes the precaution of leaving a sturdy, conscious aspect of herself behind to monitor her descent into the unconscious. When you descend into the unconscious, you may *become* unconscious. You need to leave a control figure behind to haul you back if you lose yourself.

Marlow tells his listeners that the "deliberate belief" of his *work* becomes his safeguard when he's in the realm of chaotic forces and "creepy thoughts." As his crew, composed partly of cannibals, penetrated "deeper and deeper into the heart of darkness" to Kurtz's ivory station, where it has been rumored "unsound practices" were going on, Marlow recalls how the natives along the bank were howling and gesturing at the little steamer he commanded.

> "[They were] cursing us, praying to us, welcoming us— who could tell? . . . It was unearthly and the men were. . . . No they were not inhuman. . . . They howled and leaped and spun and made horrid faces, but what thrilled you was just the thought of their humanity—like yours—the thought of your remote kinship with this wild and passionate uproar. . . . You wonder I didn't go ashore for a howl and a dance? Well, no—I didn't. Fine sentiments, you say. Fine sentiments be hanged! I had no time. I had to mess about with white-lead and strips of woolen blanket helping to put bandages on those leaky steam pipes—I tell you. I had to watch the steering and circumvent those snags and get the tin-pot along by hook or crook. There was surface truth enough in these things to save a wiser man."

What safeguard does Kurtz leave behind, as Inanna did—or take with him, as Marlow did? In Belgium, which Marlow says always makes him think of "a whited sepulchre," Kurtz has left behind one person who worships him, the lady he refers to—along with his ideas, his ivory, his great plans—as his "intended." "I had all his noble confidence," she tells Marlow later in her proud sorrow, "his goodness shone in every act." She has idolized Kurtz in her way as Marlow has seen the natives idolize him in theirs. She believes his whitewash and always will. People who believe our whitewash may provide flattering mirrors as long as we're concealed in the finery of our illusions about ourselves, as Inanna is before she's stripped, but what help is their adoration when we are stripped of the very illusions they worshiped in us? Kurtz has left no Ninshubur behind to save him.

Neither does Kurtz have Marlow's safeguard of "a deliberate belief" in the surface chores connected to hard day-to-day work; Kurtz has time to paint pictures (of a blindfolded woman with a pair of scales in her hands!) and compose pamphlets; the natives carry out Kurtz's daily dirty work for him (plundering ivory from other villages and killing the villagers); then he lets them worship him and, it is intimated to Marlow, Kurtz joins his worshipers in feasting on the dead. Afterward, he adorns the posts around his hut with the heads of the slaughtered.

Aside from the literal regression into cannibalism, Kurtz is also flaunting the very old wisdom of myths that warn us that the one thing you must not do in the underworld is eat its food or drink its water. To do so, symbolically, is to become of the same substance as the unconscious and lose any chance of differentiating yourself from it. Naciketas is instructed by his father not to eat anything in Death's

house. Persephone dooms herself from total release from the underworld by eating a pomegranate seed offered by Hades just as she is
departing from his realm.

Safe Conduct out of the Heart of Darkness

Inanna seeks enlightenment and expansion through her descent.
She, too, is ambitious, like Kurtz, but has left behind a worthy safeguard in Ninshubur. Thus, stripped of her identity in the underworld, Inanna submits, lets go of her ego, dies to herself, becomes
completely receptive (humble, like humus or dirt) to whatever must
take place between above and below so that life may remain fruitful.

And because of Inanna's descent and the resultant rescue mission
of Enki, the god of wisdom and flow, her dark sister Ereshkigal is also
transformed and revalued. The very last lines of the Inanna cycle are a
paean to the queen of the underworld: "Holy Ereskigal! Great is your
renown. Holy Ereshkigal! I sing your praises!" (And in another translation: "Hail to Ereshkigal the pure!") Ereshkigal is no longer "kept
down" and Inanna is no longer "high and mighty." A passageway has
been opened between the two realms and its queens. Thanks to
Inanna's courage and caution, an exchange of energies has taken place.

Marlow does his job. He completes his assignment, which was to
go up the river, and fetch the dying Kurtz, who does not, however,
survive the return journey. Following Kurtz's death aboard the
steamer, Marlow suffers a deathly illness himself through which he
takes on the "infection" of Kurtz. His hours spent in the company of
the dying man—and Kurtz's final damning pronouncement on himself (" 'The horror! The horror!' ")—has shaken Marlow's concept
of the simply "good" human heart. ("Kurtz discoursed. A voice! A
voice! It rang deep to the very last. It survived his strength to hide in
the magnificent folds of eloquence the barren darkness of his heart.")

During his illness, Marlow experiences Kurtz's life as his own. Just as in dreams we sometimes go through someone else's ordeal, all the while observing the action from the sidelines, Marlow enters Kurtz's hell and is yet permitted to awaken from the nightmare.

It is not my own extremity I remember best—a vision of greyness without form filled with physical pain and a careless contempt for the evanescence of all things—even of this pain itself. No. It is his extremity I seem to have lived through. True, he had stepped over the edge, while I had been permitted to draw back my hesitating foot.

Much has been written about Marlow's lie to Kurtz's fiancée when he returns to Belgium. Not long ago I sat next to a Conrad scholar at a dinner and we discoursed intensely through three courses over whether it was a serious moral lapse, proof that Marlow, *as well as Conrad*, had been corrupted by Kurtz (the scholar's view), or an act of gentlemanly kindness and allowable cowardice on Marlow's part.

When the intended asks to know Kurtz's last words, Marlow hears them all too well (" 'The horror! The horror!' "). As she stretches out her pale hands to beseech Marlow to share them, Marlow sees her gesture as mirroring that of the other woman she will never know about. He sees the outstretched arms of the grieving savage woman in Kurtz's life, his heart of darkness consort, the dark double of the sheltered fiancée, "tragic also and bedecked with powerless charms, stretching bare brown arms over the glitter of the infernal stream" as Kurtz is borne away from her. Marlow speaks his lie to Kurtz's intended: "The last word he pronounced was—your name."

It will take years for Marlow's shaken heart to absorb the experience. His desire at last to tell his story aboard a cruising yawl on the becalmed Thames seems to serve as his catharsis as well as an epiphany. He relives the experience in a circle of trusted friends, and he speaks his entire story through the added safety of quotation marks. For Conrad has fashioned the tale so that *Marlow* is not even the "I" figure. The first-person narrator, unnamed, is one of the friends who will "undergo" Marlow's story. Here is how that framing narrator sums up the group: "Between us there was as I have already said somewhere, the bond of the sea. Besides holding our hearts together through long periods of separation it had the effect of making us tolerant of each other's yarns—and even convictions."

At the end of Marlow's tale—the novella is only eighty pages long—it is the unidentified man who has been listening to Marlow's story who speaks the last words. His consciousness of the unknown has been widened—and illuminated—by Marlow's yarn. Observing the old storyteller, yellow from tropical illness but still seagoing, who seems to have achieved a kind of nirvana by shedding his tale in this circle of friendly hearts, the listener ponders thus on Marlow's dark gift:

> Marlow ceased and sat apart, indistinct and silent, in the pose of a meditating Buddha. Nobody moved for a time. "We have lost the first of the ebb," said the Director suddenly. I raised my head. The offing was barred by a black bank of clouds, and the tranquil waterway leading to the uttermost ends of the earth flowed sombre under an overcast sky—seemed to lead into the heart of an immense darkness.

Marlow and Inanna have brought back gifts of wisdom from their ordeal to share with others. Kurtz leaves behind only his ivory and his "effects," which he entrusts to Marlow: a slim packet of letters from the fiancée and Kurtz's pamphlet, "The Suppression of Savage Customs." (Marlow later tears off the "Exterminate the brutes!" postscript.) Marlow and Inanna have had their hearts enlarged and enlightened by their hearts of darkness; Kurtz has been swallowed and destroyed by his. He tells Marlow to close the shutter in his cabin because he can't bear to look at the wilderness he is leaving. "Ah, but I will wring your heart yet!" he cries out to it. Conrad's unpublished version of that cry—"Oh! but I will make you serve my ends!"—gives us a more explicit insight into Kurtz's fatal hubris: he wants to wrest pillage from the heart of darkness to serve his own ends in the world. He has used the interior journey as a means to enlarge his ego. But you cannot, in good faith, loot the heart of darkness while you are undergoing it.

"MY HEART OF DARKNESS": PERSONAL STORIES

During the writing of the first draft of this chapter, I broke off to do a three-day seminar on "Faith and Fiction" at a conference center in the western North Carolina mountains. I told the participants what I had been working on at home and invited them to contribute any insights or stories pertaining to journeys into hearts of darkness. I received a generous number of responses in notes and letters, some unsigned or with a pseudonym, left in my conference mailbox. A few sought me out and told their tales face-to-face.

Railroad Tracks

He was a fine-looking, articulate old gentleman of superior bearing. You could see at a glance that he had been used to exercising authority all his life and to this day did not suffer fools gladly. "You asked for heart of darkness stories. I have one for you," he announced, as if summoning me to the chairman's boardroom. We sat down in two of those old-fashioned green rocking chairs on the porch during a break. Other people from my "Faith and Fiction" conference were milling around, but they gave us a wide berth. I knew it was because of him and his formidable demeanor; for them I was fair game.

"I'm in my nineties now, and I never told anyone this story. Not even my children; never plan to, either. I tell it to you because you asked for heart of darkness stories. I'm familiar with Conrad's tale, of course. Strong stuff. That snaking river. I wouldn't have minded going up the Congo in my day. But the geography of my heart of darkness was flat and open, the last place you'd expect to encounter an unwelcome surprise. Marlow's curling river led into his heart of darkness, whereas mine came in the form of railroad tracks, the straightest tracks you ever did see, leading—straight away from me.

"My wife and I were newlyweds. My job had transferred us away from the eastern seaboard, which was the only home either of us had ever known, to a city in the dead center of the Dust Bowl, where we knew no one. My wife spent most of her time hanging wet sheets over the windows to keep out the dust. I was completely absorbed in my work; at the time I was more married to it than to my wife. Then she got pregnant and miscarried. She got pregnant again and to make a long story short I had to send her back east. No, there were no complications of that sort. The 'complication' was the doctor. The problem was that he was the only obstetrician in town and, to make it a lot less complicated than it was—I see no reason for going into all *that*—he made a pass at her. And then, well, she and I agreed the best thing would be for her to go back east. Of course she was going through her heart of darkness, too, but this is the story of mine. And mine was when I put her on the train and the train pulled out of the station and I stood there watching it go down those tracks, getting smaller and smaller, the line between us stretching thinner and thinner on those infernally straight tracks. Then there was a point where I couldn't be sure whether I saw it anymore or not. I couldn't be sure any longer. And with it came the realization that it was quite possible that I had seen the last of her."

He paused to take out an immaculate ironed handkerchief and apply it to his stern visage. "I'm not a demonstrative man, but you can observe for yourself that I'm still undone by it. Oh, things worked out, eventually, we got back together and had that child and another and another, but not until we had both been through our separate hells. I hadn't been what you'd call an attentive husband, and I guess I had it coming to me. I'd like to think my hell period made me a better husband afterward; she was kind enough to say so before she died. But all I have to do is remember those tracks, taking her away from me just when I realized I couldn't stand to live without her, and—as you see—I still come undone."

The story of a heart that needed to grow in darkness, told by a man who, like Marlow, kept the unbearable details from loved ones afterward. Until a neutral person showed up, years later, and asked for a tale.

Hell

After we met and talked, the young chaplain gave me his card. On the back he had printed neatly and legibly: "Gail, I invite you to join me at this home for abused and neglected children. It is a place which might help you explore the dark side. Peace." He had asked me about my heart book, and when I informed him I was currently exploring the heart of darkness, his face lit up with understanding and he said with calm simplicity, "I go there every day." As he told me about some of "his" children, I found myself pressing my open hand flat against my heart. As if to steady it from the blast of too much outrage.

"We got a new girl a couple of months ago. Seven years old, she'd had to be removed from her mother for protection. There had been severe beatings, you see. She was very subdued when she arrived at the home, but after several days when she noticed that her bruises were fading, she got more and more upset. She went into hysterics and insisted she was in hell. Things didn't improve. She really believed she was in hell, and she was terrified and inconsolable. Well, after some counseling sessions, we put it together that as far back as she could remember the child had been beaten at the end of every day as 'a precaution' to save her from going to hell during the night. While the mother was administering the blows she would chant, 'Spare the rod and spoil the child, spare the rod and spoil the child,' and sometimes they would even chant together until the child passed out. It was, if you'll excuse the irony, the bedtime prayer that put the little girl to sleep every night.

"And now that she was safe, she believed she was in hell because the 'protection' of these beatings had been taken away from her. Her whole mythology had been turned upside-down: for her the hell she had known all her life was home and this place of rescue was hell."

"And do you . . . live at the home yourself?" I asked him.

"Ah, no, no," he replied gently. "I go home at night."

For some, the heart of darkness is their chosen day job.

Afternoon Ride

I don't know whether this qualifies as a "trip to the heart of darkness" or not, but when I was sixteen something happened which darkened my heart. I still go through periods of depression because of it, even though I've been through years of therapy. And even though I'm a success-ful therapist myself now and have a wonderful relation-ship with my husband, it can still cloud over my day whenever I recall that afternoon.

My stepfather had been giving me a driving lesson one sunny spring afternoon. As we were returning home (he was at the wheel again) he suddenly turned to me and addressed me by name, in this choked, intimate voice. "Yes?" I answered, wondering why his voice sounded so strange. He said, "There is something you've repressed, and I think for your own good you should try to remember what it is." I couldn't imagine what he was talking about. "You really don't know what I'm referring to?" he asked, and I said I truly had no idea. He then told me that he and I had been having intercourse regularly, during the night, after Mother had gone to sleep. I was overcome with revul-sion and horror. "You must be crazy," I said. He said, "You deny it because you have repressed it, but it happened, and you wanted it, so it's nothing to be ashamed of."

Looking back on it, I wonder if he wanted me to believe it so that he could *make* it happen. There had been overtures, I'd wake and find him kneeling by my bed in the darkness, his hand up my nightgown, and I'd thrash and threaten to scream and he would scuttle out.

The next part is even worse. Years later I confronted him about that afternoon and he denied ever saying any such thing! You must have imagined it, he said. But he did say it, I can still hear him saying it—the word "intercourse," in that choked, unctuous voice he always used when discussing sex. And I felt—even now I feel it—my mouth dries up and my heart clenches, and I feel—as I did that afternoon and for many years after—irreversibly spoiled. The afternoon reels and turns dark. I left home one person and am now returning as somebody totally different. If the horrible word was true, then it was too late, it had all been done, and could never be undone. And I couldn't even remember it! The power of the word, that afternoon, and all those years later when he denied he said it, though no longer devastating to me, still has enough charge in it to make me turn queasy and shake my belief in who I really was and am.

> Thanks for listening,
> Darker-Hearted Than Before

Dear Darker-Hearted Than Before, do you remember Persephone? There she was on that afternoon, about the age you were, it was sunny, it was spring, she was picking flowers, innocently assuming she would pick her lovers and the events of her life in the same carefree manner. And suddenly the earth opens and Hades crashes forth in his chariot and snatches her off to the kingdom of the dead. "The afternoon reels and turns dark." Like you, she "left home one person" and everything was changed by an afternoon ride. Innocence was over.

As we know, her persistent mother finally worked out a deal with the gods so Persephone could return to earth except for the winter months, and it sounds as though you also have come through via some persistent mothering, your therapist's and your own. However, like your sister in ancient Greece, you make your "darker-hearted" perennial descents. And like Persephone, and also like *her* predecessor, the goddess Inanna, who went below of her own volition, your experience has made you larger-hearted and wiser-hearted as well. To be in touch with the underworld on a regular basis is no small thing, especially for a therapist!

You're right, the power of the word can be devastating. The words he spoke can never bring back the innocent day it was before he said them. But how fitting that you now make your living finding words that help others rebuild their hearts in darkness. "You are not alone" is what we all need to hear, and your heart of darkness journey (it damn well does qualify as one!) links you to all the other "Darker-Hearteds" who became "Larger-Hearted" from the ordeal.

A Tooth

Robert had been reading a draft of my "Heart of Darkness" chapter. During the twenty-seven years that we have shared a life, I like him to read my work in progress, whereas he likes to finish a piece of music and then play it for me accompanied by a bottle of champagne. When he reads my drafts, he takes notes, which are treasures of encouragement, insight, and loving tact. We talk about our work in the evenings, though my writing lends itself to dialogue better than his composing. Sometimes, in the middle of a conversation, when he gets very still and his eyes go distant, I will ask, "What are you thinking?" and he will say, "I wasn't thinking, I was hearing music."

"I think I can pinpoint the afternoon when I entered my heart of darkness," he said, after we had discussed my chapter in progress. "I was fourteen and when I came out of Hebrew school they were waiting for me, four of them, older boys in their neat brown uniforms, waiting for someone like me to come out of the synagogue. I fought them, but they were too many. They knocked out my front tooth, then I ran. I was a fast runner and I outran them. There was no one at home. We had no maids anymore because Jews in Vienna were forbidden by law to have them by then. When my father came home he said you did the right thing, you ran.

"Soon after, I stood in line all night to get an exit visa. You prayed to get a German and not an Austrian because the Germans were at least correct. My parents saw me off at the station. I never saw my mother again. I remember her pale face as she looked up at me from the platform, it was an awful sight. But my heart of darkness had already begun with those boys in the brown shirts. Up until then I believed that the world was a civilized place and I was safe; I grew up hearing at school that there would be no more wars, but now I saw that there was going to be a war and I was the enemy.

"I knew exactly what those boys were there for and what was coming next.

"And you know the rest. I went to Palestine; when I looked old enough I lied about my age and joined the British air force. I wanted to fight the Germans, but the air force sent me around to play the piano, and sometimes the harp, for the troops instead.

"Now I'll tell you about one of my 'Heart of Lightness' moments. I was practicing the piano, all by myself, in a concert hall in North Africa—it was a Spanish piece, I remember, quite romantic—when suddenly from outside came this surging, mighty chorus. It was the King's African Rifles squadron, working just outside the building. They were singing in their language to my music."

Once more "the afternoon reels and turns dark" for someone. A tooth is lost, and with it a whole world. An innocent person left home and never returned. But after safe conduct out of darkness comes another tale, this time accompanied by music and a surging, mighty chorus from another world, and once more the human story is enlarged for a listener.

IV. Change of Heart/ Conversion of Heart

SUDDEN, VIOLENT, DRAMATIC, RADICAL

A stingy man works late on Christmas Eve, sends his underpaid clerk home as late as possible, refuses to make a donation to the poor, turns down his only nephew's invitation to Christmas dinner, goes home to his own joyless house and eats a bowl of gruel, is visited by the warning ghost of his late business partner, followed by spirits from the past, the present, and the future—and wakes up a thankful, generous, happy man, forever changed, on Christmas morning. This well-beloved story of Scrooge's conversion, published in 1843 by a popular author who said he laughed and cried all the way through the composition of it, has become the classic example of an overnight change of heart.

A fanatic man who is obsessed with defending the laws of his ancient religion is galloping hell for leather to Damascus to continue his war against a new faith. Yet along the road he is struck down and blinded by a bright light accompanied by a voice asking him by name, "Saul, why do you persecute me?" After three days of blindness, he is healed, turns his life completely around, and, taking the new name of Paul, becomes the most powerful and eloquent proselytizer of the new faith he was determined to expunge from the face of the earth. Another famous instance of a sudden—in this case, violent—change of heart.

A thirty-nine-year-old Spanish nun with twenty years of a lukewarm vocation behind her (she took the veil because she neither wanted to marry nor go to hell) enters the chapel, wishing the hour for prayer were over, when she confronts a new statue, procured by the convent for Lent, of Jesus being scourged. For the first time the significance of the man permeates her, she feels the pain, she feels the love, her knees hit the floor, and, sobbing, she repents of her indifference and begs to be strengthened in her vocation once and for all. From that time on, she becomes more loving and charitable to her sisters, she is eager for prayer, her vocation is like a happy marriage, it is now a time of delights and raptures. The conversion of heart, she writes in her autobiography, came at that moment when she saw Christ as the very one with whom she could converse continually, "heart open to heart." Another sudden dramatic instance— Teresa always had a penchant for the dramatic—though in this case the ground had been prepared by her years of reading and spiritual disciplines, as well as her growing disgust for her inconstant nature.

Though dramatic suddenness characterizes all three conversions, the force behind each evolves directly out of the individual's personality. Scrooge is scared into a change of heart: his unconscious has given him the gift of the worst thing he can imagine: himself mocked, unloved, dead and forgotten, treated as an expendable object, the same way he has treated others. He dreams his awful fate in such vivid detail that when he wakes up he feels overpowering relief that it *was* only a dream and he gets to work immediately to redress his stinginess.

Saul/Paul is a born proselytizer. His energies just naturally flow toward fighting and arguing powerfully *against* something or *for* something. What knocks him off his horse and blinds him with its light is that the enemy against whom he has been hurling all his force suddenly speaks to him personally in a voice he cannot resist. The enemy point of view becomes his new cause.

Teresa of Avila had been boring herself praying to a distant God who was incongenial to her passionate nature. Then suddenly, through the image of a suffering man being scourged, she understands her God is one who feels things, too: here, at last, is someone she can talk to, "heart open to heart."

If you want to see a radical change of heart portrayed on-screen, spend a delightful evening watching Jack Nicholson's Academy Award–winning performance as Melvin Udall, the mean-mouthed, intolerant, health- and privacy-obsessed writer in *As Good As It Gets*. Through the catalysts of a little dog, an injured neighbor, a waitress at the corner restaurant, and her sick son, Melvin is changed from a sneering, selfish, epithet-slinging misanthrope into someone capable of generosity, compassion, and love. The waitress, played by Helen Hunt, who also won an Oscar for her role in the film, has frankly confronted him with his awfulness all along, upping the ante when he deserves it: "You don't love anything, Mr. Udall." "Do you have any control of how creepy you've allowed yourself to get?" "You absolute horror of a human being!"

Melvin's change of heart, though dramatic, is portrayed as realistically gradual. His transformation is by no means completed at the story's end, he's still edgy about stepping on sidewalk cracks, and you know he's likely to open his mouth any minute and spoil things by being his old self, but you come away feeling that if this is as good as it gets, it's miraculously better than what it might have been without those other people and the dog—who also should have gotten an Oscar. Melvin first experiences unconditional love from a dog (it would have to be unconditional, because Melvin is such a monster at the start) and that, in turn, awakens his heart to the possibility of loving a few humans.

"IT'S A PHRASE WE USE WHEN WE DON'T FEEL THE SAME ANYMORE": A BRIEF ETYMOLOGY

"Change of heart" appears for the first time in the 1828 edition of Webster's, where it is defined as conversion, in a theological or moral sense, to a different frame of mind. In popular fiction of the nineteenth and early twentieth centuries, the phrase was often shortened to having a "change." ("Do you mean to insiniwate that ye've met with a change?" said Widow Bedott to Jim Clarke, the peddler [F. M. Whitcher, *Widow Bedott*, 1847].) In revival language, religious converts were described as having "experienced a change."

On a darker note, John Ruskin in 1853 writes to a friend about his wife, the beautiful Effie Gray, whom he had married in 1848: "She passes her days in melancholy, and nothing can help her but an entire change of heart."

In 1854, the change of heart arrived on their doorstep in the attractive person of John Everett Millais, the gifted Pre-Raphaelite painter who had come to visit them in Scotland. When Effie sued for an annulment so she could marry Millais, it came out that she and

Ruskin had never consummated their marriage. Ruskin, defending himself in the suit that became the salacious scandal of its day, claimed he was virile but: "Though her face was beautiful, her person was not formed to excite passion. On the contrary there were certain circumstances in her person which completely checked it" (J. H. Whitehouse, *Vindication of John Ruskin*, 1950).

"In most men it seems theoretically possible to produce a 'change of heart,'" writes J. S. Huxley in *Essays on Popular Science* in 1926. Huxley, a scientist and proclaimed atheist, then goes on to define the concept more pragmatically, excising the religious aspect altogether. When you undergo a change of heart, according to Huxley, you "substitute new dominant ideas for old."

Orwell, in his essay "Inside the Whale," gives "change of heart" yet another twist when he says of D. H. Lawrence: "Like Dickens, he is a 'change-of-heart' man and constantly insisting that life here and now would be all right if only you looked at it a little differently."

Shakespeare, coiner of so many heart-phrases, such as "heart of hearts" ("I will wear him in my heart's core: in my heart of hearts," *Hamlet*, III, ii, 78) and "wearing one's heart on one's sleeve" ("But I will wear my heart upon my sleeve for dawes to peck at," *Othello*, I, i, 64), appears also to have been the originator of the "change of heart" conceit. In the comedy *Measure for Measure* (circa 1604), the Duke of Vienna, having cast off his friar's disguise, proposes marriage to Isabella thus:

> *Come hither, Isabella;*
> *Your friar is now your prince: as I was then*
> *Advertising and holy to your business,*
> *Not changing heart with habit, I am still*
> *Attorney'd to your service.*

When I began to work on this chapter, I asked some friends around my dinner table one night what "change of heart" meant to them. The country doctor summed it up at its simple best: "It's a phrase we use when we don't feel the same anymore," he said.

LOVERS WHO STOP LOVING

A lover's change of heart can be a gradual decompression of emotion, an aerating freeing-up of the heart, such as Lord Warburton's heart-change in Henry James's *The Portrait of a Lady* after Isabel Archer has disappointed him by marrying Mr. Osmond.

Lord Warburton is a loving and discerning man, with a wide range of privileges and interests, and he will always esteem the first woman who broke his heart, and continues to enjoy being near her, but (and here is a fine description of an ample heart on the mend): "Time had breathed upon his heart, and without chilling that organ, had freely ventilated it."

Other withdrawals of ardor strike with the lightning-flash suddenness of conversion in reverse. William James, in *The Varieties of Religious Experience* (the chapter on "The Divided Self"), relates the case of a young man violently in love with a pretty, good-humored girl "with a spirit of coquetry like a cat" with whom he shared meals at a boardinghouse. For two years he lived "in a regular fever," where he could think of nothing else. He was so afraid someone else would get her that he believed he would go insane. He understood why people murdered their sweethearts. And then, suddenly one morning, the change of heart came:

> The queer thing was, the sudden and unexpected way in
> which it all stopped. I was going to my work after break-

fast . . . thinking as usual of her and of my misery, when, just as if some outside power laid hold of me, I found myself turning round and almost running to my room, where I immediately got out all the relics of her which I possessed, including some hair, all her notes and letters and ambrotypes on glass. The former I made a fire of, the latter I crushed beneath my heel. . . . I now loathed and despised her altogether, and as for myself I felt as if a load of disease had suddenly been removed from me. That was the end. I never spoke to her or wrote to her again . . . and I have never had a single moment of loving thought towards one who for so many months entirely filled my heart. . . . From that happy morning onward I regained possession of my own proper soul.*

An extreme case, you say, bordering on the pathological? But who hasn't hoarded a swatch of hair that was later flushed down the toilet with an incredulous epithet or a shamefaced blush, or ripped up certain photographs (since we no longer have glass negatives available to stomp underfoot)—and subsequently felt vastly freed? For some reason or other, or for no reason we can fathom, our projection has been withdrawn from the carrier of it and we are ourselves again. Dr. James (the brother of novelist Henry) proposes that even the most sudden and violent changes of heart are the result of what he terms "subconscious incubation": Two levels of personality, he says, have been fighting it out underground, filling life with discord and dissatisfaction, until "at last, not gradually," some sudden crisis resolves the "unstable equilibrium" with

*Penguin Classics, 1985, p. 180.

such force that it can seem that some outside power really did lay hold.

But what about the case of Swann in Marcel Proust's *A Remembrance of Things Past* (the literal translation from the French is *In Search of Lost Time*)? Swann's obsessive and tormented love for Odette, whom he finally marries, *does* change gradually, over time, into complete disenchantment. When I was in my twenties, working in London, and suffering from unrequited love the same summer I was reading Proust, I could recite by heart in the Scott Moncrieff translation Swann's closing self-reproach: "To think that I've wasted years of my life, that I've longed to die, that I've experienced my greatest love, for a woman who didn't appeal to me, who wasn't even my type!"

How that last phrase cheered me: the person I yearned for wasn't my type either. His favorite pastime was washing his boat, and his favorite book, if he had to read one, was Robert Louis Stevenson's *Travels with a Donkey*. But if, like Odette, my unrequited should suddenly capitulate to my desire, I knew very well I would have gone right off to the registry office with him that minute. The curious part was, I could imagine *exactly* how bored I would be if I got him: the same old weekend boat trips up and down the same stretch of the Thames, our respectable married fumblings belowdecks in our bunks, the certain knowledge that he would never in a million years get through the first ten pages of *Portrait of a Lady*, or delve with me into the shady groves of the inner life. In this scenario I could picture myself, a few years hence, performing my variation of Swann's incredulous lament—and yet I enjoyed fantasizing on exactly this scene!

HEART WORK: THE HEART IN PILGRIMAGE
(RILKE, YEATS, HERBERT)

Work of the eyes is done, now
go and do heart work
on all the images imprisoned within you.
　　—Rainer Maria Rilke, "Turning Point,"
　　　The Selected Poetry of Rainer Maria Rilke,
　　　translated by Stephen Mitchell

I sought a theme and sought for it in vain,
I sought it daily for six weeks or so.
Maybe at last, being but a broken man,
I must be satisfied with my heart.
　　—W. B. Yeats, "The Circus Animals' Desertion,"
　　　Last Poems

Yet Lord restore thine image, hear my call:
And though my hard heart scarce to thee can groan,
Remember that thou once didst write in stone.
　　—George Herbert, "The Sinner"

Who would have thought my shrivel'd heart
Could have recover'd greenness?
　　—George Herbert, "The Flower"

Here are three poets who chronicled their changeovers from head work and "seeing" to heart work and loving. The writing of the poems actually served to abet the conversions of heart.

Rilke (1875–1926) was thirty-nine when, in the above-quoted poem, he sounded his own clarion call for heart-change. To his former lover, muse, and mentor, Lou Andreas-Salomé, he wrote that this latest "strange" poem, composed that very morning, signaled the turning point that had to come "if I am to stay alive."

The poem begins with a little retrospective bragging, a celebration of his artistic prowess to date. For a long time the poet had only to turn on his compelling vision and "stars would fall to their knees." His appealing urgency could tire out a god until it smiled at him in its sleep. Animals, flowers, women, and even the less visible creatures were captivated by him because he knew how to look. But one day, his waiting and his looking are no longer enough to make living poems. He sits in an "unnoticing" hotel room and hears voices in the air discussing his heart; he hears them pass judgment: the heart does not have love, and therefore "further communions" will be denied him. Apparently there is a limit to just looking. The world that is looked at, no matter how compellingly, also wants to be loved, to "flourish in love."

It is time to enter a new, heartfelt stage of poem-making. It is time to "go and do heart work," like Rilke.

Both the Yeats and the Rilke poems address the Faustian deadline theme: there comes a turning point in the production of every achiever, however brilliant and facile, beyond which the work and thought become stale, dry, and death-driven if the heart is not involved.

Yeats (1865–1939) was seventy-three, in the last full year of his life, when he summed up his heart status in "The Circus Animals' Desertion." The poem begins with a mature assessment of his life's work, a listing of favorite themes and images, his "circus animals all on show"; it then chronicles a turning-point period, during which these images, pursued over the long span of years, engender a dream that *combines thought with love*. In turn, the new dream and the poems that come out of it hint at "heart-mysteries" but remain in the end only "emblems" of what these mysteries are pointing to.

Yet in the final stanza Yeats concedes that though all his masterful images grew in "pure mind," they had their beginnings at the bottom of the ladder, in the most humble and earthy of circumstances.

> *A mound of refuse or the sweepings of a street*
> *Old kettles, old bottles, and a broken can,*
> *Old iron, old bones, old rags, that raving slut*
> *Who keeps the till. Now that my ladder's gone*
> *I must lie down where all the ladders start*
> *In the foul rag and bone shop of the heart.*

"The raving slut" that he singles out for particular tribute is his madwoman-muse for the Crazy Jane poems he wrote the decade before in a burst of uncontrollable energy and daring. Crazy Jane, probably based on a mad old woman Yeats knew in Galway who suffered from Tourette's syndrome (symptoms include a helpless propensity for obscene talk) calls things as she sees them, and the ivory tower of pure mind is not for her. In "Crazy Jane Talks with the Bishop," the bishop tells her that her breasts are fallen and it's time to live in a heavenly mansion, "not in some foul sty." Her shocking but apt rejoinder that "Love has pitched his mansion in the place of excrement" is her way of knocking the bishop off his ladder.

In "The Circus Animals' Desertion," the poet as old man acknowledges that his ladder is gone, and resolves to lie down—

indeed there is a suggestion of comfort in the prospect—in the place that will engender whatever living work he has left in him: "the foul rag and bone shop of the heart."

Rilke lived to the age of fifty-one, Yeats to seventy-four. Both were acclaimed poets during their lifetime; Yeats won the Nobel Prize when he was fifty-eight.

George Herbert (1593–1633) was a priest in the Church of England—and that only for the last three years of his short life; he died of consumption just before his fortieth birthday. Though today he is ranked as one of the great Metaphysical poets, his volume of poems, *The Temple*, was not published until some months after his death, shepherded into print by his friend Nicholas Ferrar, best known for his establishment of the Anglican community at Little Gidding.

The whole volume of *The Temple* was organized by Herbert to represent the movements of a heart in pilgrimage. In "The Altar," the speaker proposes to make an altar of his heart:

> *A broken ALTAR, Lord, thy servant rears,*
> *Made of a heart and cemented with tears . . .*

The early phase of the pilgrimage is a turbulent orgy of self-abasement; the poet seems intent on using all his powers of language to convince God of his unworthiness. His heart is so hard "it scarce to thee can groan": it is "sapless" and "full of venom," "void of love"; it is weak, it is made of clay, it is wounded by thoughts that are "a case of knives"; it is sick, peevish, shriveled, "unfit to hold thee," and drowned in sorrow; within his heart he has "made closets, and in them many a chest."

Eventually, this self-denigrating tone abates. If, as Helen Vendler points out in *The Poetry of George Herbert* (Harvard University Press,

1975), this gap between created and creator had not been closed,
Herbert's verse would have been made up only of "continual self-
reproaches, wincings, and pleas of unworthiness." Something seems
to have occurred in Herbert's life that shamed him into desisting
from his self-attentions and enlarging his sympathies—even toward
himself.

What is remarkable about Herbert's autobiography of heart work
is that you can follow along on the pilgrimage as he writes his way out
of self-involved flagellation into the enjoyment of God dwelling in his
heart. (God at last goes so far as to finish the poet's poem for him!)

> My God, what is a heart
> That thou shouldst it so eye and woo
> Pouring upon it all thy art
> As if that thou hadst nothing else to do?
> > —"Matins"

> Take a bad lodging in my heart;
> for thou canst make a debtor,
> and make it better.
> > —"The Star"

> I felt a sug'red strange delight
> Passing all cordials made by any art
> Bedew, embalm, and overrun my heart
> And take it in.
> > —"The Glance"

> The soul in paraphrase, heart in pilgrimage . . .
> > —"Prayer (I)"

Happy is he, whose heart
Hath found the art
To turn his double pains to double praise.
—"Man's Medley"

Whereas if th' heart be moved,
Although the verse be somewhat scant,
God doth supply the want.
As when th' heart says (sighing to be approved)
Oh, could I love! *and stops: God writeth,* Loved.
—"A True Hymn"

This is only a sampling from the 178 poems that comprise *The Temple.* Herbert wrote over half of them in his final three years. It must have been an extraordinarily full and demanding time: he was recently married, had the full duties of his parish, which included church and rectory repairs, as well as having taken on the care of his orphaned nieces. In his last year, when his consumption must have been debilitating, he wrote *The Country Parson,* which could be called a "handbook of the heart" for priests of the church; it is still read lovingly by clerics today. He had resolved, he said, to "set down the Form and Character of a true Pastor." There are chapters on everything from "The Parson's Library" to "The Parson's Mirth" to "The Parson in Circuit" to "The Parson's Dexterity in Applying Remedies." Here is Herbert's standard for "The Parson Preaching":

The character of his Sermon is Holiness; he is not witty, or learned, or eloquent, but Holy. . . . [This] is gained, first, by choosing texts of Devotion, not Controversy, moving and ravishing texts, whereof the scriptures are full.

Secondly, by dipping and seasoning all our words and sentences in our hearts before they come into our mouths, truly affecting, and cordially expressing all that we say; so that the auditors may plainly perceive that every word is heart-deep.

"Dipping and seasoning all our words and sentences in our hearts before they come into our mouths." Good advice. Where have we heard something like it before? In Chapter 75 of the Koran, when God, speaking through the angel Gabriel, cautions Muhammad not to move his tongue in haste, rather to let "Us" gather it in his heart and cause it to be recited as it ought to be recited.

Just imagine a single day—or a single hour—during which you and everyone you meet in that hour dips and seasons all their words and sentences in their hearts before they come into their mouths. A change-of-heart exercise in itself.

V. The Heart in Love

In my medical experience as well as my own life I have again and again been faced with the mystery of love, and have never been able to explain what it is. . . . Love is [man's] light and his darkness, whose end he cannot see.
     —C. G. Jung, *Memories, Dreams, Reflections*

Anna Sergeyevna, too, came in. She sat down in the third row, and when Gurov looked at her his heart contracted, and he understood clearly that for him there was in the whole world no creature so near, so precious, and so important to him; she, this little woman, in no way remarkable, lost in a provincial crowd, with a vulgar lorgnette in her hand, filled his whole life now, was his sorrow and his joy, the one happiness that he now desired for himself.

—Anton Chekhov,
"The Lady with the Dog,"
translated by Constance Garnett

Until a few days ago, I was going to call this chapter "The Loving Heart." I had the schema for it more or less in place. It was to be heavily indebted to Dante's "ordering of loves" in the *Purgatorio* of the *Divine Comedy*, when Virgil discourses on the kinds of loves in Cantos 17 and 18. My scholar-character Magda Danvers in *The Good Husband* had published an essay entitled "*Discrezione* and the Ordering of Loves in Dante's *Divine Comedy*"; it was going to be the first chapter of a book she didn't live to finish and probably wouldn't have finished anyway because her husband was making her too comfortable. It would have been interesting to create Magda's chapter in full, working from the bottom up through the "small loves" to the "greater loves," and see where I came out. Like most people of my era, I am fond of making lists and "prioritizing" things in order of excellence, preference, whatever. I have grown up trained in the habit of grading everything, including myself.

But somewhere during my musings on Yeats's abandonment of his ladder in the previous chapter, I decided to toss the idea of imposing any kind of ladder system on the human heart and love. I think I may have undergone a small change of heart from writing the "Change of Heart" chapter. Having recognized my tendency to impose rankings and separations on my life, I would like to try for a more circulatory, inclusive mode—a mode closer to the heart model.

On a scale of one to ten, where is your heart? No, it won't do, my old scale outline. I'm not satisfied with it, whether the scale is one that ranks the quality of my love ("Am I possessed by wanton Cupid, or am I way up the scale with Shakespeare's love that does not alter when it alteration finds, or almost to the top of Dante's elective loves, where I am finally in love with the most vigorous good, rather than second-best or slothful goods?") or whether the scale is measuring the degree of my love for something or somebody. (I once had a fiancé who admitted to me after we broke it off that during our engagement he had made a list of the attributes he'd ideally like in a wife. Then he had ranked me on each and averaged out the sum, on a scale of one to ten. "What was my overall average?" I asked. We were having the most extravagant meal of our two years together to celebrate our mutual relief that we did not have to spend our lives together. "Well, it was"—he hesitated—"it was an eight." "Eight's no good," I said, "especially at the *beginning*." "No," he agreed, blushing, and we both burst out laughing.)

I also decided to abandon categories and their implied progressions in value. Erotic love for those who can't resist sex, *agape* for those who can, *caritas* for the charitable high flyers. Rocks, plants, animals, mother, father, sweetheart, husband, wife, child, community, the planet, God. Infant love, childhood love, teenage love, conjugal love, Platonic love, merge-with-the-universe love.

"The Loving Heart" rubric no longer serves, either. It brings with it an image of a subjective heart carrying its gerund of "loving" like an overnight bag to its appointed "beloved" destinations: lover, friend, et al. But, however frequent or intense its appointments, it always *returned home to itself.* Whereas "The Heart in Love" could

not only include the "in love" state of romantic love but also encom-
pass the idea of a heart immersed in love, a heart that "has gone out
of itself." ("She's evicted me from my life!" protests Melvin Udall,
after having been transformed by love in *As Good As It Gets*.) The
heart in love is *inside* the element of love, and love is in that heart,
just as the fish is in the ocean and the ocean is in the fish.

Having cavalierly shed the traditional rankings and categories,
what do I have left? Love, of course, and the heart, which has been
the stimulus and the drive of this book: the heart as locus, as the
place to start out from; the heart as traveler, as explorer, as sentient
signaler, as guard of what truly matters to us, as the discerning organ
of our deepest values; the heart as paradigm for something in us
capable of infinite expansion; the heart as verbal shorthand and pictorial symbol for all of the above.

SHAKESPEARE'S HEART IN LOVE

What does a writer gain from working, over and over, in
one sub genre? My brief answer is that Shakespeare
learned to find strategies to enact feeling in form. . . . No
poet has ever found more linguistic forms by which to repli-
cate human responses than Shakespeare in the Sonnets.
—Helen Vendler, *The Art of Shakespeare's Sonnets*

Since we are communing through the written word here, I can find
no better beginning than William Shakespeare (1564–1616), that
incomparable tracker of heart movements and word-coiner of states
of the heart in our shared language.

In 1592, bubonic plague closed the London theaters and Shake-

speare, out of a job, needed a patron. Probably between 1593 and
1601, in his late twenties and early thirties, the playwright wrote 154
sonnets, linked by theme and imagery and having a story line: that of
a heart in love. In the past the main argument was as to whether the
beloved was a man or a woman (a nervous early printer of the sonnets replaced all the "he"s with "she"s); now the consensus is that
the poems were addressed first to a young man, then a lady, and that,
during the writing of the sonnets, the two real-life beloveds got
together and abandoned the poet. These days, the big flirtation in the
Shakespeare industry is with the possibility that both the sonnets
and plays were written by someone else with a finer education and
nobler connections than a mere genius-commoner from Stratford.

The sonnets fall into two groups. Sonnets 1–126 are addressed to
the dear friend, a handsome and noble young man; Sonnets
127–152 to a malign but fascinating "Dark Lady," loved by the poet
despite himself and in spite of her unworthiness. The nobleman was
probably Shakespeare's young patron during the plague years, Henry
Wriothesley, third earl of Southampton. The identity of the Dark
Lady has more candidates, but the first choice is Elizabeth Vernon,
Southampton's mistress, later his wife after she became pregnant.
Further speculations need not concern us here. We are interested in
how language—in this case our own, without the perils of translation—*can* transmit certain universal movements of love.

Here are three sonnets. The first two (46 and 47) make up a pair,
dramatizing an evolving interior quarrel between the eye and the
heart of the lover. Which mode of loving, the aesthetic or the affective, he is asking, should have pride of place? The third (116) accepts
the challenge of defining, in fourteen rhymed lines in iambic pen-
tameter, the human heart in a state of true love. Since I was assigned
to memorize 116 in eighth grade, long before I ever attempted to fig-

ure out what a "marriage of true minds" was, I have recited its opening lines countless times (it is great for insomnia, whether you fall
asleep or not) and am still working toward a heartfelt comprehension of its complete design.

The debate in the earlier twin sonnets between the eye and the
heart is probably as old as when the first caveperson inwardly wondered, "What is it about this other upright creature that makes my
heart gallop in my breast? Is it in here for me to feel, or is it out there
for me to see?" But how does an authority on human passions, a
master of the word during the peak period of Elizabethan eloquence,
convey this perplexity?

SONNET 46

Mine eye and heart are at a mortal war,
How to divide the conquest of thy sight:
Mine eye my heart thy picture's sight would bar,
My heart mine eye the freedom of that right.
My heart doth plead that thou in him dost lie
(A closet never pierced with crystal eyes),
But the defendant doth that plea deny,
And says in him thy fair appearance lies.
To [de]'cide this title is impanelled
A quest of thoughts, all tenants to the heart,
And by their verdict is determined
Thy clear eye's moiety and the dear heart's part,
And thus: mine eye's due is thy outward part,
And my heart's right thy inward love of heart.

The best way to appreciate the sonnets is to hear them recited by
someone who studies and loves them and knows where the

emphases fall. (Helen Vendler's publishers have included a compact
disc of her reading a selection of them.) The next-best way is to
speak them aloud yourself until the intricate word-dance yields up
the sonnet's inner logic. Since our vocabulary has shrunk and meanings have changed since Shakespeare's day, some words may have to
be looked up in dictionaries or commentaries. (Elizabethan scholar
A. L. Rowse, in *Shakespeare's Sonnets: The Problems Solved*, thus
adumbrates lines 10–13: "Contemporary life is reflected [in Sonnet
46] in the image of impaneling the jury, the tenants of the manor:
their verdict was to award a *moiety* . . . one-half to each. We still
retain the word 'quest' in local country speech: a 'crowner's quest'
means coroner's inquest.")

Speed-reading is the quickest way to drain a sonnet of its heart's
blood.

SONNET 47

Betwixt mine eye and heart a league is took,
And each doth good turns now unto the other:
When that mine eye is famished for a look,
Or heart in love with sighs himself doth smother,
With my love's picture then my eye doth feast,
And to the painted banquet bids my heart;
Another time mine eye is my heart's guest
And in his thoughts of love doth share a part.
So, either by thy picture or my love,
Thyself away art present still with me;
For thou not farther than my thoughts canst move,
And I am still with them and they with thee.
Or, if they sleep, thy picture in my sight
Awakes my heart to heart's and eye's delight.

Here a compromise, beneficial to both, has been reached between eye and heart. This newly formed "league" of mutual hospitality has diminished the pain and enlarged the comforts of both. When the eye and heart alternate in doing "good turns" to each other, the eye giving its pictures to the heart, the heart sharing with the eye its thoughts of love, the overall effect is to keep the absent lover more constantly present to the speaker than if the eye and the heart had remained separate and in competition.

The eye-heart reciprocity worked out in this sonnet has the power to awaken the poet-speaker's own heart to increased solace and delight. Just as George Herbert wrote his way out of self-flagellation and into the enjoyment of God dwelling in his heart, Shakespeare makes room in his heart for a reconciliation between two anguished aspects of his love through the discipline of his art.

SONNET 116

Let me not to the marriage of true minds
Admit impediments; love is not love
Which alters when it alteration finds,
Or bends with the remover to remove.
O no, it is an ever-fixed mark
That looks on tempests and is never shaken;
It is the star to every wandering bark,
Whose worth's unknown, although his height be taken.
Love's not Time's fool, though rosy lips and cheeks
Within his bending sickle's compass come;
Love alters not with his brief hours and weeks,
But bears it out even to the edge of doom.
If this be error and upon me proved,
I never writ, nor no man ever loved.

Throughout the entire sequence of the sonnets, Shakespeare plays on the theme of what the tyrant of time does to youth, beauty, lovers, things, buildings, human relationships. This sonnet, one of the most famous, seeks to define true love. In the first quatrain, it declares what love *isn't* by refuting all excuses of "impediments" (an allusion to the line in the marriage service in the 1549 English Prayer Book, which charged the couple to declare "as you will answer on the dreadful day of judgement, when the secrets of all hearts shall be disclosed" whether there was any impediment to their being joined together in matrimony). Neither does it alter when it perceives alterations in the other person, nor does it remove itself when something is removed from the other person.

The second quatrain, after a fervent "O no," abandons negative definitions and abstract language ("impediments," "alterations") for clear pictorial emblems and positive refutation: love is the "fixed mark" of navigation—the North Star. Though a small sailing boat may wander, it is never permanently lost while under the guiding eye of this steady star who sees through storms: a star whose ultimate worth surpasses our comprehension even though we as mariners can measure its altitude.

The final quatrain returns to a scolding "it is not": love is *not* "Time's fool," love does *not* alter according to time's "hours and weeks," or when the beloved's youth fades. Love bears it out (as in St. Paul's "love beareth all things" in Corinthians 13) even to the edge of both persons' eventual extinction.

In the final couplet, which in the Shakespearean sonnet (named after him because he is its finest practitioner) serves as an epigram or a summing-up, the poet goes so far as to declare that if he has erred in his definition of true love, then *he never wrote anything.* And, furthermore, *nobody* ever loved.

The implications of this final couplet are pretty staggering. If what it claims is accurate, then true love is a much rarer achievement than we commonly assume. What about someone who loved a spouse, and then later fell out of love, and divorced? Is Shakespeare saying that it was never true love? I think he is saying that.

And what is the marriage of true *minds*? What role does the heart play in such a marriage? Where could we glimpse such a marriage so we at least know what it looks like?

TWO OLD HEARTS, STILL ENTWINED: BAUCIS AND PHILEMON

The Roman poet Ovid's (43 B.C.–A.D. ?17) *Metamorphoses* is the only source of this story of the devoted old couple, who certainly would have qualified for Shakespeare's definition of "a marriage of true minds." Though the tale starts off as the adventure of two gods in search of entertainment, it finds its true inspiration in the loving details of two humble lives, firmly situated in what Yeats would call "the rag and bone shop of the heart," and also, I believe, a worthy example of the marriage of true minds as well as hearts.

Here is their story, which I have extrapolated from several sources—mainly Mary M. Innes's translation of the *Metamorphoses* (Penguin Classics) with a little flavoring from Thomas Bulfinch's and Edith Hamilton's renditions—and then recast in my own style.

BAUCIS AND PHILEMON

In the hill country of Phrygia [now central Turkey], two trees, a linden and an oak, grew extremely close together, their branches entwined like bodies embracing. The sight

was a source of wonderment to the local people and visitors. Here is how this phenomenon came about, back in
the time of the gods.

Jupiter frequently got bored with his god-life in Olym-
pus and would put on the appearance of a human and go
looking for adventures. His favorite companion on these
jaunts was Mercury, the swiftest, shrewdest, and most
fun to travel with. On this occasion, Jupiter, the patron-
protector of all strangers in foreign lands, set out with
Mercury to find out how hospitable the people of Phrygia were.

Disguised as two poor wayfarers, they knocked on a
thousand doors and were turned away a thousand times,
until at last they came to a hut on a hill, where Baucis and
Philemon, united when very young, had grown old
together.

As soon as the disguised gods knocked, two cheerful
cracked voices bade them enter. The visitors had to stoop
to pass through a low entrance, but inside the room was
clean and snug. A kindly old man and woman bustled
about excitedly, heaping the unexpected guests with comforts. The old man, Philemon, set a bench near the fire.
Baucis spread a cushion stuffed with seaweed on the
bench. They introduced themselves by name, explaining
that they had lived here their whole married life. "We're
poor," the old lady Baucis said, "but it's not so bad when
you own up to it. And a kindly disposition greatly helps."

She fanned the ashes to life in the hearth, hung a water
kettle on a hook above the fire. Her husband returned

from the garden with vegetables and some fresh herbs, which she shredded from the stalks and threw into the boiling water. Philemon cut a piece of bacon from the long-cherished flitch hanging in the chimney and that went in, too. Baucis had filled a beechwood bowl with warm water so the guests could wash. One of the table legs was too short, so they propped it up with a piece of broken dish. Then the old woman rubbed the table with sweet-smelling herbs, and set down olives, radishes, cheese, and several eggs which she had cooked in the ashes. When the stew was placed, smoking hot, on the table, the old man proudly brought forth a flagon of wine of no great age and plentifully diluted with water to make it go around.

The old couple were so pleased with the hospitality they had managed to scrape together that it took a while for them to realize that the flagon of wine remained brimful no matter how much the guests drank. Then they exchanged a look of terror and began to pray. They understood that these were no ordinary visitors. Philemon beseeched them to let him kill the old goose they kept for a companion so that he could offer them a proper meal. Jupiter and Mercury watched in good fun as the old couple chased the goose around and around. When it finally took shelter between the gods, they forbade it to be killed and decided the time had come to reveal themselves.

Jupiter and Mercury then washed out the inhospitable countryside with a flood, sparing only the old couple and their little hut on its hill. Baucis and Philemon were so kindhearted they wept out of compassion for their drowned neighbors, even though the neighbors had always treated them shabbily. When they dried their eyes, they saw that their hut had been transformed into a beautiful temple. "Now, good people," said Jupiter, "ask whatever you want and it shall be yours." The old couple conferred by themselves for a minute, and then Philemon said: "Let us be the caretakers of your temple, and, since we have lived so long together, grant that we might die at the same time so that I may never have to witness my wife's funeral and she will not have to bury me."

The gods, charmed and pleased by the old couple's request, promised it should be so. So Baucis and Philemon faithfully served the temple for the remainder of their lives. One day they were reminiscing about former times in their cozy little hut with the cheerful fire, when suddenly each saw the other putting forth leaves. They had only time to cry, "Good-bye, dear heart," and then the bark grew all around them until they became the linden and the oak entwined in each other's branches.

Two Old Hearts Survive Swiftian Satire

The story of Baucis and Philemon was recast as dyspeptic burlesque by Jonathan Swift (1667–1745) during a period when he was feeling particularly cantankerous about religious excesses. (The author who would later write his biting satire about humanity, *Gulliver's Travels*, was also an Anglican priest, though not a happy one.)

In Swift's "Baucis and Philemon," the gods are replaced by "Two Brother Hermits, Saints by Trade," who "stroll about, but hide their Quality, To try good People's Hospitality." The two saints go begging door-to-door unsuccessfully in Kent until they come at last to

Philemon, an honest old yeoman, and his Goody Baucis, who invite them to spend the night and immediately get to work with the "Flitch of Bacon off the Hook," and the jug of wine ("'Twas still replenish'd to the Top, As if they ne'er had touch'd a Drop"). Swift having set his poem in English wintertime, all traces of olives, herbs, and fresh vegetables have been excised; there is no goose chase, either.

After the saints flood the inhospitable surroundings of "that Pack of churlish Boors, Not fit to live on Christian Ground," the body of the poem devotes itself to a detailed transformation of the couple's humble cottage into a church. ("The Chimney widen'd and grew higher, became a Steeple with a Spire . . . the groaning Chair began to crawl Like an huge Snail along the Wall; There stuck aloft in pub-lick View, And with small change, a Pulpit grew.")

You get the feeling that Parson Swift tremendously enjoyed him-self as he composed this part of the poem.

Having completed the church, the saints ask their old host to make a wish, and Philemon replies, "My house has grown so fine, Methinks I still would call it mine: I'm old, and fain would live at Ease, Make me the Parson, if you please." Philemon's grazier's coat promptly becomes a cassock with pudding sleeves, and "His Talk was now of *Tythes and Dues*, He smok'd his Pipe and read the News . . . At Christ'nings well could act his Part, And had the Ser-vice all by Heart."

Though Dame Baucis gets a better hairdo and a grosgrain gown and is now called Madam, their love for each other is allowed to sur-vive even the mocking poet's lampoon. "Philemon was in great Sur-prize, and hardly could believe his Eyes, Amazed to see her look so prim; And she admir'd as much at him."

They continue "happy in their Change of Life," until one day while walking together in the churchyard Baucis exclaims, "My Dear I see your Forehead sprout!" whereupon Parson Philemon replies, "And really, Yours is budding too—Nay,—now I cannot stir my Foot: It feels as if t'were taking Root."

They are both turned to yews and are admired and pointed out as "Baucis and Philemon" for many years after, until eventually a new parson cuts "Baucis" down to mend his barn. At which, " 'tis hard to be believ'd, How much the other Tree was griev'd, Grew scrubby, dy'd a-top, was stunted: So, the next Parson stubbed and burnt it."

Two Old Hearts, Evicted by Faust
the Land Developer, Are Incinerated

A century and a quarter after Swift wrote his "Baucis and Philemon" parody, Johann Wolfgang von Goethe (1749–1832), completing his two-part tragedy of *Faust* in the year before his death, revived the old couple yet again in order to emphasize a sinister and prophetic insight about human "development" during the modern age. He told his secretary Eckermann, with whom he often discussed his work in progress, that he had purposely taken the names of this renowned mythical couple because the persons and their relations bore resemblances to those in his story and the use of those elevated names would intensify the effect.

Goethe had been working on *Faust* for over sixty years, compelled by the subject ever since he saw a Faust puppet show in his youth about the legendary figure who promises his soul to Mephistopheles in return for all human knowledge and experience.

In Part I of Goethe's rendering, completed in his early fifties, Mephistopheles has renewed Faust's youth and granted him the full enjoyment of human love with Gretchen, in all its earthly erotic and idealistic aspects—although Gretchen is destroyed by the union.

In Part II, begun when Goethe was in his late seventies and sealed away by him to be published only after his death, Mephistopheles grants Faust the opportunity to accomplish some great deed in the world. Faust decides he will reclaim land from the sea in order to create an ideal kingdom over which he will be lord. The only trouble is, having drained the land and built his palace, Faust complains bitterly to Mephistopheles that "my heart is stabbed and stabbed," because an old couple on a hill, with ancient rights to a thatched hut, tiny chapel, and a clump of mature linden trees, will not let him buy them out and move them to a handsome little farm so that he can complete his masterpiece of development.

I'm ashamed of it, he admits to Mephistopheles, echoing many a land grabber before and after, *but those few trees that are not my own, ruin my possession of the world.*

Why do you scruple and torture yourself, scoffs Mephistopheles, don't you know how to colonize? *You* go and clear them out, orders Faust. Settle them in that farmhouse I built for them.

But Mephistopheles and his henchmen prove too heavy-handed for the old folks. Baucis and Philemon die of simultaneous heart attacks as their door is being battered down, and their untended fire kills a sleeping wayfarer to whom they had given hospitality.

Like many a fastidious dictator who has delegated his dirty work, Faust curses Mephistopheles (I didn't mean for you to go *that* far in violating human rights!) and then suffers deep remorse for his act ("Too rashly commanded, too rashly obeyed!") when he climbs to his tower and witnesses the conflagration on the hill and the charred and mutilated lindens.

The loving pair has been destroyed at last by the achievements of an industrial revolution, which brought with it an imbalance between head and heart. It is appropriate that Oswald Spengler (1880–1936) in *The Decline of the West* christened our ceaselessly striving, ceaselessly dissatisfied Western culture "Faustian," after his fellow countryman's *Faust*.

How did Baucis and Philemon achieve that rare balance of head and heart that makes possible "a marriage of true minds"? Ovid and Swift leave us a few clues. In Ovid's tale, there is Baucis's testimony to the disguised gods that "a kindly disposition helps." She seems to speak of this disposition as a joint quality, it is neither "mine" nor "his," but something they have acquired by being together. Then there is their obvious enjoyment of giving hospitality. However poor they may be, they have found such abundance in their mutual relationship to have surplus left over to offer others. And they are conscious of this abundance and *can articulate it*; that's where mind comes into play. Swift has them ("on a Day which prov'd their last") taking a walk together in the churchyard, "discoursing o'er old Stories past," when their foreheads begin to sprout leaves. And when Baucis as tree is cut down, even though her tree-husband has left his human mind and its articulative powers behind, "'tis hard to be believed, How much the other Tree was griev'd."

A hard act to follow for most of us, but I do think that's what Shakespeare had in mind in Sonnet 116.

Two Old Hearts Leave Us a Legacy

You have hit the mark absolutely: all of a sudden and with terror it became clear to me that I have taken over

Faust as my heritage, and moreover as the advocate and avenger of Philemon and Baucis, who, unlike Faust the Superman, are the hosts of the gods in a ruthless and god-forsaken age.

—Letter from C. G. Jung to Paul Schmitt,
5 January 1942*

When he was a boy, Jung (1875–1961) often heard it bruited proudly behind family walls that his paternal grandfather was an illegitimate son of Goethe. Though the mature psychiatrist demoted the wishful speculation to the more likely probability that his great-grandmother Sophie Jung, the friend of many German writers, simply had a "transference" to Goethe, Jung continued to look upon the author of *Faust* as his spiritual ancestor.

Having early discovered himself to be the possessor of a "Number 1" and a "Number 2" personality (Number 1 being the striving, not-always-successful schoolboy, the son of his parents; Number 2, an old, skeptical, remote, solitary "other," who knew himself worthy and was at peace with himself), Jung said that he, like Faust, could claim that "two souls, alas, are housed within my breast." All Jung's life he was fascinated by *Faust,* at first because he felt Goethe had dramatized his very own inner contradictions. Faust the purblind philosopher encounters his shadow, Mephistopheles, who, in spite of his negating disposition, represents the spirit of life as opposed to the aridity of the scholar, who is close to suicide.

*From *C. G. Jung Letters,* selected and edited by Gerhard Adler and Aniela Jaffe, translated by R. F. C. Hull (Bollingen/Princeton University Press, 1973).

The dichotomy of Faust-Mephistopheles came together within myself into a single person and I was that person. . . . I was directly struck and recognized that this was my fate. Hence, all the crises of the drama affected me personally; at one point I had passionately to agree, at another to oppose. No solution could be a matter of indifference to me (*Memories, Dreams, Reflections*, pp. 234–35).

It was only during and after the debacle that led to World War II that Jung realized that Goethe's myth had prophetically anticipated the fate of the German people. But long before he understood that *Faust* had dramatized a collective experience beyond his own, he had already accepted the atonement for Faust as his personal task.

I felt personally implicated, and when Faust caused the murder of Philemon and Baucis, I felt guilty, quite as if I myself in the past had helped commit the murder of the two old people. This strange idea alarmed me, and I regarded it as my responsibility to atone for this crime, or to prevent its repetition (p. 234).

In later years Jung consciously came to link his own life work to redeeming "what Faust had passed over," the negligence of which had led to human rights crimes like the incineration of Baucis and Philemon to get them out of the way for "development"; what needed to be reinstated were "respect for the eternal rights of man, recognition of 'the ancient,' and the continuity of culture and intellectual history." He recognized that our bodies and souls have an intensely historical character, and that the loss of connection with our ancient parts gives rise to the discontents dramatized in *Faust*. We rush impetuously into "new developments," driven by a frantic sense of insufficiency and restlessness; we no longer "live on what we have," like the old couple with their love and radishes and hospitality and evening walks and talks.

When Jung built his tower at Bollingen, on the upper Lake of Zurich, where he frequently retreated to rest his body and refresh his mind, he constructed it so that the dead would feel at home. If a man in the sixteenth century were to move into the house, Jung claimed, only the kerosene lamp and the matches would be new to him.

> Moreover, my ancestors' souls are sustained by the atmosphere of the house, since I answer for them the questions that their lives once left behind. I carve out rough answers as best I can. I have even drawn them on the walls. It is as if a silent, greater family, stretching down the centuries, were peopling the house. There I live in my second personality and see life in the round, as something forever coming into being and passing on (p. 237).

Over the entrance to Jung's tower are carved the words:

PHILEMONIS SACRUM– FAUSTI POENITENTIA
[Shrine of Philemon–Repentance of Faust]

HOLY EROS: THE MYSTIC HEART IN LOVE
TERESA OF AVILA (1515–82)

Saint Teresa is a synonym for the heart.
> –E. M. Cioran, *Tears and Saints*,
> translated by Ilinca Zarifopol-Johnston

Love is the extremely difficult realization that something other than oneself is real.
> –Iris Murdoch, "The Sublime and the Good," *Chicago Review*, 1959

She is the classic example of that complete flowering of personality in which the life of contemplation does not tend to specialism, but supports and enhances a strenuous active career. To write a series of works which are at once among the glories of Spanish literature, and the best and most exact of guides to the mysteries of the inner life; to practice and describe with an unequaled realism, the highest degrees of prayer and contemplation; to found numerous convents in the face of insuperable difficulties; to reform a great religious Order in spite of the opposition of those pious conservatives whom she was accustomed to call pussy-cats; to control at once the financial and spiritual situations of her enterprise, and to do all this in spite of persistent ill-health in a spirit of unfailing common sense, of gaiety, of dedicated love—this, which is far from exhausting the list of St. Teresa's activities, seems a sufficient program for one soul.
> –Evelyn Underhill, *The Mystics of the Church*

When last we glimpsed her in the "Change of Heart" chapter, Teresa was on her way to chapel for a bout of dutiful prayer, a thirty-nine-year-old Spanish nun who had taken the veil at twenty because she didn't want to marry and accept some man as her lord and master for life, and yet feared the sheer power of her own abundant erotic vitality. As she neither wished to disgrace her family (as she came close to doing in a hushed-up dalliance when she was sixteen) nor to spend eternity in hell, she had chosen to put herself out of danger behind convent walls. She still could fall in love, and did, frequently. She hated sermons, but could fall in love with a priest who delivered one.

High-spirited and extremely good-looking (her convent sisters and priest-confessors have left descriptions: glossy black hair and eyes, perfect skin and teeth, shapely figure, elegant carriage, and light, buoyant step), she was the irresistible drawing card of the convent parlor (the *locutorio*) during visitation hours with relatives and friends and friends of friends, including a number of gallant *hidalgos*, used to making physical conquests, who relished the added *frisson* of a "spiritual flirtation" with a handsome, witty, well-bred nun. Although the Spanish Inquisition was in full swing, her Carmelite convent was under "mitigated" rule and quite permissive in certain aspects. If a nun's family could afford it, she could decorate her cell and private oratorio with fine paintings and furniture, wear jewelry and scent, hoard her own stash of gourmet treats, even organize, "in the name of her favorite saint," little parties and musicals where the nuns could wear their prettiest adornments and show off their singing voices.

Being a person who admired exuberance and high courage, she was distraught about her tepidity in her chosen vocation. Her inner conflict had precipitated two illnesses that forced her to be sent home from the convent, the second one so severe that she was in a coma and paralyzed for three years after: she had to learn to crawl before she could walk again. During both convalescences, she read books on how to pray and meditate. With shame, she had witnessed her own father in his last years become a passionate man of prayer just as she had reached the stage where she could no longer pray.

Such was her state as she approached the chapel for yet another dutiful round of orisons. Her soul had become weary, she tells us in her *Life*, but it couldn't rest because of the wretched habits she had contracted. But today, as she enters the oratory, there is a new statue, procured by the convent for Lent, that literally knocks her off her feet.

It is the figure of Jesus being scourged before his crucifixion, "so terribly wounded" that her heart "seems to break" when she considers the poor return she has made for those wounds. She collapses on the floor, weeping, and, "abandoning all trust in herself," she tells God she will not rise until he gives her the strength to do better. Apparently God could not resist her, either, because she got up and began to grow into one of the most loving and lovable mystics the reading world has ever known, and the foundress of seventeen reformed monasteries that returned the Carmelite order to the focused rule of its beginnings. Her two books on prayer and the spiritual life, *The Way of Perfection* and *The Interior Castle*, and her disarmingly candid autobiography have become universal classics.

I have not been able to find a more detailed account of the statue that opened Teresa's heart—or even better, a picture of it, or its type—but, given the religious art of sixteenth-century Spain, unsurpassed in its grisly depictions of human suffering, the figure most likely would have borne the bloody open gashes from the scourges (leather thongs filled with bones or spikes), and the face and body, perhaps beautifully elongated in form and feature in the style of El Greco, would have been contorted into an expression of agony. But whatever its particular lineaments, its sudden presence was the magnet needed to gather the nun's scattered energies into a single dedicated love powerful enough to contain—and express—her amplitude of gifts.

"From then on," she reports in her *Life*, "I began greatly to improve." An understatement indeed, when you consider all she accomplished in the remaining twenty-eight years of her life.

In his chapter on mysticism (the simplest definition of a mystic being "one who knows God by experience") in *The Varieties of Religious Experience* (Penguin Classics), William James elaborates on what this "improvement" of Teresa's entailed. "A formation of a new center of spiritual energy" had taken place, he suggests.

Though James crowned Teresa "the expert of experts" in describing experiences that lead to new depths of love, he personally deplored that "one of the ablest women who has left a written record of herself" should have squandered her extraordinary abilities on religion. Because of his declared skepticism, we value James's assessment of her abilities all the more:

> She had a powerful intellect of the practical order. She wrote admirable descriptive psychology, possessed a will equal to any emergency, great talent for politics and business, a buoyant disposition, and a first-rate literary style. She was tenaciously aspiring, and put her whole life at the service of her religious ideals. Yet so paltry were these, according to our present way of thinking, that (although I know that others have been moved differently) I confess my only feeling in reading her has been pity that so much vitality of soul should have found such poor employment (p. 346).

And yet, though the Father of Pragmatism was the first to admit that his own constitution shut him out "entirely from the enjoyment of all mystical states," he did choose to compile a massive, comprehensive, and extremely readable survey of the experiences of others and even to stipulate the "four marks" of a valid mystical experience (pp. 380–82):

1. *Ineffability*. Must be directly experienced, involves feeling more than intellect: "Lacking the heart or ear," James says, "we cannot interpret the musician or the lover justly."

2. *Noetic quality*. Although similar to a state of feeling, a state of knowledge is involved, the person receives an insight into "depths of truth unplumbed by the discursive intellect," and as a rule the revelation carries with it "a curious sense of authority for aftertime."

3. *Transiency*. Can't be sustained for long, "half an hour, or at most an hour or two," except in rare instances. *But when these experiences recur they are recognized*, and each recurrence brings continuous development "in what is felt as inner richness and importance."

4. *Passivity*. Although the mystical state may have been facilitated by previous disciplines and practices, the person undergoing the actual experience feels as if her will is in abeyance. Mystical states, however, are never merely interruptive. They leave behind a residue that modifies the inner life of the person.

How She Changed

The important thing is not to think much, but to love much; and so do that which bestirs you to love.

—*The Interior Castle* 4, 1, 7,
translated by Kieran Kavanaugh, O.C.D.,
and Otilio Rodriguez, O.C.D.

Her heart from the beginning was passionate and robust in its ardors. When she was seven, she talked her eleven-year-old brother Roderigo into walking to Africa so they could get themselves beheaded by Moors, become instant martyrs, and go straight to heaven. (An uncle stopped them at the bridge and sent them home, where they played instead at being saintly hermits.) Before her radical conversion, she had loved father, mother, brothers, sisters, cousins, nieces, friends, priests and confessors, animals, nature, cooking and eating good food, dancing, playing the tambourine, reading, writing, and lively conversation. Although she had trouble praying, she enjoyed talking enthusiastically about her favorite manual on the practice of mental prayer, *The Third Spiritual Alphabet*, written by a Franciscan. Afterward, these loves remained but they began to fall into place in a new pattern and increasingly to bear fruit. The radical experience in front of the statue had somehow collected the many loves and galvanized her energies toward one great love. From the center of this new integrated love radiated a powerful creative freedom produced by a *concentration of heart*.

Though more steadily focused than before, she was never to lose her gift for intimacy. Her prayer, formerly an arid duty, was now a joy because it was a dialogue *with both the object and the source of her love*. Now she can say (in Chapter 8 of her *Life*), "Affective prayer is nothing but an ultimate friendship, a frequent conversation, heart to heart, with one we know to be our lover." All the books she will write will impart the feeling of an intimate conversation. She is always addressing someone, either her nuns ("And so you see, sisters . . ." "I know you can do this!" "Well, now, my daughters, where was I?") or the spiritual director who has ordered her to write the book ("I shall have to make use of some comparison here,

although I should like to excuse myself, but seeing so much stupid-
ity will provide some recreation for your Reverence"). She converses
with God, and reports back to her sisters or director ("Today I complained to His Majesty, I said to Him, how is it when there is so little
time to enjoy Your presence You hide from me?").

Her final years during her later sixties were harrowing. In ill
health, plagued by frequent "little heart attacks" (probably increasingly severe recurrences of angina), carrying around an arm so badly
broken it was useless, she nevertheless endured constant travel on
treacherous roads to found new convents, sleeping in lice-infested
inns; she endured lawsuits, malicious gossip by the jealous and
resentful, denunciations to the Inquisition by former "friends," neg-
lect by her dearest spiritual adviser, Father Gracian, who backed out
at the last minute from accompanying her on a much-looked-
forward-to mission. Yet her large heart not only found accommodation for these trials and disappointments, but bathed them in humor.
When a carriage broke down and tumbled her into the mud, she
cried out to God, "If this is the way you treat your friends, no wonder you have so few!" When Gracian let her down, she wrote to him,
wryly, that he had done her a service by reminding her that God is
the only one you can safely trust.

As soon as she was dead, her convents began fighting over who
would get the beloved body. The Father Provincial, none other than
her beloved Gracian, cut off her left hand to keep as a saintly relic.
Everyone wanted a piece of her: her remains were disinterred,
hacked up some more, "kidnapped," driven hither and yonder in the
dead of night, reinterred. By the time it reached its final resting place,
the oft-pillaged saintly husk was without the rest of the left arm
Father Gracian had started on, the right foot, some fingers from the

right hand, some ribs, most of the neck, part of the jaw, the left eye, and the heart. (Generalissimo Franco kept her left hand by his bedside until he died; now it has been returned to Avila; in the gift shop at the Convent of St. Teresa in Avila, reproductions of a Teresan finger can still be purchased.)

Remember, in Part I, "The Great Heart Split of the Seventeenth Century: St. Teresa's Heart Preserved in Alcohol," when the Belgian cardiologist Dr. Boyadjian visited the convent in Alba de Tormes to see Teresa's heart in its jeweled urn, noticed its deep split, and diagnosed coronary thrombosis with rupture of the heart as a probable cause of her death? Well, here is one more story about the saint's heart, which I found in Vita Sackville-West's joint biography of Saints Teresa of Avila and Thérèse of Lisieux, *The Eagle and the Dove: A Study in Contrasts.*

At one time, mysterious little "thorns" began sprouting at the base of the urn that housed Teresa's heart. Onlookers could see them through the openings of the reliquary. Every time the Church passed through another crisis, it was believed, another thorn appeared. Finally the Bishop of Salamanca called for an investigation. The thorns turned out to be bits of feather brush from cumulative dustings. How Teresa, who shuddered when people put her on a saintly pedestal, and who loved a good laugh, would have enjoyed that one.

COMPLETING LOVE'S GUEST LIST: LOVE OF SELF

Better is a dinner of herbs where love is than a fatted ox and hatred with it.

—Proverbs, 15:17

Thou shalt love thy neighbor as thyself.

—Leviticus 19:18

He shall gird himself, and make them to sit down to
meat, and will come forth and serve them.

—Luke 12:37

Well, let's see now, as Teresa might have said, where are we? We
have compiled a few stories and utterances of hearts in love. Not
ranking, ordering, separating, or laddering from bottom to top, but
just looking around for memorable instances of human hearts in
the state, or element, of love: a playwright out of work distilling
love's aches and oscillations into the clarity of sonnets; a timeless
old couple who never seem to get enough of each other, no matter
who is reimagining their story; a great-hearted woman whose capacity for love, once focused on an object ample enough to contain all
her passions, feels limitless and alive to us four centuries later.

Who wouldn't be comforted to know we'd transformed our love-
sufferings into something balanced and beautiful, as Shakespeare
did? What Baucis wouldn't hope to grow old with her Philemon,
once found; or what Philemon with his Baucis, once found? Who
wouldn't like to be more intimate with God and go from strength to
creative strength in the freedom of that great love?

Is there anything we've left out of this chapter on the heart in
love? Is there anybody we've overlooked?

Love your neighbor as yourself rolls glibly off the tongue. We are
trained from an early age to concentrate on the "neighbor" part with
the not very surprising result that it may not occur to us until years
later that the dictum rests on the premise that I *do* love myself. Yet

true love of self is hard to come by; I venture to say the majority of us will never fully experience it. The behaviors of those about whom we most vehemently complain, "Boy, is he ever in love with himself! . . . Does she think the universe revolves around *her*?" are usually fueled by something quite the opposite from pure delight in themselves, something closer to an uneasy admixture of fear and angry pride and little leaden deposits of self-hatred.

I have known only a handful of people who, I believe, have come to love themselves. The one I've known the longest died last month. Except for one of them, who I suspect has never given a thought to whether he "loves" himself, the others have had to work at it and slowly grow into it. All are/were focused, disciplined people; all have a firm grip on their world. They tend to love their work, whether it is teaching or nursing or running a fruit and vegetable market or staying at home and taking good care of themselves and those they love. They share a certain detachment from trivialities, and a peculiar readiness to stop whatever they are doing and do something else, if needed or asked.

In monastic life, this highly valued quality of allowing oneself to be distracted goes by the paradoxical-sounding rubric "guard of the heart." It seems to be in direct contradiction to focus and discipline, but ultimately it isn't. As near as I can understand it, it's a willing giving over of yourself because you know you're part of a larger whole and are of specific and vital use to that whole—and also you know there is more of you where that came from, so you don't need to hoard. As a friend put it, thoughtfully choosing her words to describe a self-loving person she knew, "She's got exquisite boundaries, but they're *permeable* when necessary." All the self-lovers I have known are what you'd call receptive personalities, whether extroverted or introverted. They are extremely good listeners, and yet enjoy telling you about themselves. All without exception have a well-developed sense of humor.

In his last poem in *The Temple*, George Herbert, whom we saw struggling with his unworthy self in verse after verse in the "Change of Heart" chapter, finally reaches the point where he can acknowledge he is lovable enough to sit down at Love's table and be Love's honored guest.

If I ever memorize another poem, to go with Shakespeare's "Love is not love which alters when it alteration finds," it will be Herbert's "Love III." You can actually follow his progress in the poem. (I have put Love's speeches in a different type to distinguish the voices, though ultimately they are one voice: the voice of the beloved, the "I," who has learned to speak to himself in Love's voice.)

LOVE III

Love bade me welcome: yet my soul drew back
Guiltie of dust and sinne.
But quick-eyed Love, observing me grow slack
From my first entrance in,
Drew nearer to me, sweetly questioning
If I lack'd anything.

A guest, I answered, worthy to be here:
Love said, You shall be he.
I the unkinde, ungratefull? Ah, my deare,
I cannot look on thee.
Love took my hand, and smiling did reply,
Who made the eyes but I?

Truth Lord, but I have marr'd them: let my shame
Go where it doth deserve.
And know you not, *sayes Love, who bore the blame?*
My deare, then I will serve.
You must sit down, *sayes Love,* and taste my meat:
So I did sit and eat.

Line by line, the distance between the enticed and the enticer shrinks, though up to the poem's last line the speaker, like a mistrustful animal confronted with a friendly domestic hand, balks and defers. But Love persists in the welcome ("drew nearer," "took my hand"). Love is personified as a relaxed, conversational, kind, and alert host: "quick-eyed," observant, "smiling," solicitous, and generous ("sweetly questioning if I lacked anything"). Yet when the speaker has protested enough, Love declares with simple firmness: "You *shall* be he." The protester is not even allowed to serve. "You must sit down and taste my meat."

Enough is enough. Our self-denigrator is at last silenced, and we capitulate along with him. Like travelers who have come a long way, we, too, approach the table that has been rubbed down with love and sweet-smelling herbs. With overwhelming relief the beloved in us graciously sits down and eats.

PART THREE
Hospitality of Heart

I. Heather's Parties

When I first met Heather, she wasn't long out of medical school. She had come south to work in a rural clinic in the Smoky Mountains. She stayed on in Asheville, married another doctor in public health, went on to specialize in emergency medicine, and eventually became director of the emergency room at one of the two hospitals in the city. I will be forever grateful to her for doing something nobody else could have done for me on the night of December 30, 1989, and in a style uniquely her own. At first, it may seem to you that this story is a long way from the subject of parties, but it goes to the very bedrock of hospitality, and thus heart.

At noon that day, my mother had been killed while driving alone. Apparently she had suffered a heart attack, veered across the median, and crashed into another car. By the time I could fly from Albany to Asheville, it was midnight, but I wanted to see my mother's body one last time before it was taken to the funeral home. Heather got out of bed and met me at the hospital. She'd already made the necessary official arrangements, but first she grabbed hold of my hand and pulled me into a softly lit room, and, looking me over, and then talking fast, as she always does, prepared me for what I was going to see, using medical terms like *septum* to muffle the impact of picturing my mother's face smashing against the steering wheel. She kept walking me around the room, zigzagging between sofas and chairs, holding tight to my hand, giving me quick glances, and talking a mile a minute. She told me she had treated the two people in the car Mother smashed into, set the man's leg and stitched up the wife's forehead—they were both going to be all right, she reassured me, though the wife would still need some plastic surgery—but Heather hadn't known who the person in the other car was because the body had been brought in already covered.

At last we went down a hall and into a room. Two official-looking people, a man and a woman, hovered discreetly by the door. My best friend, Pat, who had driven me to the hospital, was also there. Inside, on a gurney in the middle of the room, was a black body bag.

"In case I faint or something," I told Heather, "please just take this and put it in her hand." In what seemed like a single unbroken motion, Heather unzipped the bag and deftly wound the blue rosary between the fingers.

I looked at my mother's body. The straight nose was divided and had a marked tilt, as if someone had playfully mashed it upward into a ski-jump nose. You could see the exposed bone and cartilage. The lips were ajar, in an expression of surprise. Some front tooth caps were gone and only the posts remained. The eyes were open but death had drained them of their lively periwinkle blue; now they were a lusterless yellow-green. Her makeup was still visible and her hair looked the way it did right after she had used the hot curlers, brushed it into shape, and sprayed it firmly into place. She had on one of her two favorite blouses and her teal green wool suit. The little half-moon diamond-and-sapphire brooch she always wore on her lapel had been removed and put in the safe with her purse by the hospital chaplain, a dear friend of hers.

I touched the face, which bore similarities to the one I had known intimately through its successive phases of adulthood, but was also the face of a formal stranger. I traced my finger around the hairline of this nice-looking, well-groomed lady who had dressed to go somewhere and had arrived somewhere else that day. I was never further from fainting in my life. I felt enclosed in a prickly, astringent alertness as I stood beside the body that had contained my mother's life. "I love you," I said aloud to the body, because it felt right for the occasion, in front of these other people. But I knew as I heard the words—and have known ever since, thanks to the inestimable gift of Heather's midnight hospitality—that my mother's complex personality and valiant heart no longer dwelled in what I touched and would not be embalmed or buried.

A few years later, Heather stepped down from her post as ER director and entered private practice. "I used to save a life and never see the person again," she said. "Now I see the same people and all their symptoms, over and over again. Is it different? Yes. The other was exhilarating, but it would have eventually killed me. Now I work regular hours, I can even have lunch uptown with Charles and go home at six and work in the garden."

Then Heather started giving the parties. Solstice parties. Halloween parties. New Year's. Valentine's. Friends' birthdays. *Equinox* parties. Elaborate, time- and energy-consuming events involving dozens of people and their contributions: recipes from her brother the caterer, who would fly down and be chef along with herself and more friends as sous-chefs; invitations and decorations from her printer and designer friends; carpenter and electrician friends to build a covered outdoor dance floor with carnival atmosphere lighting; her husband and his musician friends to provide live piano and strings.

What is she doing? people asked. Yes, the very ones who responded to the beautifully designed and printed invitations, and admitted afterward they'd never been to such a glorious bash, but . . . why is she wasting all that energy on such an ephemeral thing as a *party*? I mean, there were lights all over the night, and someone must have spent hours hanging those antique wheelbarrows up in that old tree, and I haven't danced like that in years, nor have I ever been to a sit-down dinner for seventy-five people, but what does she get out of it, a smart, successful person like herself, a medical doctor, for God's sake, washing up seventy-five place settings afterward, and planning the next extravaganza, no doubt.

I have never been to one of Heather's parties. My visits to Asheville usually take place in early October and during Passiontide, thereby just missing Halloween and the spring equinox, but she always sends me the beautiful invitations anyway. I am looking at one right now. Against a background of crimson there is an eye superimposed on some barely discernible Greek and Latin, or pretend Greek and Latin, words (*horum* and *accipe* are the only ones I can guess at; I have a feeling she and Charles had fun concocting the other ones), and below the eye is a quote from T. S. Eliot: "*at the still point, there the dance is.*" You open the card and inside in a small square is a picture of an old tree similar to the one the wheelbarrows were hanging in. And below:

COME DINE AND DANCE
BY MIDSUMMER LIGHT
SATURDAY, JUNE 20
Festivities begin at 5
Supper at 7
Dancing thereafter
RSVP

If that isn't enough, the artwork continues on the back of the card: an astronomer's drawing of the planet marked up correctly for summer solstice. The only place name on the planet large enough to read is *Asheville*.

My friend Pat was giving me a blow-by-blow of Heather's most recent party. "For a long time, I didn't understand the parties," said Pat, "but I'm beginning to. Look, for years she ran the emergency room. You know what she used to tell her co-workers? 'When a new patient comes in you have exactly one minute to gauge what *response* that person needs from you.' That's what she'd tell them: 'You have one minute to look them over and decide whether they'll do best with Spartan professionalism or down-home reassurance or a bit of joking along, *and then you have to start giving them what they need.*' Heather is used to delegating, and I think that's what she's doing with all her friends chop-chopping and building and cooking and wiring. Only now instead of performing triage together she assembles her team to do parties."

"Pat told me about what you used to say in the ER about having one minute to gauge what response each new patient needs," I said to Heather the next time we were together. "I was really impressed by that. It's so . . . human."

Heather blushed, she's awkward with compliments. "Yes, I did say that, but it wasn't a minute. A minute would be far too long. I told them fifteen seconds."

Of course, I thought, remembering that midnight when she gave me her quick once-over and then pulled me into the low-lit room and walked me around and around the furniture talking a mile a minute about my mother's septum and the people in the other car who were going to be all right and the unidentified stranger who came in already covered and no longer needed her help.

Heather wrote me in one of her dashed-off missives torn out of her Levenger notebook:

> May Day was last Friday. The Sunday before, while "power-weeding," I was inspired to throw a May Day party *sans* pole. Charles's only request was that I not get frantic. This was accomplished by planning a menu with my brother's phone assistance that could be entirely ready at the guests' arrival, and getting food preparation help. Thursday evening three friends came over for a slice-and-dice pre-party. I had the kitchen organized with 4 work stations, each with the recipe, food, and tools for that particular dish. Friday we fed 18 at tables of 6 with Fiesta Ware and flowers from my friend Perry. Everyone brought something to do with May Day: a rock, a morel, poems, stories, spoonerisms, and songs were offered as we madly applauded each person's gift. It was magical and certainly part of my answer to your question "so what is it about these parties?" It's an art form (of sorts): creating experiences together. You must get Charles to describe, as he is so much better at that. Anyway, solstice is 6 weeks away. I would like to celebrate with my tribe/community all 8 holidays per year, 4 cross-quarter days and 2 equinoxes, 2 solstices. Your questions are always so challenging and I will continue to work on my answer.

II. Toward More
Consciousness of Heart

Two years ago, after I called my agent back and said yes, I would like to do this book on the heart, I made an outline. "The Heart Through Time," "Heart Themes in Life and Art"—and then what? Where did we go after that? I settled on "Notes Toward a New Consciousness of Heart" for my conclusion. The title promises a little something more, yet at the same time it protects itself. "Notes" are not a dissertation. "Toward" something can't be expected to have arrived there. "New," of course, is always seductive, as in Ezra Pound's "MAKE IT NEW." In our quick-change, self-improving culture we take "new" seriously, just as we prize "consciousness" as a desirable commodity, something we like to think we're busily accumulating more and more of.

But now after all these months spent in the School of the Heart, I realize my course of study has led me somewhere, after all. As I followed the heart through time, and looked at manifestations, both in life and art, of heartbreak, heart-absence, hearts of darkness, heart-changes, and hearts in love, I did arrive at an idea of what we need to train for next if we are to develop more consciousness of heart. And that training school is the School of Hospitality in its myriad aspects, from Baucis and Philemon's welcoming table with the short leg propped up, to Heather's finely tuned imagination for what is needed by a traumatized patient in the ER. Or even Heather's parties for overworked and underplayful friends in want of a festive communal gathering—a place to celebrate the earth's turning and recall them to that still point "where the dance is."

Hospitality is having ready what is needed (as when Mrs. Hawkins had the nasturtiums ready on the winter night a woman intended to drown herself); hospitality is making room in yourself for the new and the strange and the *other*, like Muhammad's ardent curiosity about the beliefs of strangers met during his caravan runs; hospitality is stretching your intellectual boundaries, as we will see priest-scientist Teilhard de Chardin doing, to include the larger picture, with all its contradictions and loose ends, rather than dividing life into security-tight compartments that keep things neat and unthreatening and familiar. (Religion over here, science over there; matter down here, spirit up there.)

Hospitality derives from the Latin *hospes*, which not only meant guest, visitor, or stranger, but also host. What was being stressed here was the concept of human exchange, so the same word could serve whether you were on the giving or receiving end. *Hospitium* was both entertainment and inn. In the early Middle Ages, a hospice, or hospital, was a place where pilgrims and travelers were received and entertained; only later was the word narrowed down to mean an institution for the care of the sick or the wounded. (An interesting reversal of Heather's hospitality, which began with emergency healing and expanded into healing entertainment!)

Hospitality of heart calls for a special kind of imagination that concentrates on how another creature might be feeling. When my cousin Sophie's beloved Jim, her twenty-five-year-old horse, had to go to the hospital for an eye operation, a friend not only supplied the horse van to take him there but, knowing of Jim's van terrors, loaded her own horse, Jim's friend, to ride with him to the hospital.

When my friend Frances, the architect, was designing a couple of courthouses in the Deep South, she came up with the idea of making the now-required surveillance borders—those places where you are

stopped and checked for concealed weapons—into interim court-
yards with flower borders and trees and fountains. "While you are
being x-rayed, you can at least feel you're being welcomed into a spot
of refreshment and beauty."

The Sufis, a mystical branch of Islam, have a word, *himma*, which
means a concentration of heart that can produce a creative energy
powerful enough to give objective body to the heart's intentions.
Frances's surveillance "borders," which came out of her heart's
imagination, will soon be growing real flowers in real soil.

III. A Jesuit Scientist and His "Converging Hearts": Pierre Teilhard de Chardin (1881–1955)

Here life is very peaceful, in a very beautiful setting, he writes to his
friend Lucile Swan, who, he claims, gives him "force and élan." *I have
started a new essay, "The Heart of Matter," an analysis of my interior evolution since my childhood.* He's sixty-nine, still depleted from the life-
threatening heart attack he suffered three years before, and
depressed by continual rebuffs from his superiors in Rome, who will
not let him publish his ideas that matter and spirit are inseparable.
Now, spending some restful time in the ancient French province of
Auvergne with family members, he is moved to begin this most lucid
and personal statement of his life's work and of his own internal
evolving, *The Heart of Matter*, a small book of around 17,000 words.

He had died and the first of his "forbidden" books had recently been published when in my twenties I discovered him. I would say I understood an average of one sentence in every third paragraph, but I knew his ideas were important to me. I felt they could keep me connected to my spiritual imagination as I entered the vale of rational doubt, from which some of us never emerge. Today when I read him, I understand most of the sentences in most of the paragraphs, but by no means all. Part of the problem is that he uses a scientist's vocabulary to work out his philosophical ideas; but the other part of the problem is that he invented the most dauntingly abstruse terms to describe the converging process going on in the universe. My apologies in advance if my rendering of his ideas turns out to be as reader-inhospitable as his. Nevertheless, he saved my spiritual life from extinction—he, along with Dr. Jung—and I want to pay homage.

Also, for the purposes of this book about the heart, he is a prime exemplar of someone who was capable of practicing a sweeping hospitality to contradictions, even though they almost tore him apart as he tried to reconcile his scientific vocation with his religious one. "It is utterly impossible for me not to see (and say) what I see," he wrote to Lucile Swan when he sent her the completed personal essay, *The Heart of Matter*. "And I am sure that God cannot be smaller than our biggest and wildest conceptions!" Now that is a "hospitality of heart" declaration if I ever heard one.

He joined the Jesuits just before his eighteenth birthday and kept his vows until his life's end, though not without struggles. He went wherever on the globe his order sent him, and he did not publish his controversial ideas (although he asked permission to do so every year).

And he remained celibate. ("Don't forget, never, that what sweetness I force myself not to give you . . . I do it in order to be more worthy of you," he wrote to Lucile Swan in 1934, five years after they had met in Peking, she a newly divorced artist of thirty-nine, he already an internationally recognized paleontologist of forty-eight.) During his lifetime, he would write her over two hundred letters, most in English, some in French, often a mixture of both, as they each traveled the world, often missing each other by mere days. Lucile liked him to write about his personal doings in French because she claimed he wrote more intimately. In his letters he addressed her as "dear friend," then "Lucile dear," then "dearest," and signed himself "P.T." under "yours," then "yours ever," then "so much yours," "yours so deeply," and "yours more deeply than ever." She called him "P.T." for "Precious Teilhard." Their letters, edited by Thomas M. King, a Jesuit, and Mary Wood Gilbert, Lucile's cousin, were published in 1993 by Georgetown University Press.

In *The Heart of Matter*, unlike the recondite *Phenomenon of Man*, Teilhard makes no attempt to work out a "scientific theology," but simply chronicles his psychological experience. In a personal, accessible style, he relates how his deep love of the world and its precious Matter (which he always capitalizes) gradually caught fire for him and burst into flames, enfolding him in "a great luminous mass, lit from within." He calls this merger of world and spirit "The Diaphany of the Divine at the heart of a glowing Universe." The transparent God lives for him at the heart of the universe.

As a child of six or seven, he already felt irresistibly drawn to Matter, "or, more correctly, by something which 'shone' at the heart of Matter" (his first intimation of the transparent God he would struggle to bring words to). He first fell in love with the metal iron (he calls it his "iron god") because it was hard, heavy, durable, concentrated . . . absolute. From the beginning, he says, he was after the absolute. When he was in the country, he kept the lockpin of a plough as his "idol"; in the city he venerated the hexagonal head of a metal bolt. When, to his dismay, he found out that iron could be scratched, pitted, or rusted, he transferred his adoration to blue flame, then to glittering fragments of chalcedony and quartz. The substitution of rocks for iron, he says, was an immense turning point for his spiritual evolution. Metal had kept him attached to objects that were manufactured, mere pieces of the whole; "Mineral, on the other hand, set me on the road to the 'planetary.'"

When the Jesuits sent him, at twenty-eight, to teach elementary physics in Cairo, his passionate love of the universe, abetted by the new kind of light, the deserts, the exotic vegetation and fauna, began to smolder in him, but "without as yet the power to burst into open flame." Now he had *Matter, Nature,* and the *Energy* of his beloved physics as the "three inflammable elements that had slowly piled up in my soul over a period of thirty years." But something was still needed to light the fire.

This fuel came in the form of Bergson's *Creative Evolution,* which Teilhard read when he was back in England, studying for his theology degree at the Jesuit scholasticate.

Until that time, he tells us candidly, his education and his religion had led him obediently to accept a fundamental difference between Matter and Spirit, Body and Soul, Conscious and Unconscious. Matter ("My Divine Matter!") was forced to be the humble servant, "if not, indeed, its enemy" of Spirit, which was, for him, up until that time, a mere shadow that he was compelled to venerate, "but emotionally and intellectually speaking, I did not in fact have any live interest in it."

But, now: "that magic word 'evolution' . . . haunted my thoughts like a tune."

> You can well imagine, accordingly, how strong was my inner feeling of release and expansion when I took my first still hesitant steps into an "evolutive" Universe, and saw that the dualism in which I had hitherto been enclosed was disappearing like the mist before the rising sun. Matter and Spirit: these were no longer two things, but two states or two aspects of one and the same cosmic Stuff.*

The "alleged barrier" separating the Within from the Without had now toppled for the young Jesuit-scientist, but it would take him a whole lifetime to work out these implications of evolution. Paleontology, the study of prehistoric forms of life, was to convince him that the progressive spiritualization of Matter was an irreversible process. "Spirit was by no means the enemy or the opposite pole of the Tangibility which I was seeking to attain: rather was in its very heart" (italics added).

Brought up on physics before quanta, relativity, or atomic structure, he had more work to do before he could recognize "the amaz-

---

*The Heart of Matter, translated by René Hague [Harcourt Brace/Harvest, p. 26].

ing attributes of universal curvature," which led to his theory of human "convergence." However, it was joyful work.

"I find it difficult to express," he would eventually confide in *The Heart of Matter*, "how much I feel at home in precisely this world of electrons, nuclei, waves, and what a sense of plenitude and comfort it gives me."

"THE HEART GROWS A NEW SKIN"

But he had to experience the "spiritual shock" of World War I in the trenches as a soldier before the idea of "the earth's thinking enve-lope" of humankind could germinate in his mind. With his creden-tials he was entitled to the rank of officer and army chaplain, but he chose to join up as an ordinary soldier. Throughout the war he worked as a stretcher bearer of the wounded at the front. Most of the soldiers in his unit were Muslims from Morocco and Algeria, and, since the unit had no chaplain, he consoled the dying and suffering as best he could. The men called him Sidi Marabout, a title of great esteem, since *Sidi* means a North African settled in France, and *Marabout* comes from the Arab *murabit*, which means someone closely bound to God.

In the trenches he found himself fulfilling a function beyond the merely personal, and becoming fully conscious of this new state. Yet he was still the soldier who took night walks in the devastated land-scapes of France, where the smell from the last gas attack lingered in the hollows under the poplars, the man who heard the crickets chirping right through the mortar bombs, the man who kept a diary and wrote letters to his soul-mate cousin, Marguerite, when he wasn't consoling the wounded and carrying away the dead. It was just that (he wrote in his wartime essay, "Nostalgia for the Front"):

"the irksome and nagging envelope of small and great worries, of health, of one's family, of success, of the future . . . slides off the soul by itself, like an old coat. *The heart grows a new skin*" (italics added).

"The Human million," with its psychic temperature and its internal energy, became as real for him in the trenches as "a giant molecule of protein." Increasingly it became clear to him that if the individual human being is composed of a "corpuscular magnitude," then the human being himself must be subject to the same development as every other species of corpuscles in the world. And that meant "that he must coalesce into physical relationships and groupings that belong to a higher order than his." During this time in the trenches, Teilhard's convergence theory was born.

THE HEART OF "THE HEART OF THINGS"

He still had to work out what he calls in *The Heart of Matter* "the most advanced stage of my inner exploration in search of the Heart of things." This has to do with the Biosphere's "thinking envelope," (which he named the Noosphere), composed of the thoughts and the "psychic temperature" of the Human-millions since the beginning of time.

This concept alone is breathtaking in its implications, but there is still more to come: Teilhard's breakthrough was to understand that this thinking envelope is *also evolving*—undergoing "Noogenesis." As the earth grows more populated and humankind becomes more compressed upon itself, and more complex in its individual elements, he compares its thinking mass to a vast phylum, whose branches, instead of diverging, as they normally do in space, are folding in upon one another ever more closely ("like an enormous flower folding in on itself"), creating a "mass Cerebration," a "collective Reflection." (Teilhard's capital letters are important: more often than not, for him, they signify God's presence at the heart of the thing being capitalized.)

"Writing in the year 1950," he concludes, "I can say that the evolution of my inner vision culminates in the acceptance of this evident fact, that there is a 'creative' tide which (as a strict statistic consequence of their increasing powers of self-determination) is carrying the human 'mega-molecules' towards an almost unbelievable quasi 'mono-molecular' state." Each ego, he predicted, was destined to be forced convulsively beyond itself into some mysterious focal point of maturity. He called this eventual ultramaturity in Humankind the "Omega Point."

The Omega Point, for him, was the ultimate "piece of iron" that he had loved as a small boy. The Omega point was the Consistence of the Universe "that I now hold, concentrated (whether above me or, rather, in the depths of my being, I cannot say) into one single indestructible center, WHICH I CAN LOVE."

To the introduction of his autobiographical essay, he has appended a haiku-like poetic summation of his lifetime findings:

> *At the heart of Matter*
> *A World-heart*
> *The Heart of a God.*

His hospitality to contradictions has embraced more and more of the universe until it admits the ultimate Guest who has been at the heart of things all along.

IV. An All-around Heart: Paul Klee (1879–1940)

When Robert is angry or troubled, he gets out his Bach Society edition of *The Well-Tempered Clavier*, sits down at his Yamaha grand piano, and, scarcely having to turn the pages anymore, lets the book fall open to the C-sharp Minor Prelude. He plays that prelude—or "enters it" would be closer to the reality—then continues with the E-flat Minor Prelude ("really a sarabande"), and, though he is usually calm by then, tarries a bit longer in Bach's kingdom of sublime sanity with the B-flat Minor.

Until the last two years of Paul Klee's life, when scleroderma, a hardening of the body's connective tissues, had stiffened his fingers beyond his music, though not beyond his art, he played the violin (Bach, Mozart, Haydn) for an hour before he began to paint.

When I am fearful or melancholy, or petulant over something, I can take up a volume of Klee's paintings and drawings and, like Robert with his Bach, immediately enter a better place. Klee's world is an inexhaustible realm of things caught in revelatory moments, rendered in such a way as to summon astonished recognition, tender feelings, or snorts of laughter. With a few lively strokes, he was uncannily able to illustrate the essence of his subject: "the governess," a "group with fleeing scold," "a super sycophant"—a cat with a bird so much on its mind that the captured bird is already imprinted in the cat's forehead.

The titles of his pictures were important to him and he made every effort to preserve them. In the same way the chapter titles of the Koran evoke stories and shapes in one's imagination ("The Cloaked One," "He Frowned," "The Nightly Visitor," "She Who Pleaded"), Klee's titles by themselves call up ideas and pictures:

Witch with Comb
Timid Brute
Angel Still Groping
Departure of the Ghost
Relapse of a Convert
Romantic Park
Little Fool in a Trance
Ceramic, Erotic, Religious
Child Consecrated to Suffering
Overladen Devil
The Chair-Animal
Menagerie Goes for a Walk
Sick Man Making Plans
Centipede in an Enclosure
Spook Going Too Far

Klee was the living embodiment of a Person of Heart. That he was a first-rate artist makes him all the rarer. Creative people are expected to be selfish beasts who wouldn't hesitate to "sacrifice their grand-mother" for their art. Rilke, in his monograph on Cézanne, reported that the great painter did not attend his mother's funeral because he didn't want to interrupt his painting; Rilke, however, was later to pass up his daughter's wedding because he was afraid he'd lose his momen-tum with his poetry. The great Tolstoy at age eighty-three left home for the monastery without saying good-bye to his wife, who threw her-self in the pond when she found out; when, days later, he was dying of pneumonia at the train station, he refused to let her see him.

So it is with surprise and awe that, having fallen in love with Klee's art, you go and get the diaries and the notebooks and fall in love with the man.

He knew from early on that the heart was his vital principle. At age twenty-one, in the diaries, he writes about his painting style: "Some will not recognize the truthfulness of my mirror. Let them remember that I am not here to reflect the surface (this can be done by the photographic plate), but must penetrate inside. My mirror probes down to the heart."

At twenty-seven, he records an important dream: "I flew home, where the beginning lies. It started with brooding and chewing of fingers. Then I smelled or tasted something. The scent freed me. I was completely freed at once and melted away like a piece of sugar in water. My heart too was involved; it had been far too large for a long time, now it was blown up to inordinate size. But not a trace of oppression. It was borne to places where one no longer seeks voluptuousness."

Of van Gogh, he writes: "I develop more and more confidence in him . . . he was able to reach deep, very deep, into his own heart."

He married Lily Stumpf, a pianist several years older than himself. She taught music and he stayed home and painted and cooked and took care of their only child, Felix, whose lovingly watched development is meticulously recorded in *The Diaries of Paul Klee*, edited and introduced by Felix Klee, University of California Press, 1964. Here are just a few excerpts:

> November 30, 1907 [date of Felix's birth]. When the child arrived, "a boy," I was astonished . . . that everybody didn't disband quietly, but instead a new center of attention was formed. And what a center, as I was to learn

hourly and thoroughly from then on. The first to leave
were the doctors. . . . Then the midwife . . . and now we
were alone, a real little family. Perhaps this reads like a
bucolic novel, and yet it was a stirring moment; indeed
one hovered close to emotion, but then back again to the
grossly practical . . . when a "*rabah, rabah,*" penetrated my
sleep and I had to resurrect from a deathlike state, heat
some water, add some milk, press the bottle against my
eye, and then shove it into the open gateway! How the fellow guzzled. But then he left us in peace again.

February 19, 1908. Bites and screeches. Begins to be able
to hold his head up.

November 2, 1908. Says *oli-yoli-yoli, togedo, togay-dodo,
toh dyay-doh* (are irritation from teeth and learning to
speak somehow connected?).

March 1–17, 1909. Felix's temperature chart (up to
105.8 degrees) recorded three times daily during the
child's serious illness.

June–October 1909. He holds clocks to his ear and
laughs with pleasure. . . . He enjoys having his nails
cut. . . . He won't sit on his training stool, and will only
be held over it. It's called *sss.* . . . Gradually he stops
plucking flowers to pieces. . . . He turns the pages of
books skillfully and doesn't vandalize them. But if one
shows a little damage he destroys it completely. . . .
Spoons are his enemy. . . . He jokes by squinting and wip-
ing his mouth and by wanting to whistle and not being
able because he is laughing.

When Felix was a little older, Klee made him toy trains, a cardboard railway station, and a puppet theater, sewing the costumes himself. (When Klee was serving in World War I, he sewed himself a pair of gloves.) He seemed to be able to do everything with artistry (make virtuoso music, paint, draw, write poetry, teach, cook, do mathematics, be father, husband, and friend: he could write and draw with both hands, though he preferred to draw with the left; Felix remembered him drawing with both hands at the same time).

His hospitable heart drew everything—even Felix's temperature chart—into his work rather than separating the work from the rest of his life. In his "Creative Credo," written in 1918, and later used in his teaching at the Bauhaus (what an interesting teacher he must have been), he encourages artists to "draw up a topographical plan and take a little journey to the land of better understanding." He first narrates a possible journey (river, boat, field, wood, a nervous companion, fog, basket weavers, flash of lightning, stars, until, at last, we come to our lodging) and then goes on to describe the draftsman's lines ("the psyche of the line") that would illustrate this particular journey.

And then, at the end of the journey, a quick narrative summary of everyman's night thoughts: impressions of the journey, permeated with personal reflections of one's life lived up until now:

> Before we fall asleep, a number of memories comes back to us . . . all sorts of lines. Spots. Dots . . . shaded surfaces. Wavy movement . . . Counter-movement. Network and Weaving. Brickwork, fish-scales . . . A line losing itself, a line growing stronger . . .
>
> The happy equanimity of the first stretch, then the inhibitions, the nervousness! Restrained trembling, the caress of hopeful breezes. Before the storm, the gadflies'

attack. The fury, the murder. The good cause a guiding
thread even in the thick of twilight. *The lightning shaped
like a fever curve. Of a sick child . . . long ago.*
—Paul Klee *Notebooks: Volume One, The Thinking Eye*
(London: Lund Humphries, 1961)

THE "HEART PICTURES"

I know this is not a picture book, but I want to see how far words can
go in describing some of Paul Klee's most striking pictorial represen-
tations of the heart. From his earliest to his last compositions, hearts
appear frequently and always significantly in his art: the heart as centerpiece and subject; as sly or satirical commentary in a drawing; as
the single telling splash of color in a monochrome landscape; as indi-
cation of the true creative source of life—or, conversely, as the heart
gone wrong, pointing to disaster and evil.

"Portrait of Mrs. P. in the South" shows a merry widow on vacation,
wearing her heart-shaped heart in the center of her dress. "The Shep-
herd" portrays a wide-eyed keeper of sheep looking both ways at once,
his large heart glowing like a beacon for his flock. "In the Magic Mirror," the face, bisected from head to thorax by a wavery, crooked line,
wears a sinister, untrustworthy smirk; though the small black heart is
anatomically correct in its location, it serves as a warning cipher.

In the colorful "Puppet Theatre," the large central human figure
has a heart-shaped face and a striped heart for her upper body. In the
predominantly brown "Arab Song" (Klee's imagination was stimulated by his trips to Tunis and Egypt), the downward smile of a
burnoosed face painted on burlap culminates in a heart: the heart is
the extension of the smile.

The mysterious "Ab Ovo" seems to be about creation itself, with the pink heart centered against a background of pointed purple and black shapes. In "Cat and Bird," a close-up of a cat's face as he dreams of a bird, the cat's nose is a wetly shining red heart. In both "Twins" and "Brother and Sister," two figures share one heart. In the water-color lithograph "Genie Serving a Small Breakfast (Angel Fulfilling a Wish)," a light-footed winged figure in motion, bearing a huge over-spilling red heart at its midpoint, carrying a tray with a champagne glass and a kettle with an overflowing spout, as well as other goodies, rushes toward the edge of the picture. In "Female Artist," one of my favorites, her heart is white-hot (a word Klee often used about himself during the act of intense perception) surrounded by a red glow.

Conversely, "Irma Rossa, the Tamer," the witchy, orange-haired tamer of animals bears her heart upside-down and on the wrong side. In "Who Kills Whom," a determined insectlike figure aims a black arrow straight into the red teardrop-shaped heart of a passive reclining figure.

One of his last great paintings, "Hibernation" (1937), was done when he was suffering from what is now called progressive systemic sclerosis, an excessive buildup of fibrous connective tissue that was gradually petrifying his body. It is a 31-inch by 49-inch mixed media and watercolor of a humanized landscape. The world is depicted as a female figure, slumbering in its own rounded curves. Judging from the cool blues and unleafy lines, the time of year appears to be deep winter. But the orange-gold highlights on the curves of the figure suggest sunrise—and, beyond the sunrise, the coming warmth of summer. There is a single red heart shape in the nature-creature's womb.

The painting would serve wonderfully as cover art for Teilhard's *The Heart of Matter.*

When you read in the 1916 diary about Air Force Reserve Engineer Klee's feelings upon escorting a transport of German fighter planes through Belgium into occupied France—toward where we just left French soldier Teilhard collecting the dead from the trenches—when you contemplate the idea of these two contemporaries, who had so much in common, being on opposite sides, the absurdity of war hits you solidly in the same place it hit Klee:

> *La douce France.* What a way to meet again! Shattering. Coming from the north along a sinister path and not toward the heart! Illegal. Poor, degraded country! The past, a ruthless line drawn under yesterday. A glittering blade striking deeply into the heart's core.

During a short leave in Munich in 1916, Klee wrote the following reflection on himself as a human being and an artist:

> My fire is more like the dead or the unborn.... Everything Faustian is alien to me. I place myself at a remote starting point of creation, whence I divine a sort of formula for men, beasts, plants, stones and the elements, and for all the whirling forces. A thousand questions subside as if they had been solved. Neither orthodoxies or heresies exist there. The possibilities are too endless, and the belief in them is all that lives creatively in me.... I seek a place for myself only with God.... I cannot be understood in purely earthly terms. For I can live as well with the dead as with the unborn. Somewhat nearer to the heart of Creation than is usual. But still far from being near enough.

He died in Switzerland in 1940, because the Nazis had made it unbearable for him in Germany. The final cause of death was paralysis of the heart. His remains were cremated in Lugano and buried in Schlosshalde cemetery in Berne, where his wife, Lily, would later be interred beside him. Lily and Felix had the following inscribed on his gravestone:

Here Rests the Painter
PAUL KLEE
Born on December 18, 1879
Died on June 29, 1940
I cannot be grasped in the here and now
For I live just as well with the dead as with the unborn
Somewhat closer to the heart of creation
Than usual
But far from close enough

EPILOGUE

Today is Independence Day. Ambrose and I took a short walk before I began work this morning. The first nasturtium is out: a deep orange color. "I wanted to watch the tall ships," grumbled Robert, who had turned on the television to see the coverage of the ships entering the harbor, "but they were interviewing some woman who complained she couldn't tell one ship from another. That is *not* news."

Before my brother Rebel left for Manila, where he's doing contract work for the IMF, he came up to Woodstock from Washington and reprogrammed my "heart" files on the computer so I wouldn't have to be coached by telephone each time I began a new section. I sat beside him, admiring his straight back—he is the only person I know who doesn't *hunch* in front of the screen—and we set up files for all the sections I hadn't written yet. He made me title each section and write a few opening lines, so that later, when I opened a brand-new file, I would never have to face a blank page. A characteristic example of his hospitality of heart.

And so, this morning, having at long last reached C:\heart\Part. Four.Epilogue.wpd, I open that file and find:

EPILOGUE
Now we come, ha, ha, to the END!

I'm going to leave them there undeleted, the words of my projected exultation, typed while straight-backed brother looked on and laughed.

Our view from the house has changed since I began this project. A storm called Floyd hit Woodstock last September. Robert and Ambrose and I sat in the darkening living room, thoroughly chastened by the power of nature, and listened to the hardwood trees cracking and crashing to the ground outside the house. By morning, most of Woodstock's roads were blocked with huge fallen trees, still in leaf. We lost forty big trees. But another person in town lost fifty and another person three hundred. So around our house there is more open landscape now. And that's not all. I can look out my study window and see the roof of a house going up just below us.

When I first heard the whine of the chain saws, I was beside myself. ("I knew we should have bought that good-for-nothing lot down below . . . and now look!") I left a message for the building inspector about the possibility of a variance so we could erase the house with a nine-foot-high fence, but he didn't return my call. I woke up feeling my peace encroached upon when I heard the hammers starting at eight sharp in the morning. I felt like Faust, after he has drained his land and built his palace and then looks out and sees old Baucis and Philemon's little house and line of linden trees right smack in the middle of his private view and complains to Mephistopheles:

> *Die wenig Baume, nicht mein eigen,*
> *Verderben mir den Weltbesitz.*
> *(Those few trees not my own*
> *Ruin my possession of the world.)*

Luckily, I do not live with Mephistopheles but with Robert, who one day cut off my contumely with an interesting suggestion: "Why don't we invite our new neighbor for a drink?"

Robert found out how to reach him and left a message. The new neighbor called back and left another message saying he'd like to come, and they finally exchanged a live phone conversation. And so he came. It was Philemon, but without his Baucis. Baucis had died, after a long bout with cancer, a few months after they had begun construction on what was to have been their retirement house. Robert built a fire, and I made my very best smoked salmon sandwiches with the crusts cut off, and we provided our guest of honor's alcoholic substance of choice, which also happened to be mine. For an hour we got acquainted: his talk was mostly about his departed love, how they had met (she was in a strict boarding school, he showed up as an actor in a visiting theatrical group), how they had lived, where they had traveled, how they had fought together to preserve her life, how she had finally given up the struggle. But her symbol, he told us proudly, had always been the butterfly. He wrote us a thank-you note on her butterfly notepaper. We expect him to move in by Labor Day.

Writing this book has broadened my education immensely. I

would go so far as to say it has given me a remedial education. Our era encourages us to "specialize" and "prioritize," and I have been a dutiful child of my time. I "chose my major," developed my most promising skills (even regretfully choosing between them at certain junctures in my life, because there was only so much time to become outstanding at something), and remained abysmally ignorant of huge portions of reality. I was loaded with information about the Christian mystics, for instance, but had never so much as opened the Koran. I sort of knew what Buddhists did, and could quote you several elusive Zen *koans*, but I had yet to discover the generous-hearted attributes of the Bodhisattva, the person who has attained enlightenment, but postpones nirvana in order to help others attain it.

I would like to think that immersing myself in heart lore for two years has made me more of a person of heart. I can report that whenever I came up against a place in the writing that felt drudge-heavy or dead, it usually turned out to be because I had neglected to consult Heart. The discriminating, differentiating intellect can and must do a great deal when you organize a book around any theme, but it is *heart*, which always relates to the whole, that must infuse the voice if it is to make the living connections and keep the circulation between all the parts moving.

Writing *Heart* has made me quicker in recognizing the presence of heart—as well as its pervasive absence—and has made me sharper in identifying the outward manifestations of both people and situations. It certainly has made me more aware of the inner qualities of my experiences—the feelings and emotions eddying below the surface, the affective connections between things that previously appeared unrelated. (Having learned, for instance, in my research that Teilhard de Chardin is buried in the cemetery of a monastery just across the Hudson River from me, I will go and walk there some

afternoon. And now, whenever I pause at Felix's grave in the mornings with Ambrose, I remember the young woman who carved
Felix's stone telling me about the marble stones she carved for the
monks and priests in those Hudson River grave sites: Felix and Teilhard now tumble around together in my heart-thoughts.)

A last local story about hearts and hospitality. This spring I went
with Tom, our priest at St. Gregory's Episcopal Church in Woodstock, to an evening service up at the Tibetan Buddhist monastery. I
had picked up a schedule in the monastery gift shop, but we had only
the vaguest idea of what the "service" would be like. We expected
some chanting by monks in maroon, like in the two recent Tibetan
films (one of which used the Woodstock shrine for its interiors),
and I had driven up to the top of Mead Mountain Road several times
to browse in the gift shop and buy a colorful *thangka* (a religious
painting mounted on a scroll of silk brocade) of the Green Tara goddess for a friend to hang on the wall above her treadmill. And of
course both Tom and I had heard the Woodstock buzz about the
dramatic December escape from Tibet of the seventeenth Karmapa
Lama, who was expected to take up residence any time now in this
monastery, designed to be his North American home. We even
knew that the strapping fourteen-year-old leader of the Karma
Kagyu Buddhists, who in his escape had crossed some of the wildest
reaches of Nepal on horseback, had already outgrown the Asian
couch-bed prepared for him in Woodstock, and that a longer one
had to be found.

We arrived ten minutes early. It was almost dark on top of the
mountain, but the sky was in that translucent green holdover stage
that immediately follows sunset. In the mystical Shangri-La light, the
luminous white buildings with their red trim and authentic Tibetan
artwork (the sixty-seven-year-old artist, seventh-generation in a

Tibetan family of artists, is in residence here), surrounded by flags of deities fluttering in the mountain breeze, might just as well have been in Tibet.

We asked someone coming out of the main entrance for directions, and made our way across the compound and up the stairs into the shrine building. Inside was a cloakroom with pairs of sandals and shoes on the floor and a sign asking us please to remove ours. The left door opened into a small darkened shrine room with purple mats and red pillows and the *thangka* wall hangings around three sides and a gold Buddha in front, flanked by shelves and tables crammed with smaller figures and offerings. It seemed impertinent just to go in and sit down all by ourselves, so we retreated to the cloakroom and then tried the other door, which led into lamplit living quarters. An old monk who looked like the ones from the movies came forward out of the gloom to meet us.

"Is it all right if we come to your service at seven?"

He bowed and gestured us to a room. "Please. Go in." He turned on a light in what turned out to be the same little shrine room. "Please. Sit." His casual, sweeping gesture seemed to indicate that anywhere would be all right.

We chose seats to the rear and arranged ourselves cross-legged on the mats and pillows. Tom was more agile with his ankle work. Presently, a young Western woman in tights and tunic, who moved like a dancer, entered, performed two graceful prostrations, and greeted us. Another came in, then another: the women offered us scripts bound in plastic (Tibetan words in Sanskrit, with transliteration below, and the English translation below that) so we could follow the evening practice if we wished to. The dancer-woman explained that they would be meditating and doing visualization on the deity of Supreme Compassion, Amitabha (she pointed to his

likeness on a *thangka* painting) and on one of Amitabha's manifestations, the compassionate bodhisattva Avalokiteshvara (a four-armed
figure who sat cross-legged just beneath him). The mantra would
sound familiar to us, she said, it was a well-known one: *Om Mani
Padme Hum*. It means "O Jewel Lotus," a name given to Avalokiteshvara the Enlightened One (comparable to a saint), represented on
the *thangka* by the four-armed figure who holds a crystal rosary in
his right hand, a lotus blossom in his left, while his two other hands
clasp a jewel to his heart. The jewel pressed to the heart symbolizes
Avalokiteshvara's vow to relieve all sentient beings of suffering and
to bestow temporary and ultimate benefit and bliss.

By seven o'clock eleven of us had gathered. Only two of the group
were Tibetans. Most of the Westerners carried little plastic bottles of
distilled water. One of the last to enter, with rosary and water bottle,
was a tall American woman dressed in monk's robes and a maroon
shawl. She settled in next to us and, in the manner of a hostess
assuring her guests that they must make themselves completely at
home, smilingly told us, "You can either follow along with us in the
booklets, or just relax and enjoy the singing."

A man in shorts struck a gong, and the chant began. Tom was the
first to put down the booklet on the little shelf in front, fold his
glasses on top, and close his eyes. I persevered for about five more
minutes, losing my place in the text several times before I abandoned
the effort—whom did I need to impress with my diligence? Certainly
not the deity of compassion, or the compassionate bodhisattva pressing the jewel to his heart and praying for our release! I closed my
eyes like Tom for a while, until my left foot went to sleep. After having noticed that the impressive woman in the monk's robe beside me
rearranged herself without fuss from time to time, I discreetly shifted
my legs to a more comfortable position.

Then my back started to ache. Then I began to worry that I would cough. I glanced covertly around at the chanters, all of whom appeared set to go on through the night. I wondered how long this "practice" lasted, and then was ashamed of my time-bound mentality. But why, at least, hadn't I read the brochure more carefully, to know what I was in for? Why exactly was I here? Looking for more heart-stuff, frankly. See if there was something more I could add to the book. That, besides my inveterate curiosity, was mainly why I had come. All those Buddhist books I'd riffled through with "Heart" in the title: *The Good Heart, The Heart of Understanding: Commentaries on the Heart Sutra*—good old diligent Gail, always on the job. My right foot went to sleep. What if I had to get up and leave the room? What if this went on for two or three more *hours*? What if I fainted?

Now two of the women were swinging their prayer wheels to the chant. Faster and faster the little chains on top went flying around. Then a pause. Did that mean we were wrapping things up?

No.

The chant shifted into something hymnlike, then segued into another session of chant. I decided to take my mind off my aching back by visualizing my bed at home, the open window, the coming night in the valley of Woodstock where I soon would be stretched supine under the eiderdown, surrounded by my books and my thoughts: I would *be there presently;* I was there *now* in my visualization. Assured by the peaceable projection, I could relish the recurring part of the chant I liked best, when they came back to the mantra, *Om Mani Padme Hum,* and different people would trail off in their own soft echoes of it, setting the room abuzz with mantra solos, like bees asserting their individuality in a hive.

And then, after I had gone beyond thinking about when it would end, all sound suddenly ceased. Several people drank from their plastic water bottles; they had been singing nonstop for a whole hour. The American woman in the monk's robe and shawl gathered up her beads and turned to us, smiling. She said something so natural and appropriate to the moment that I've forgotten it. She introduced herself simply as Kathy. Later, when I finally did read the brochure, I learned that she was a lama herself—which means a teacher of the highest rank—and that we had inadvertently "dropped in" on a week of intensive meditations for advanced practitioners. Yet nobody had made us feel that we were anything but expected! Upon hearing that Tom was an Episcopal priest, she immediately slipped into his language and likened these meditations to the liturgy of the hours. The one we had just completed was a restful one, she explained, to prepare for sleeping, similar to our compline, with its plea to an eternally changeless God to grant us a peaceful night and a perfect end. The meditation at five in the morning would be more energetic, to prepare for the day's vigorous challenges. The one at five in the afternoon was also full of vigor because the bad stuff *from* the day needed to be cleared away.

The dancer-woman took apart her prayer wheel for us, a small cylinder pierced by a rod, one end of which is fixed in a wooden handle. Inside was a tiny, thick paper scroll with prayers. "When we spin it, we are sending out prayers to everyone in the world, everyone in Woodstock," she said. "Billions and billions of prayers," someone else chimed in, laughing. "And all those flags you see flying outside," said the man who had sounded the gong, "are wafting blessings down to you in the valley of Woodstock."

"Come back anytime!" they urged us. And we invited them, in turn, to come down to us at St. Gregory's, in the valley.

The moon was not up yet, but the sky was full of stars. As Tom cautiously took the hairpin curves of the steep descent in low gear, we mused some about our shared hour, but the interior of the car felt swathed in our yet unformed reflections. When he delivered me to the house, I said, "Well, I have to go in and think about this."

"No, don't think" was Tom's bemused reply.

Later, around eleven, when the moon was bright outside my window, having achieved my previously visualized bed, I could in supine comfort project myself back into the mountaintop shrine room, alive and alight with its buzzing mantra solos, its "billions and billions" of prayers flung extravagantly into the night. However much I had been afraid I wouldn't make it physically through the hour, the ultimate effect of our exchange with them had been like a "cordial," that lovely old heart-based word for a glass of spirits at the end of the day for the purpose of "stimulating the heart." The hour with the Tibetans on the mountain had restored my human spirits and enlarged my heart's imagination.

On the morrow I would read, in another one of my Buddhist "heart books" piled on the bed, that the saintly bodhisattva Avalokiteshvara, who vowed he would not rest until he had helped all beings reach the bliss of enlightenment, created a mantra for his own use. Regarded as the essence of Buddhist teaching, it is daily recited in temples and practice centers throughout the world.

It is known universally as "the Heart Mantra," and perfectly expresses the ultimate aim of the heart's hospitality, as well as my parting wish for all of us:

Gate gate paragate parasamgate bodhi svaha

Which means, "Gone, gone, gone all the way over, everyone gone to the other shore, enlightenment, Welcome!"

700
G

Godwin, Gail.

Heart.

$20.01